MANAGING CORPORATE LIQUIDITY

An Introduction to Working Capital Management

MANAGING CORPORATE LIQUIDITY

An Introduction to Working Capital Management

James H. Vander Weide
Steven F. Maier

JOHN WILEY & SONS

New York   Chichester   Brisbane   Toronto   Singapore

Copyright © 1985 by John Wiley & Sons, Inc.

All rights reserved. Published simultaneously in Canada.

Reproduction or translation of any part of
this work beyond that permitted by Sections
107 and 108 of the 1976 United States Copyright
Act without the permission of the copyright
owner is unlawful. Requests for permission
or further information should be addressed to
the Permissions Department, John Wiley & Sons.

Library of Congress Cataloging in Publication Data:

Vander Weide, James H.
  Managing corporate liquidity.

  Includes index.
  1. Cash management. 2. Working capital. 3. Corporations—Finance. I. Maier, Steven F. II. Title.
HG4028.C45V36 1985   658.1'52   84-13232
ISBN 0-471-87770-0

Printed in the United States of America

10 9 8 7 6 5 4 3 2 1

PREFACE

The field of corporate finance can be divided into two areas. One relates to a group of decisions that affect the firm's value primarily in the long run, including decisions about the firm's capital budget, capital structure and dividends, as well as mergers and acquisitions, lease financing, and business reorganization. The second area relates to a group of decisions that affect the firm's value primarily in the short run, including management of the firm's receivables, inventory management, management of the firm's marketable securities portfolio, cash management, and management of the firm's short-term sources of finance.

In recent years, financial theory has been concerned primarily with advancing the frontiers of knowledge relating to long-term financial decision making. Debates about the relevance or irrelevance of the firm's capital structure and dividend policy decisions, the proper method of adjusting for risk in capital budgeting decisions and the value of pursuing mergers for the sake of diversification dominate the academic literature in corporate finance. Very little attention has been devoted to the theoretical issues involved with making financial decisions in the short run, primarily because an adequate theory of corporate liquidity has yet to emerge.

It is interesting that the *practice* of corporate finance has evolved along different lines. With interest rates at unusually high levels for most of the last 15 years, practitioners of corporate finance have devoted their attention to improving the art and science of cash management (broadly defined), receivables management, and inventory management. Because the profits from improvements in these areas have been so large, banks, accounting firms, and independent consulting firms have also been very active in providing advice and developing decision techniques for improving short-run financial decisions. Hence, the practice has come before the theory.

Awareness of the importance of making sound financial decisions in the short run has grown to such an extent that the National Corporate Cash Management Association was formed in 1980 to encourage the advancement of knowledge and the sharing of ideas relating to short-run financial decision making. This organization now has over 2800 members, sponsors a widely read journal, *The Journal of Cash Management,* and organizes a national association meeting. In addition, there has been widespread participation by financial managers within a local area in regional corporate cash managers associations.

This book is intended to serve as a bridge between academic thinking and the practice of corporate finance. Although it offers no new theory of why firms hold liquidity, it introduces much of the academic work that does exist in short-term corporate finance to the beginning student. The book mixes institutional knowledge and modeling skills that are most relevant to the practice of financial decision making in the short run.

The notes for this book were prepared for distribution to students taking an elective course in the M.B.A. program at the Fuqua School of Business at Duke University. Since this course was introduced into the curriculum in the fall of 1975, student interest in the course has grown to the point that it is the most heavily enrolled course in the program. We wish to thank the many students who shared their enthusiasm for the subject, stimulated our thinking, and encouraged us to develop new materials for this course.

In addition to the many students who have taken our course in short-run financial management over the years, we specifically acknowledge the support of the following individuals. Dr. David Robinson is a colleague who has made significant contributions to our thinking in corporate finance in recent years. He has coauthored several research papers with us in this area and has worked with us closely in the practical application of many of the techniques described in the text. Larry Forman, Marc Mitchell, Mark Friedman, Jim Jeck, Randy Partin, Russell Kessler, and Steve Schmoll have provided examples, questions at the end of the chapters, and editorial suggestions that have significantly improved our pedagogy. Barbara Webb has done an outstanding job in typing the original manuscript and its many revisions. Finally, Ann Vander Weide provided invaluable editorial assistance.

The quality of this book has been significantly enhanced by the helpful criticisms and suggestions of several very competent referees. In this regard we wish to acknowledge the help of William Beranek, University of Georgia; Allan Frankle, University of Tulsa; James A. Gentry, University of Illinois, Urbana-Champaign; Ned C. Hill, University of Indiana; Keith V. Smith, Purdue University; and Ralph Collins Walter, III, Northeastern Illinois University. Finally, we think it only appropriate to acknowledge our debt to Bernell K. Stone, whose many contributions to the practice and theory of working capital management are indicated by the number of references to his work in this book.

James H. Vander Weide
Steven F. Maier

CONTENTS

SECTION I

INTRODUCTION

CHAPTER 1

Working Capital Management: Basic Concepts

Management of the firm's short-term assets and liabilities is commonly known as working capital management. The study of working capital management is important because decisions regarding the firm's short-term assets and liabilities have a significant impact on both the firm's profitability and its risk. Working capital decisions affect the firm's profits through their impact on sales, operating costs, and interest expense. They affect the firm's risk through their impact on the variability of the firm's cash flows, the probability of not receiving the cash flows, and the ability to generate cash in a crisis. The literature is replete with examples of firms that developed successful long-term competitive strategies, but failed because of a lack of attention to working capital management.

We begin our discussion of working capital management with an introduction to the basic concepts that govern working capital decisions. In particular, we discuss the scope of working capital management, the responsibilities and goals of working capital management, and the economic factors that most affect working capital decisions. Later chapters will discuss concepts and decision frameworks for individual working capital decisions in great depth. Our intent here is to give the student a broad overview of what working capital management is all about and, at the same time, to introduce her/him to some of the basic concepts of this important subject.

SCOPE OF WORKING CAPITAL MANAGEMENT

Before we begin our study of working capital management, it is helpful to have some notion of the nature and scope of working capital decisions. This section describes the scope of working capital management in three ways: it discusses which assets and

3

liabilities come under the control of working capital managers and provides data on the typical size of the firm's working capital position relative to its total assets, it explores the major cash flows of the firm to illustrate the basic nature of working capital decisions and how they relate to the firm's production and marketing decisions, and it provides a compendium of working capital decisions that will be discussed in greater depth in the remainder of this book.

The Balance Sheet Approach

The scope of working capital management may be described in terms of a representative balance sheet such as the one shown in Figure 1.1. This balance sheet is divided into two sections. The upper section contains asset and liability items that typically turn over in a short time period, perhaps a year, while the lower section contains assets and liabilities that normally remain on the firm's balance sheet for many years. Working capital management is concerned with the principles governing the management of the firm's short-term assets and liabilities. It includes cash management, management of the firm's marketable securities portfolio, receivables management, inventory management, and management of the firm's short-term sources of credit.

To provide some understanding of the importance of working capital management, it is helpful to study Table 1.1, which displays various working capital accounts as a percentage of total assets for the S&P 400. We see that firms in the S&P 400 typically maintain inventories worth 20% to 25% of their total assets, receivables worth 15% to 20% of their total assets, and cash and marketable securities worth between 7% to 10% of their total assets. The working capital accounts represent about half of the total assets of nonfinancial corporations.

Assets	Liabilities and Stockholders' Equity
Current Assets	**Current Liabilities**
Cash	Accounts payable
Marketable securities	Notes payable
Receivables	Wages payable
Inventories	Commercial paper
Prepaid expenses	Current maturities of long-term debt
Noncurrent Assets	**Noncurrent Liabilities**
Land	Long-term debt
Buildings	
Furniture and fixtures	**Stockholders' Equity**
Equipment	Preferred stock
	Common stock
	Reinvested earnings

Figure 1.1 Balance sheet of a nonfinancial corporation.

Table 1.1 Working Capital Accounts as a Percentage of Total Assets for the S&P 400 (firms equally weighted, 1978–1982)

	1978	**1979**	**1980**	**1981**	**1982**
Cash and S-T Investments	9.2%	7.9%	7.1%	7.0%	7.2%
Accounts Receivable	19.7	19.8	19.1	18.2	17.1
Inventories	24.1	24.0	22.8	21.6	20.0
Other	2.7	2.5	2.2	2.0	2.4
Current Assets	55.7%	54.2%	51.2%	48.8%	46.7%
Accounts Payable	10.4%	10.5%	9.9%	9.3%	8.6%
Debt in Current Liabilities	4.8	4.8	4.1	4.0	3.7
Income Taxes Payable	3.9	3.6	3.0	2.3	2.0
Other	12.5	12.2	11.0	10.8	11.2
Current Liabilities	31.6%	31.1%	28.0%	26.4%	25.5%
Net Working Capital	24.1%	23.1%	23.2%	22.4%	21.2%

Source: Standard and Poor's Compustat Tapes.

The Flow-of-Funds Approach

The scope of working capital management may also be described in terms of the typical firm's flow of funds. A diagramatic representation of the flow of funds through a typical firm is shown in Figure 1.2. At the top of the diagram, we see how the firm's current operations and capital investments represent both a source and use of funds. Cash sales, collection of receivables, and the sale of assets generate funds; payments to suppliers for raw materials, inventories, labor, and plant and equipment use funds. The circular flow of cash from raw materials to inventories, to receivables, and finally back to cash is sometimes called The Operating Cash Cycle.

In addition to its cash flow from operations and investments in physical capital, the firm both receives funds from and sends funds to the money and capital markets. The firm receives funds from the money and capital markets through new issues of debt and equity, borrowings from banks and other financial institutions and the earning of interest on short-term investments. The firm provides funds to the money and capital markets when it pays dividends and interest, purchases short-term securities, repays lenders, and repurchases its shares.

The flow-of-funds approach is helpful in illustrating how the financial manager's responsibilities relate to those of other corporate officers. Decisions made in marketing, production, personnel, corporate planning, and credit management can have a profound impact on the firm's cash position. The financial manager must forecast this effect and discuss it with other corporate officers so that they can consider changing their policies when the firm's cash position is threatened.

It also illustrates how the financial manager interacts with the external financial environment, especially the money and capital markets and the banking system. The financial manager is responsible for investing the firm's excess funds in the money

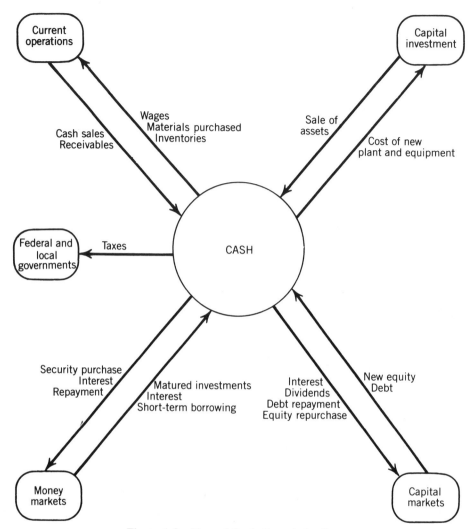

Figure 1.2 Flow-of-funds through the firm.

market, as well as for borrowing additional short-term funds when the firm is temporarily short of cash. In addition, the financial manager is responsible for directing the flow of funds through the firm's banking system on both the collections and disbursements sides. Both aspects of the financial manager's responsibility will be discussed in detail later in this book.

Finally, the flow-of-funds approach illustrates how the financial manager's responsibilities for working capital are distinct from, but also related to, his responsibilities for managing the firm's capital investment program and long-term financial structure. The cash flows on the left of Figure 1.2 are typically identified as being directly related to working capital management. However, since the firm's capital investment and capital structure decisions both impact the firm's pool of cash (shown at the center of the diagram) and cash management falls within the scope of working capital management, the firm's working capital decisions are clearly related to its long-run capital investment strategy and its capital structure.

Decision-Making Approach

Third, we may describe the scope of working capital management in terms of the major working capital decisions that affect the firm's profits. These may be broken into six areas:

1. *Collections and disbursements.* The financial manager in charge of the firm's working capital is responsible for managing the process of collecting funds from customers and disbursing funds to vendors. This frequently includes the implementation of a cash and check collection system and of a system of disbursement banks.
2. *Cash concentrations.* The financial manager is responsible for designing and managing a system for transferring funds from regional banks to the money-center banks where funds are concentrated for the purpose of investment. This includes decisions about the method of cash transfers, the timing of the transfers, and the choice of concentration banks.
3. *Liquidity management.* The financial manager is responsible for managing the firm's liquid (i.e., short-term) assets and liabilities. Liquidity management includes decisions regarding the aggregate amount of the firm's short-term portfolio of money market securities, and the type and maturity structure of the firm's short-term borrowings.
4. *Bank relations.* The financial manager is responsible for designing the firm's banking network and managing bank relations. This category includes the choice of banks the firm will do business with and the services the firm will buy from each bank.
5. *Receivables management.* The financial manager is responsible for managing the firm's credit policy and the resulting accounts receivable. This involves decisions about the firm's overall investment in accounts receivable, its customer credit selection policies, and its systems for monitoring accounts receivable performance.
6. *Inventory management.* The financial manager is responsible for evaluating the firm's investments in inventories. This requires the development of information systems for determining how much inventory is available and analysis systems for determining the optimal level of inventories.

Thus, the financial manager in charge of working capital decisions is primarily concerned with the operational aspects of the firm's financial area. Major strategic decisions such as capital budgeting, mergers and acquisitions, dividend policy, and the firm's mix between long-term debt and equity are made by a combination of the firm's chief financial officer, president, and board of directors. Although these latter decisions have a significant impact on the firm's market value, a person entering the field of corporate finance will not be directly concerned with them for many years. However, he or she must be cognizant of these decisions and aware of their implications on working capital management.

RESPONSIBILITY AND GOALS OF WORKING CAPITAL MANAGEMENT

We have discussed the management of the firm's current assets and liabilities as falling within the responsibilities of the firm's (chief) financial officer. Because the task of managing the firm's current assets and liabilities is complex, day-to-day responsibility for management is frequently delegated to other individuals within the firm. For instance, a large firm might have a treasurer who is responsible for managing short-term borrowings and bank relations, a cash manager who is responsible for managing the firm's cash and marketable securities position, a credit manager who is responsible for managing the firm's receivables, and a purchasing manager who is responsible for managing the firm's trade credit. Responsibility for managing inventories is generally shared by someone in marketing, production, and finance.

In carrying out their responsibilities, the firm's financial managers should seek to maximize the market value of the firm. Two implications of the market value goal are relevant for managing working capital. First, the financial manager should assess investments in working capital assets such as receivables and inventories in the same manner as he assesses investments in the firm's capital assets. In short, he should determine the cash flows associated with these decisions and make that choice which maximizes their present value. Second, the financial manager should assess decisions regarding the firm's cash and marketable securities positions in terms of their effect on the firm's ability to generate cash in times of crisis, as well as their effect on the present value of the firm's cash flows. The ability to generate cash in times of crisis (or perhaps in times of opportunity) is an important aspect of the concept of liquidity.

Demand for Working Capital

Before we proceed too far in our discussion of working capital management, it is desirable to resolve a conflict regarding the demand for working capital. Many economists have wondered why firms that desire to maximize the market value of their shares need to hold positive amounts of short-term assets and liabilities. As these economists have demonstrated,[1] in a world of perfect markets where there are no transactions costs, no time delays in the production, marketing and check clearing systems, no bankruptcy costs, and no differences in the borrowing rates of individuals and firms, the value of the firm does not depend on the firm's working capital decisions. Thus, there is no need to study working capital decisions, as we are doing here.

From our earlier discussion of the scope of working capital management, however, it is obvious that the conclusions reached from such perfect economic models do not seem to apply in practice. Not only do firms hold considerable amounts of short-term assets and liabilities, but financial managers seem to devote a significant amount of time to the working capital management process. In fact, practical interest in working capital management has risen to such an extent that there is now a national organization

---

[1]See Richard A. Cohn and John J. Pringle, "Steps Toward an Integration of Corporate Financial Theory," Reading 3 in *Readings on the Management of Working Capital,* Keith V. Smith (ed.), West Publishing Company, St. Paul, 1980.

called the National Corporate Cash Managers' Association that sponsors a journal devoted to working capital management, holds annual meetings at which working capital decisions are discussed, and is about to organize a national exam for the purpose of certifying competence in working capital decision making. It is highly unlikely that practicing financial managers would devote so much attention to a subject that had no effect on their firm's market value.

The apparent conflict between theory and practice can be resolved once we recognize that many of the perfect market assumptions on which the working capital irrelevance conclusions rest do not hold in practice. In this section, we shall briefly consider several factors that we believe have a significant impact on practical working capital decisions, but that are absent in many economic models of these decisions. In particular, we shall consider the effect of transactions costs, time delays in the production, marketing and collection processes, bankruptcy costs, and differences in the borrowing rates experienced by firms and individuals.

Transaction Costs   In economics, a transactions cost is a dollar outlay associated with the purchase or sale of a good or service. Transactions costs may take one of two forms. The first may be thought of as a "brokerage fee" that consists of either a dollar payment to a third party for bringing the buyer and seller together, or an internal cost for arranging the transaction. The second is more difficult to define, but is familiar to anyone who has tried to sell a house on very short notice. It consists of a loss in market value that results when the seller does not have the luxury to search the market carefully to obtain the best price.

Transactions costs are an important element in working capital decisions. Financial managers frequently hold significant quantities of cash and near-cash assets simply because the "transactions costs" involved in converting other assets to cash in times of emergency are prohibitively high. In fact, financial managers often rank various assets on the basis of their "liquidity," which is an expression for the ability to convert assets into cash on short notice with little or no loss in value. Cash, of course, is the most liquid of all assets, while property, plant, and equipment are the least liquid, because of the significant loss in value that occurs when property, plant, and equipment must be sold on short notice.

Time Delays   Time delays in the production, marketing, and cash collection processes also play an important role in working capital decisions. Figures 1.3 and 1.4 display typical time delays in these processes. Consider first the time delay between the receipt of an order and the crediting of the firm's account. We see that this is associated with the need to order and/or manufacture finished goods, the need to invoice customers and allow some time before payment is due, the need to send the customer's check through the mail, and the need to present the check for payment to the customer's bank.

To reduce this delay between the receipt of an order and the crediting of the firm's account, the financial manager can take one or more of four actions:

1. Maintain finished goods inventories.
2. Improve the processing of orders and invoices.

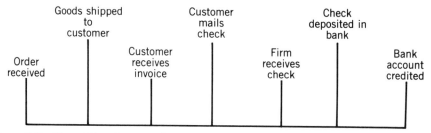

Figure 1.3 Time delays between the receipt of an order and the crediting of the firm's bank account.

3. Offer discounts for more rapid payment.
4. Take steps to reduce the mail time, internal processing time, and bank availability time on the customers's check.

Each of these steps, however, involves a cost as well as a benefit, and so the financial manager must evaluate these working capital decisions with great care.

Consider next the delay between the placing of an order and the debiting of the firm's account. We see that this is associated with the need to process the order and transport the raw materials, the need to give the firm some time to pay the bill, and the need to present the check to the firm's bank for collection. Once again, the financial manager can take actions that affect the time delay in the disbursement of funds. Furthermore, the choices she makes affect both the level of the firm's working capital balances and its profits.

Bankruptcy Costs   Bankruptcy costs are another important element in working capital decisions. Although bankruptcy costs are somewhat difficult to measure, they refer to the very real expenses in the form of legal fees, court costs, managerial time, and so on that a firm incurs when it is forced into bankruptcy by its creditors. Because of the high costs that most financial managers associate with bankruptcy, they keep a significant amount of liquid balances, even though these balances earn a low rate of return compared to the firm's fixed assets.

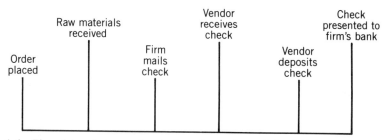

Figure 1.4   Time delays between the placing of an order and the debiting of the firm's bank account.

Differences in Borrowing Rates Economists sometimes ask why the firm extends credit to its customers. Certainly there is no need to do so if the customer can borrow funds as cheaply as the firm can. However, in practice this is rarely the case. Large firms can frequently borrow at lower rates than their customers because (1) they can tap the national money markets and bypass the cost of financial intermediation, and (2) the transactions cost of obtaining funds in large amounts is smaller than that associated with many small individual borrowings. Thus, the extension of customer credit is a natural attempt to reduce the costs of customer financing.

ANALYSIS OF WORKING CAPITAL DECISIONS

Since working capital decisions cannot at this time be related in a simple manner via economic theory to the market value of the firm's shares, it may seem that we will have to abandon economic analysis altogether in our study of working capital decisions. Nothing could be farther from the truth. Throughout this book, we shall rely extensively on the traditional concepts of economic analysis wherever possible. However, we will also recognize that there are some factors which affect working capital decisions in practice that are not amenable to the simplifications required in the economic models. There is still much room for user judgment in working capital decision making.

Our approach in this book will be to treat working capital decisions as having two influences on market value. The first influence is through the effect that working capital decisions have on the present value of the firm's cash flows. The second influence is through the effect that working capital decisions have on the firm's risk and liquidity. Thus, in each instance, we will begin by identifying the cash flows associated with a particular working capital decision and evaluating their present value. We will then discuss, where appropriate, the implications of this decision on the firm's risk or liquidity.

To elaborate on this approach, let us briefly consider how it can be applied to each of the six major decision areas that we earlier noted were under the province of working capital management.

Managing Cash Collections and Disbursements Looking at Figures 1.3 and 1.4, it is clear that the time delays inherent in the collection and disbursement systems are a major element in managing the firm's cash collections and disbursements. Through use of the techniques discussed in Chapters 3, 4, and 5, the financial manager can significantly shorten the time required for cash collections and significantly lengthen the time for cash disbursements. The use of these techniques, however, involves a cost in the form of fees, bank balances, and management time. The decision to use these techniques can be evaluated using present value analysis. If the present value of the investment in these techniques is positive, then the financial manager should obviously give strong consideration to their use. However, he must balance the results of the present value analysis with an assessment of the resulting risk. A method for trading off risk and return resulting from the design of cash disbursement systems is described in Chapter 5.

Cash Concentrations   The financial manager can frequently realize significant benefits by designing a system for rapid transfer of funds from regional bank accounts to a central account in a money center bank. A present value analysis of the various alternative cash concentration systems helps the financial manager make decisions about the appropriate method of cash transfers, the timing of transfers and the choice of concentration banks. However, some cash concentration systems may differ from others in terms of the risk of having insufficient funds in the regional bank account. The financial manager must obviously weigh these risks in making her final decision.

Liquidity Management   In managing the firm's portfolio of money market securities, the financial manager would like to choose securities that maximize the present value of interest income to the firm, given the manager's forecast of the firm's cash requirements. However, the portfolio that maximizes the present value of interest income may involve substantial risk, both in terms of the chance that a particular security will default and in terms of the overall liquidity of the portfolio. In Chapter 10, we describe a computer model that helps the financial manager to evaluate the risk and return of various portfolio strategies. Although this model does not relate the risk and return in a unique fashion to the market value of the firm, it does provide the manager with quantitative information about the risks and returns of various strategies, so that he can make his choice with the best available information.

Receivables Management   Decisions regarding the firm's customer credit policies, like those regarding the money market portfolio, affect the firm's profits, its liquidity, and its risk of loss from individual credit decisions. Once again, it is difficult to analyze these three elements of credit policy within a single economic model of the firm's market value. However, as shown in Chapter 13, it is possible to employ economic analysis to analyze each of these elements separately. In particular, we can employ present value analysis to evaluate the impact of alternative credit policies on the present value of the firm's cash flows, and we can then assess whether the decisions with the highest present value have an adverse impact on the firm's credit risk and its liquidity.

Inventory Management   In discussing Figure 1.3, we noted that the firm could significantly reduce the time between the receipt of an order and the shipment of goods by maintaining an inventory sufficient to meet customer demand. In Chapter 14, we analyze the decision to maintain inventories primarily in terms of the effect on the present value of the firm's cash flows. Once again, however, the financial manager should recognize that inventory decisions can have a significant impact on the variance of the firm's cash flows as well as on its liquidity. The final decision requires accurate information on the effect of inventories on each of these three elements that affect market value and the application of judgement to reach a final decision.

OUTLINE OF THIS BOOK

This book is divided into seven sections. Section I contains two chapters. The first introduces the student to the basic concepts of working capital management and the second provides background information on the operations of commercial banks and the Federal Reserve System that is important in managing the firm's bank relations, its cash collection and disbursement system, and its marketable securities portfolio.

Section II contains three chapters that deal with topics normally falling under the title "cash management." Chapter 3 treats the design of check collection systems, Chapter 4 deals with the problem of designing disbursement systems, and Chapter 5 discusses the design of cash concentration systems. These chapters should be of interest both to students pursuing a career in corporate cash management and to students interested in banking, since cash management consulting is a major product of the nations leading banks.

Section III contains three chapters dealing with cash forecasting and financial planning. The techniques discussed in these chapters are essential to the management of the firm's marketable securities portfolio. They are also important for analyzing the firm's receivables and inventory policies. Although these chapters are more oriented toward learning techniques than toward making decisions, the techniques that are learned are crucial to sound working capital management.

The economics of managing the firm's marketable securities portfolio is discussed in the four chapters comprising Section IV. The first chapter in this section, Chapter 9, provides background information on the characteristics of the marketable securities that are often found in a firm's marketable securities portfolio and the markets in which they are traded. The second chapter in Section IV describes a number of strategies that portfolio managers have found useful in making short-run investment decisions. The final two chapters of Section IV introduce the student to the possibility of using futures contracts to hedge the interest rate risk involved in short-run investment and borrowing decisions. Although futures contracts are not currently in widespread use among corporate working capital managers, we feel that they are potentially of great use in this area. Our decision to devote two chapters to futures contracts is a function primarily of the difficulty of the topic and the potential for future use, rather than its importance in practice.

Section V is devoted to receivables management. The relative magnitude of the typical firm's investment in receivables indicates that this is a very important topic of working capital management. In Chapter 13, we discuss three aspects of receivables management: the overall investment in accounts receivable management, the evaluation of individual credit applicants, and the monitoring of accounts receivable performance. Chapter 13 presents a number of techniques that financial managers have found useful in making accounts receivable decisions.

The final section of this book discusses some of the financial aspects of inventory management. A progression of models involving the important elements of inventory management decisions is reviewed so that the financial manager can appreciate which economic factors are most relevant to making inventory decisions. Because the complexities of inventory management are usually covered in courses in production or operations management, we have decided to treat only the basic topics in inventory management here.

SUMMARY

Working capital management is concerned with the management of the firm's short-term assets and liabilities. It includes cash management, management of the firm's marketable securities portfolio, receivables management, inventory management, and management of the firm's short-term sources of credit. This book provides the institutional knowledge and analytical skills required to manage these areas more effectively.

The study of working capital management is important because working capital decisions can have a significant impact on both the firm's profitability and its risk. Working capital decisions affect the firm's profits through their impact on sales, operating costs, and interest expense. They affect the firm's risk through their impact on the variability of the firm's cash flows and its liquidity. The financial manager needs to consider each of these impacts when making working capital decisions.

Although working capital decisions have a significant impact on the firm's profitability and risk, their impact on the firm's market value is not self-evident. In a world of perfect markets where there are no transactions costs, no time delays in the production, marketing, and check clearing systems, no bankruptcy costs, and no differences in the borrowing rates of individuals and firms, the value of the firm is very likely independent of the firm's working capital decisions. However, none of these conditions is true of the practical world of financial management. Thus, the study of working capital management is important for practitioners and scholars alike.

DISCUSSION QUESTIONS

1. What assets and liabilities are generally included in the definition of working capital?
2. How large are the working capital accounts in relation to total assets for the firms in the S&P 400?
3. Name several industries where firms would normally have very significant investments in working capital assets.
4. Name several industries where firms would normally hold very small amounts of working capital in relation to total assets.
5. Describe the flow of funds from operations for a typical manufacturing firm.
6. How are the financial manager's responsibilities for working capital related to her responsibilities for managing the firm's capital investment program and long-term financial structure?
7. What major decisions does the financial manager have to make in regard to the firm's working capital?
8. What are the major goals of working capital management?

9. How do working capital decisions affect the value of the firm's shares?
10. Why are transactions costs important in working capital management?
11. Describe the major time delays in the production, marketing, and cash collection processes.
12. What actions can the firm take to reduce these delays?
13. Why do firms grant credit to their customers?
14. Describe how working capital decisions can be analyzed using present value analysis.
15. What factors does the present value analysis ignore?

ADDITIONAL READINGS

1. Paul J. Behler, *Contemporary Cash Management,* Wiley, New York, 1983.
2. Dileep R. Mehta, *Working Capital Management,* Prentice-Hall, Inc., Englewood Cliffs, N.J., 1974.
3. Keith V. Smith, *Guide to Working Capital Management,* McGraw-Hill, New York, 1979.
4. Keith V. Smith, *Readings on the Management of Working Capital,* 2nd ed., West Publishing Company, St. Paul, 1980.
5. James H. Vander Weide, "Financial Management in the Short Run," Chapter 23 in *The Handbook of Modern Finance,* Dennis E. Logue (ed.), Warren, Gorham & Lamont, New York, 1984.

CHAPTER 2

COMMERCIAL BANKS

Commercial banks play an important part in the life of the financial manager. In addition to being a major supplier of financial services, commercial banks have a significant effect on the level of interest rates and the supply of credit in the money markets. A sound understanding of commercial banks and their role in the economy is a prerequisite to effective financial management performance.

COMMERCIAL BANK STRUCTURE

The U.S. banking industry contains approximately 15,000 firms that vary considerably in size and the range of financial services they provide. At one end of the spectrum are a few large banks located in money center cities such as New York, Chicago, and San Francisco that provide a full range of financial services and compete in both the national and international market for loans. Unlike many smaller banks, the money center banks do not rely on demand and time deposits as their major source of funds. Instead, they purchase large quantities of funds in the money markets by issuing debt securities or borrowing from other banks and financial institutions.

In addition to their borrowing and lending activities, most money center banks offer financial services and consulting of interest to the financial manager. The services include the evaluation and design of cash management systems, dealing in money market securities, serving as a transfer agent for corporate securities, foreign exchange trading, lease financing and pension fund supervision. To assist in the decision making activities of the financial manager, money center banks also maintain consulting staffs in areas such as cash management, economic forecasting, international finance and tax planning.

At the other end of the U.S. banking spectrum are thousands of banks that compete on a purely local basis. Local banks rely primarily on deposits as a source of funds, and they lend almost exclusively to individuals and firms in their local areas. To provide financial services such as check clearing, financial expertise, trust, and access to the money markets, local banks establish a correspondent banking relationship with money center or large regional banks. The local banks maintain deposit balances with the large banks to pay for financial services, and the large banks then use these deposits to fund their lending activities.

In between the large money center and small local banks are both large and small regional banks. Large regional banks serve the financial needs of corporations in their geographical area, but play only a minor role in the national and international loan markets. These regional banks have considerable consulting expertise, especially in corporate areas such as cash management, that helps them attract a national clientele for their consulting services. Regional banks are more actively engaged in consumer and real estate lending and rely to a much greater extent on demand deposits as a source of funds than their money center counterparts. In recent years, large regional banks have begun to rely more extensively on "purchased" money such as federal funds and repurchase agreements,[1] but they do not rely on such funds quite as extensively as the money center banks. Some large regional banks have begun to operate as dealers in money market securities, and to compete in the international market for loans.

Small regional banks behave much more like local banks. They rely more heavily on demand deposits and less heavily on the money market as a source of funds than do their large regional counterparts. On the investment side, they place a large percentage of their interest-earning assets in real estate and personal loans, as opposed to commercial and industrial loans. The corporate service offerings of the smaller regional banks are limited.

Tables 2.1 and 2.2 provide some indication of the magnitude of the differences between various bank categories. Focusing first on the two extreme categories, local and money center banks, we note five major differences:

1. Over 60% of local bank assets are concentrated in the three categories: securities, real estate loans and personal loans, while only 20% of money center bank assets are in these categories.
2. One third of money center bank assets are concentrated in commercial and industrial loans, while only 13% of local bank assets are in this category.
3. Money market liabilities are 67% of total assets for money center banks, and only 13% for local banks.
4. Demand deposits represent 19% of total assets of local banks; they represent only 11% of the total assets of money center banks.
5. Money center banks hold a relatively high percentage (11.7%) of interest-bearing deposits in their portfolio of assets, while local banks hold a relatively low percentage of such deposits (2.6%). Furthermore, although the figures are not available to verify this, one would expect a difference in the form of these deposits: the interest-

---

[1]These are described in detail on pages 27 and 28.

Table 2.1   Asset Composition of Local, Regional, and Money Center Banks, EOY 1982 (Selected asset items as percentage of average consolidated assets.)

Item	Local	Regional	Large Banks	Money Center
Interest-earning assets	91.0%	89.0%	83.0%	81.4%
Loans	52.5	53.4	55.1	61.0
Comm. and industrial	12.9	16.9	21.8	33.6
Real Estate	18.4	19.4	14.6	8.1
Personal	12.9	13.2	9.3	4.3
Securities	29.6	25.3	13.8	6.3
U.S. Treasury	9.8	8.0	4.1	1.7
U.S. gov't. agencies	8.4	5.5	2.1	.7
State and local governments	10.9	11.1	7.1	2.7
Other bonds and stocks	0.4	0.7	0.5	1.2
Gross fed. funds sold and Securities purchased under repurchase agreements	6.4	5.9	4.3	2.4
Interest-bearing deposits	2.6	4.4	9.8	11.7

Local: Banks with less than $100 million in assets
Regional: Banks with $100 million to $1 billion in assets
Large: Banks with more than $1 billion in assets other than money center banks
Money Center: Banks with more than $1 billion in assets with headquarters in New York, Chicago, or San Francisco

Source: Federal Reserve Bulletin, July 1983.

bearing deposits of money center banks are likely to be Eurodollar deposits, while those of local banks are most likely large time deposits (CD's) in major U.S. banks.

Turning to the remaining two categories, small regional banks and large banks in other than money center cities, we note that their asset and liability structures fall clearly in between the two extremes. Large banks in other than money center cities invest heavily in commercial and industrial loans (almost 22% of their assets), but their investments in this category are still significantly less than those of money center banks (33.6%). Furthermore, although the money market liabilities of large banks represent 43% of their assets, this is also significantly less than the corresponding percentage (67.1%) for money center banks. Small regional banks seem to behave very much like local banks, except that they obtain a significantly larger percentage of funds from the money market (23% versus 13%).

COMMERCIAL BANK REGULATION

Commercial banks are one of the most heavily regulated industries in the U.S. economy. At least four agencies have a hand in controlling their activities—the Federal Reserve System, the Federal Deposit Insurance Corporation, the Comptroller of the Currency, and the various state banking commissions.

Table 2.2 Composition of Financial Claims of Local, Regional, Large and Money Center Banks, End of Year, 1982 (Selected financial claim items as percent of average consolidated assets.)

Items	Local	Regional	Large	Money Center
Financial Claims	89.5%	90.6%	88.8%	87.2%
Demand deposits	19.0	21.3	19.7	11.1
Interest-bearing claims	70.3	69.2	68.8	74.8
Time and saving deposits	68.1	61.6	54.4	61.4
Large time	10.7	15.4	17.7	15.7
In foreign offices		.2	11.0	38.0
Other domestic dep.	57.5	46.0	25.7	7.7
MMCs and 91-day	23.1	16.6	8.4	2.5
NOW accounts	6.2	5.2	3.2	.9
Subordinated notes and debentures	.1	.4	.5	.2
Other borrowings	.3	.8	2.2	4.6

Gross fed. funds purchased and
  securities sold under repurchase
  agreements
	1.7	6.5	11.7	8.6

Memo: Money market liabilities	12.8	23.2	43.0	67.1

Local:	Banks with less than $100 million in assets
Regional:	Banks with $100 million to $1 billion in assets
Large:	Banks with more than $1 billion in assets other than money center banks
Money Center:	Banks with more than $1 billion in assets with headquarters in New York, Chicago, or San Francisco

Source: Federal Reserve Bulletin, July 1983.

The Federal Reserve System

The Federal Reserve System established by the Federal Reserve Act of 1913 consists of the Board of Governors, the Federal Open Market Committee, the Federal Advisory Council, the twelve Federal Reserve Banks and their branches and all member commercial banks. Its purpose is to promote a consistently high level of economic activity and assure the health of the nation's banking system. It is important to note that the Federal Reserve System is intended to be a largely independent organization within the federal government that can conduct its business without the interference of political considerations.

The Board of Governors

The Board of Governors is the primary governing body of the Federal Reserve System. It consists of seven individuals appointed by the President of the U.S. to a 14-year term. The appointments are staggered so that one term expires every 2 years. One member of the Board is selected by the President to be Chairman, and he is the chief spokesman for the system's policies.

With the help of its large staff of economists, the Board of Governors conducts studies of economic and financial conditions, and designs policies intended to encourage high employment, low inflation and strong growth in the U.S. economy. The Board pursues these objectives in three ways. First, it regulates the percentage of each class of deposits that banks must hold as non-interest bearing reserves (i.e., it specifies "reserve requirements"). Second, it sets targets, through its controlling membership on the Federal Open Market Committee, for the activities of the Federal Open Market Trading Desk of the Federal Reserve Bank of New York. The Trading Desk influences the supply of credit and the level of bank reserves (i.e., the amount of funds that banks keep as non-interest bearing reserves) through the purchase and sale of government securities. The level of bank reserves in turn affects the growth in the nation's money supply and the level of interest rates. Third, it influences the cost of credit through its ability to review the discount rates set by the 12 Federal Reserve district banks.[2]

In addition to its role in the conduct of monetary policy, the Board of Governors makes recommendations to Congress concerning bank legislation.

The Federal Open Market Committee   The Federal Open Market Committee (FOMC) sets the Federal Reserve's targets for growth in the money supply, interest rates and availability of credit. The Committee includes the seven members of the Board of Governors, a representative of the Federal Reserve Bank of New York and four representatives from the eleven remaining Federal Reserve Banks who serve on a rotating basis. The FOMC meets on the third Tuesday of every month and its minutes are made available to the public on the following Friday. There is frequently wide speculation in the financial community about the stance the FOMC will take at its next meeting, since this stance greatly affects interest rates and other money market conditions.

The 12 Federal Reserve Banks   The Federal Reserve Act of 1913 divides the country into 12 Federal Reserve districts, and dictates that there be one Federal Reserve bank in each district. The district banks have the primary responsibility for the examination and supervision of member banks in their district. In addition, they maintain check collection and wire transfer facilities, supply notes and currency, safekeep securities and perform a great many services for the Treasury and other government agencies.

The Federal Deposit Insurance Corporation (FDIC)

The Federal Deposit Insurance Corporation (FDIC) provides insurance on deposits at commercial banks. Any bank that chooses to contribute one half of 1% on all deposits it accepts can obtain FDIC insurance. Approximately 98% of all U.S. commercial banks are currently covered by the FDIC. The present maximum FDIC insurance coverage is $100,000 per depositor.

To assure the integrity of bank deposits, the FDIC has legal authority to examine all

---

[2]The discount rate is the rate of interest that the 12 Federal Reserve district banks charge their member banks for loans.

insured banks. In practice, the FDIC examines only those banks that are not nationally chartered. It works closely with the state banking authorities to avoid duplication of effort. In the event of a bank insolvency, the FDIC acts as receiver to protect the interest of depositors.

Comptroller of the Currency

The Office of the Comptroller of the Currency issues national charters to new commercial banks that appear to be qualified for the banking business. In addition to providing charters, the agency conducts an annual examination of the loan quality, capital adequacy and management competence of the banks it charters. (These are generally called national banks.) In reviewing applications for new branch offices, the Comptroller of the Currency must conform to state branching laws.

The State Banking Commissions

Banks that choose not to obtain a national charter from the Office of the Comptroller of the Currency are chartered by their State Banking Commission. The State Banking Commission conducts regular examinations of banks chartered in that state, and has authority to approve or disapprove any mergers or holding company acquisitions. State chartered banks may choose whether or not they want to become members of the Federal Reserve System (all national banks must be members). For many years, most state banks chose not to become members of the Federal Reserve System because state reserve requirements were considerably easier to meet than those of the Federal Reserve System. This advantage of nonmembership was eliminated as a result of the Depository Institutions Deregulation and Monetary Control Act of 1980 (DIDMCA).

COMMERCIAL BANKS AND MONETARY POLICY

The Federal Reserve System (the ''Fed'') is charged with the responsibility of pursuing monetary policies that help the nation achieve its economic goals of full employment, high growth, and low inflation. The Fed pursues these goals primarily through its control of commercial bank reserves. When commercial bank reserves are in excess of those required by the Fed, commercial banks generally seek to expand their loans, which tends to reduce interest rates. When the reverse is true, commercial banks seek to contract loans, which has the opposite effect on interest rates. In the first case, economic activity is stimulated, and in the second, it is discouraged.

The Fed controls member bank reserves by its decisions regarding reserve requirements, discount window policy and open market operations. It is instructive to briefly consider each of these three tools of Federal Reserve monetary policy.

Reserve Requirements

The Fed has the power to fix the percentage of various types of deposits that banks must hold in reserve. If the reserve requirement for a certain type of deposit is fixed at 10%, then commercial banks must keep 10% of the total amount of that type of deposit either in cash, or on deposit at a Federal Reserve district bank. The remaining 90% may be used to acquire securities or make loans. The difference between a commercial bank's actual reserves and its required reserves is termed excess reserves.

The ability to control reserve requirements can be a powerful tool of monetary policy. When the Fed lowers commercial bank reserve requirements (say from 12% to 8%), those banks that previously had zero excess reserves now find themselves in a position of positive excess reserves. Since these new excess reserves earn no interest, banks have an incentive to eliminate them by purchasing securities or making loans. The efforts of commercial banks to eliminate excess reserves stimulates economic activity.

Reserve policy is generally considered to be a blunt tool for the purpose of controlling economic activity. Slight changes in reserve requirements have an impact on a commercial bank's ability to extend loans that is frequently greater than that which the Federal Reserve intended. For that reason, changes in reserve requirements are an infrequently used tool of monetary control.

Discount Window Policy

The term "discount policy" refers to the Fed's ability to control the amounts that commercial banks borrow from regional Federal Reserve banks. Member commercial banks are given the privilege of borrowing at the Fed to soften the impact of rapid changes in bank excess reserves and to avoid the disruption in the financial markets caused by banks refusing to extend loans. However, if banks borrow too freely from the Fed, the Fed's intended monetary stance may have no effect at all on bank loan activity. The Fed discourages overuse of the discount window through its control of the interest rate charged on loans to commercial banks and through its policy of treating commercial bank loans at the Fed as a privilege rather than a right. Those banks who borrow too frequently at the Fed's discount window are warned that further loans will not be granted.

The efficiency of discount policy as a monetary tool has been seriously questioned in recent years. To the extent that banks borrow at the discount window to meet reserve requirements, they are avoiding the actions the Fed hoped they would take in response to changes in their nonborrowed reserves. However, there is some evidence that a change in the discount rate can be an important signal to the credit markets about the direction of Federal Reserve policy. In this sense, its value may be largely informational.

Open Market Operations

The Fed conducts open market operations by instructing its agent at the Open Market Trading Desk at the Federal Reserve Bank of New York to purchase and sell securities in the open market for the Fed's account. The agent pays for security purchases with a check drawn on the Federal Reserve that clears through normal channels.[3] When the check arrives at a Federal Reserve district bank, it becomes a reserve deposit of the

---

[3]In essence, the agent is creating money.

commercial bank in that district at which it was deposited. This leads to an increase in excess reserves, and eventually to increased economic activity and lower interest rates. When the agent at the trading desk sells securities, on the other hand, excess reserves decline and economic activity eventually contracts.

Open market operations have become the primary tool of Federal Reserve monetary policy in recent years. Because the Fed can purchase or sell any amount of securities it desires over any length of time, it can exert a fairly precise degree of control on bank reserves through its open market operations.

Illustration   The effects of Federal Reserve open market operations may be illustrated with an example. Suppose the Fed purchases $10 million of Treasury bills in the open market at a time when the excess reserves of commercial banks in the aggregate are zero. For the sake of illustration, let us assume (1) reserve requirements are 10% of all deposits and (2) reserves are held only as deposits at the Fed. As shown in Figure 2.1, the Fed's purchase of $10 million in securities increases bank deposits and reserves, and produces excess reserves for commercial banks. When the banks see they have excess reserves, they extend an additional $90 million in loans to their customers. The additional loans are recorded as an increase in customers' deposit balances, and the banks achieve a new equilibrium between actual and excess reserves. It is notewor-

Step One: The Fed purchases $10 million of securities from securities dealers.

Fed		Banks		Securities Firm
Securities	Member bank	Reserves	Deposits	Bank Deposits
+10	deposits +10	+10	+10	+10
				Securities
				−10

Banks' Reserve Position

Deposits	$10 million
Req. Reserves	1 million
Excess Reserves	9 million

Step Two: Commercial banks expand loans and create new deposit balances for customers.

Fed		Banks		Securities Firm
Securities	Member bank	Reserves	Deposits	Bank Deposits
+10	deposits +10	+10	+10	+10
		Loans	+90	Securities
		+90		−10

Banks' Reserve Position

Deposits	$100 million
Req. Reserves	10 million
Excess Reserves	0

Figure 2.1   Effects of Open Market Purchase of Securities

thy that the increase in commercial bank lending is nine times the amount of the initial Federal Reserve purchase of securities. This multiplier results from the fractional nature of the assumed reserve requirements.

COMMERCIAL BANK ASSET AND LIABILITY ACCOUNTS

In this section, we use the aggregate balance sheet for all commercial banks in the United States, as a vehicle for describing the activities of commercial banks. The asset accounts, shown in Table 2.3, represent the major uses of bank funds and the liability accounts, shown in Table 2.5 (p. 30), represent their major funding sources.

Cash Assets

In December, 1982, commercial banks held over $200 billion in cash assets. This represented almost 10% of the total assets of commercial banks at that time. The surprisingly large bank investment in non-interest earning cash assets reflects the dual role of commercial banks in the nation's financial system. They are the primary providers of the nation's payment mechanisms and they play a key role in the implementation of Federal Reserve monetary policy.

For the purpose of understanding why banks hold such a large amount of cash assets, it is instructive to divide the cash account into four subcategories: currency and coin, reserves with Federal Reserve Banks, balances with depository institutions, and cash items in the process of collection.

Table 2.3   Assets of Commercial Banking Institutions, December 1982

	(billions of dollars)
Cash Assets, total	$ 200.7
Currency and coin	23.0
Reserves with Federal Reserve Banks	26.8
Balances with depository institutions	81.4
Cash items in process of collection	69.4
U.S. Treasury securities	132.8
Other securities	242.1
Loans, excluding interbank	1,054.9
Commercial and industrial	396.5
Other	658.4
Other assets	341.7
Total assets	1,972.2

Source: Federal Reserve Bulletin.

Currency and Coin   At the end of 1982, banks held 10% of their cash assets in the form of currency and coin. Although much has been written in recent years about the coming of a "cashless society," the general public prefers to transact much of its business in cash. Banks hold currency and coin primarily to meet the transaction needs of their customers. Thus, the total amount of currency and coin held by banks tends to fluctuate with the general level of business activity. For instance, the December total is somewhat higher than usual because of the level of holiday spending. The cost to the bank of holding currency and coin is somewhat reduced by the fact that such holdings are included in reserves meeting the bank's reserve requirements.

Reserves with Federal Reserve Banks   Commercial banks are required to keep a certain percentage of their deposits either on deposit in one of the twelve Federal Reserve Banks or in the form of currency and coin. Originally, the reserve requirements were intended as a safety reserve against a depositor run on the bank. With the establishment of the Federal Deposit Insurance Corporation in 1933, however, depositor runs on banks have been far less common. Today, member bank reserves serve primarily to facilitate the conduct of monetary policy.

Until the passage of the Depository Institutions Deregulation and Monetary Control Act of 1980 (DIDMCA), the Fed's reserve requirements applied only to those commercial banks that were members of the Federal Reserve System. This gave an unfair competitive advantage to those banks that were not members of the Federal Reserve System, since they did not need to tie up such a large proportion of their assets in noninterest bearing accounts. With the passage of DIDMCA, the Fed's reserve requirements were extended to all financial institutions offering transaction balances. This includes all accounts on which checks may be written.

Balances with Depository Institutions   Commercial banks frequently hold demand deposit balances in other commercial banks with which they have a correspondent banking relationship. The depositor bank uses the deposit to obtain services, such as check clearing, consulting, trust and securities trading that it may not be able to provide itself.

In addition to serving as a means of compensating for services, correspondent accounts are the vehicle through which local banks lend excess reserves to money center banks that are often in a reserve-deficit position. The market for such excess reserves, known as the Federal Funds Market, will be discussed at some length in Chapter 11.

Cash Items in the Process of Collection   Cash items in the process of collection is a large item in the cash account. To describe this item, it is necessary to describe first how a typical check is cleared through the banking system.

When a check is deposited in someone's account in a commercial bank, the bank must send the check for collection to the bank on which it is drawn (i.e., the drawee bank). It can do this in one of four ways.

1. If the check is drawn on itself, the bank can simply send the check to the bookkeeping department, where the appropriate accounts will be debited and credited.
2. If the check is drawn on another local bank, the bank of deposit will send the check to the local clearing house. The clearing house is simply a local place where banks meet on a daily basis to exchange checks drawn on each other.
3. If the check is drawn on a nonlocal bank, the bank of deposit may send the check to the nearest Federal Reserve office. This office then either sends the check directly to the drawee bank or sends it on to another Federal Reserve office, depending on the drawee bank's Federal Reserve district.
4. Alternatively, if the check is drawn on a nonlocal bank, the bank of deposit may send it to a correspondent bank in another city for collection. The correspondent bank then collects it from the drawee bank.

In cases 3 and 4 above, the correspondent bank or the Federal Reserve Bank may grant credit to the bank of deposit before the check is actually collected from the drawee bank. Credit is granted by increasing the balance in the demand account which the bank of deposit holds with the Federal Reserve or correspondent bank. Since the demand deposit is a liability of either the Federal Reserve Bank or the correspondent bank, there must be a corresponding asset to balance the books. The corresponding asset is called "cash items in the process of collection."

Securities Portfolio

The securities portfolio is the second major asset category for commercial banks. It consists of investments in U.S. Treasury securities, obligations of other U.S. government agencies, obligations of state and political subdivisions, various other securities, and federal funds sold and repurchase agreements. At the end of 1982, banks had security portfolios valued on their books at approximately $375 billion.

In addition to their direct investments in securities of various types, banks hold some securities as part of their dealer activities in the securities markets. An understanding of the banks' dealer activities is especially important to the financial manager, because she frequently interacts with banks in this role. These activities will be discussed in more detail in Chapter 3.

U.S. Treasury Securities   U.S. Treasury securities consist of Treasury bills, Treasury notes, and Treasury bonds. A Treasury bill is a short-term obligation of the U.S. government that is sold at a discount through competitive bidding. On a weekly basis, 91- and 182-day Treasury bills are sold at auction by the Treasury. Fifty-two-week bills are sold at auction once a month.

Commercial banks invest in Treasury bills because they are a safe and highly liquid vehicle for earning interest on money not currently needed for loans. Bank investment in Treasury bills tends to fluctuate with the business cycle. In a period when business activity is high and loan activity is brisk, commercial banks reduce their investment in Treasury bills so that they can accommodate the loan demand of their business customers. The excellent liquidity of Treasury bills is especially important at these times, because they can be sold quickly with little loss in value. In times when business activity is slow, bank investment in Treasury bills increases.

In addition to their holdings of Treasury bills, banks sometimes invest in Treasury notes and bonds. Treasury notes are obligations of the U.S. government whose maturity ranges from 1 to 10 years and Treasury bonds are obligations of the U.S. government with maturities of over 10 years.

Treasury notes and bonds are somewhat less desirable as bank investments, because they expose the bank to a much greater degree of interest rate risk. Banks who purchase Treasury notes and bonds at times when excess reserves are plentiful and interest rates are low, and sell them when loan demand is heavy and interest rates are high, can take large capital losses on their security portfolio.

Obligations of Other U.S. Government Agencies Banks are also heavy purchasers of the securities of the various agencies of the U.S. government. In order to provide credit on easy terms to certain special classes of borrowers, the U.S. Congress has periodically established a federal agency whose purpose is to supply credit at the lowest possible cost to a particular borrower group. Federal agencies act as financial intermediaries in the sense that they issue securities to the general public, and use the proceeds to extend credit to this special class of borrowers. The securities of the federal agencies are generally not backed by the full faith and credit of the U.S. government, but the likelihood of their default is extremely small. Federal agency securities are at times an attractive investment, because their yields exceed those on U.S. Treasury securities.

Obligations of State and Political Subdivisions Banks also invest heavily in the securities of state and local governments. These securities are attractive for two reasons. First, since the income on state and local government securities is exempt from federal income taxes, the after-tax yield frequently exceeds that available on U.S. Treasury securities by a substantial margin. Second, state and local governments sometimes keep large deposits in commercial banks that earn little or no interest. Banks compete actively for these deposits by agreeing with the state and local government involved to purchase substantial amounts of their securities. In some instances, banks are actually required to keep investments in state and local government securities as reserves on their deposits.

Federal Funds Sold and Securities Purchased Under Repurchase Agreement
Federal funds sold and securities purchased under repurchase agreement is the final category in commercial banks' securities portfolios. Although the two items in this category are similar in many ways, it is helpful to define them separately.

Federal funds are unsecured overnight loans from one financial institution to another in a group of financial institutions that includes commercial banks, savings and loan associations, mutual savings banks, federal agencies, and domestic agencies and branches of foreign banks. This group is special because the Federal Reserve Board has ruled that commercial bank borrowings from any one of these financial institutions are exempt from reserve requirements. Federal funds transactions are frequently negotiated through federal funds brokers and are settled in immediately available funds. (Immediately available funds are deposit liabilities that may be transferred or withdrawn within one business day. For most practical purposes, they include deposits at federal reserve banks and certain types of deposits at correspondent banks.)

To understand why there is a large volume of federal funds on both the asset and the liability sides of the aggregate commercial bank balance sheet, it is helpful to recall the differences between small local banks and large money-center banks. Smaller banks in rural areas acquire large amounts of deposits, but have a limited demand for loans. Large banks in major metropolitan areas have a large loan demand, but have limited access to new deposits. It is natural for rural banks to lend their deposits to commercial banks in major metropolitan areas to help them satisfy their loan demand. Thus, federal funds are typically on the asset side of the balance sheet of rural banks and on the liability side of the balance sheet of large metropolitan banks.

A repurchase agreement is an agreement to buy a security, usually a Treasury bill or a federal agency security, and to resell it at a specified price at a later date. Since the agreement to repurchase the security is made at the same time it is sold, it is clear that repurchase agreements are really a loan from the buyer to the seller. The term of repurchase agreements is typically one day, but it is not uncommon for them to be sold with maturities of up to 30 days. Repurchase agreements are an attractive source of financing for commercial banks because they already have a large portfolio of T-bills and federal agency securities to sell, and borrowings made under repurchase agreements are exempt from reserve requirements of the Federal Reserve System. The small amount of repurchase agreements that appear on the asset side of the aggregate commercial bank balance sheet is probably part of the bank's dealer operations. At times it will be profitable for a bank, in its role as a securities dealer, to "work both sides of the street," simultaneously borrowing and lending in the repurchase agreement market.

Loans

Loans are the most significant asset category on the commercial bank balance sheet. At the end of 1982, aggregate loans totaled $1055 billion, or approximately 54% of commercial bank assets.

As shown in Table 2.4, commercial bank loans take a variety of forms. The aggregate balance sheet shows (1) commercial and industrial loans, (2) real estate loans, (3) loans to individuals, (4) security loans, (5) loans to financial institutions, (6) agricultural loans, and (7) all other loans.

Commercial and Industrial Loans   Commercial and industrial (C&I) loans are a very important source of income to most banks. Although the terms of C&I loans are negotiable, most tend to fall into one of four categories: lines of credit, revolving credit agreements, term loans, and variable-rate term loans.

A line of credit is an agreement between a firm and a bank, usually renegotiated once a year, whereby the firm can borrow up to a stated maximum amount of funds at any time. The company that negotiates a bank line of credit usually compensates the

Table 2.4 Loans of Commercial Banks, December 1982

	(billions of dollars)
Total loans and leases	$1,042.0
Commercial and industrial loans	392.4
Real estate loans	303.2
Loans to individuals	191.8
Security loans	24.7
Loans to non-bank financial institutions	31.1
Agricultural loans	36.1
Lease financing receivables	13.1
All other loans	49.7

Source: Federal Reserve Bulletin.

bank in two ways. First, it pays a rate of interest for the amount actually borrowed that depends on its credit standing and its credit relationship with the bank. The rate is often stated on the basis of a prime rate plus a negotiated percentage over prime, where the prime rate is the rate of interest on loans to the bank's most credit-worthy customers. Second, the borrowing firm pays the bank by maintaining compensating balances that depend on both the amount of the line (i.e., the maximum amount that can be borrowed) and the usage of the line. A typical compensating balance requirement states that the firm must maintain compensating balances equal to 10% of the credit line plus 10% of the amount actually borrowed. (*Note.* In recent years some banks have allowed firms to pay for the line with fees instead of balances.)

A firm borrowing under a line of credit should recognize that the bank may have no legal commitment to extend credit. If the firm's financial condition deteriorates during the course of the year, the bank may reconsider and not extend the loan. Since the loss of goodwill is substantial when they do this, however, banks do not exercise this privilege indiscriminantly. Under most line of credit agreements, the firm is required to clear its books at least part of the year.

The revolving credit agreement is similar to a line of credit in that the bank agrees to extend credit up to a maximum amount. The primary difference is that the revolving credit agreement frequently extends beyond a 1-year period, is usually collateralized by receivables or inventories, and is a legal commitment on the part of the bank. In addition, the firm may not be required to bring its debt balances down to zero during at least one time period of the year.

A term loan is a loan from the bank to the firm with a maturity greater than one year; most frequently it is in the range of 2 to 7 years. Term loans are repayable in periodic installments which may not be equal and are scheduled to coincide with the firm's period of greatest cash inflow.

In recent years, many banks have begun to extend variable-rate term loans that differ from ordinary term loans in that the rate of interest is adjusted periodically to conform more closely with other interest rates then available in the money markets. Various schemes for adjusting the rate have been used; some call for no adjustment during an initial period of as much as a year, and then periodic adjustments on a semiannual or quarterly basis.

Real Estate Loans Banks are also very active in extending real estate loans of various kinds. Part of the total outstanding in this category is for construction and land development loans. These are loans to finance builders and others in the construction trades during the period when the project is in progress. They are thus of relatively short duration, but play an important role in this industry. Another part of the total outstanding real estate loans is in the form of long-term mortgages on individual and commercial properties. Bank loans in this area are generally conventional; that is, they are not insured by the Federal Housing Authority or the Veterans Administration.

Loans to Individuals Consumer loans are the third largest category in the aggregate commercial bank loan portfolio. These loans are primarily for the purpose of financing consumer durable goods or the remodeling of residential properties. Consumer loans have variable maturities, and are often paid back in installments. In recent years, there has been a tremendous increase in bank loans associated with credit cards.

Loans to Financial Institutions Banks frequently make loans to other banks and financial institutions. The list of borrowers includes finance companies, mortgage companies, commercial banks, real estate investment trusts, and brokers and dealers.

Agricultural Loans Although agricultural loans represent only a small total of the aggregate bank loan portfolio, they can represent a large share of the total loans of banks located in rural areas.

Demand Deposits

Demand deposits are the first item on the liability side of the aggregate commercial bank balance sheet shown in Table 2.5. These represent the total dollar amounts deposited in the checking accounts of individuals, partnerships and corporations (IPC).

Table 2.5 Liabilities of Commercial Banking Institutions, December 1982

	(billions of dollars)
Deposits	$1,409.7
Demand	376.2
Time	296.7
Savings	736.7
Borrowings	278.3
Other liabilities	148.4
Residual (assets less liabilities)	135.8

Source: Federal Reserve Bulletin.

They are used primarily as transactions balances, although, as we have previously noted, a substantial portion is also in the form of idle balances that compensate banks for loans and services rendered. Because banks have traditionally not been allowed to pay interest on demand deposits, this source of funds tends to dry up in periods of high interest rates.[4] Competition from other financial institutions and money market funds that offer interest bearing transactions accounts has also severely limited the growth of demand deposits.

Time and Savings Deposits

Time and savings deposits have been a major source of bank funds throughout U.S. banking history. For many years, this category was dominated by deposits in passbook savings accounts held by individuals. Passbook savings accounts are a safe and highly liquid form of savings for many small investors. However, the interest rate on passbook savings accounts is limited by the Federal Reserve under Regulation Q. Currently, interest rates on passbook savings accounts are limited to be no more than 5¼%, although this limit is scheduled to rise over the next several years and to be eliminated by 1986.

Because of the interest rate ceiling on passbook savings accounts, banks tended to suffer from large-scale deposit withdrawals in periods when market interest rates rose above the Regulation Q limits. When this occurred in 1970, the Federal Reserve removed the interest ceilings on large certificates of deposits (CD's) with maturities less than 90 days. Gradually the Federal Reserve removed the interest ceilings on certificates of deposit of all maturities and investments in CD's have grown considerably in recent years.

Since CD's were only available in amounts greater than $100,000 the lifting of interest ceilings on CD's did not help banks attract deposits from small depositors in periods of high interest rates. Then, in June 1978, the Federal Reserve allowed banks to introduce a new "Money Market Certificate" whose yield is tied to the yield on U.S. Treasury Bills. These certificates are available in minimum denominations of $10,000; they have a maturity of six months. Since then, the growth in Money Market Certificates has been phenomenal.

The surprisingly large total in the account titled "IPC Dep. in Foreign Offices" represents the deposits of individuals, partnerships and corporations in foreign branches or foreign offices of U.S. domestic banks. Traditionally, deposits in this account were an especially attractive source of funds for banks because they were exempt from both reserve requirements and interest rate ceilings. Although a 3% reserve requirement on deposits in this account has been imposed by the Monetary Control Act of 1980, these deposits have not declined substantially. Many foreign governments and firms prefer to hold dollar denominated deposits in foreign branches of U.S. banks because they are less subject to the control of the U.S. government.

---

[4]This aspect of demand deposits changed significantly on November 15, 1982, when the Depository Institution Deregulation Committee, a committee created by the Monetary Control Act of 1980 to administer the deregulation of interest rates, authorized banks to create a new money market depository account (MMDA) that has no interest rate restrictions, but does limit the number of monthly transfers.

Federal Funds Purchased and Securities Sold

Federal funds purchased and securities sold under repurchase agreements are a major source of funding to many banks. From the bank's point of view, federal funds and repurchase agreements are attractive because they are not subject to reserve requirements. Since we have already discussed both federal funds and repurchase agreements above, we will not treat them in more detail here.

Equity Accounts

The equity accounts of commercial banks represent only a small percentage of their total liabilities plus net worth. The Federal Reserve is concerned with the capital adequacy of banks as measured by the percentage of equity in their capital structure. It has established a set of guidelines that banks can follow to determine capital adequacy. Banks that stray too far from the Federal Reserve's guidelines are placed on a list of "problem banks" that the Federal Reserve then monitors with great care.

MAJOR CHANGES IN THE BANKING INDUSTRY

During the last two decades, commercial banks have operated in an economic environment of high interest rates, rapid technological innovation, and frequent changes in banking regulations. This environment has had a significant impact on the range of financial services that banks offer and the prices they charge. Some of the more significant changes in the banking industry are described in the following sections.

Liability Management

High interest rates encourage bank customers to minimize non-interest bearing balances held in checking accounts, and to shift liquidity balances into investments that offer a higher yield than banks are allowed to pay on time and savings deposits under Regulation Q. Because of these forces, bank demand and time deposits have not kept pace with the demand for bank loans, forcing banks to seek alternative means of financing their loan portfolios.

The process of actively seeking funds in the open market, as opposed to passively accepting time and demand deposits, is known as liability management. Banks who practice liability management finance their loan and securities portfolios, at least in part, by (1) purchasing federal funds from other banks and financial institutions, (2) selling securities under repurchase agreements, (3) selling large denomination, negotiable CD's, (4) floating commercial paper, and (5) purchasing Eurodollar deposits in the international marketplace.[5]

Although liability management allows banks to maintain and even increase their

[5]In late 1982, commercial banks and other financial institutions were given additional flexibility in practicing liability management. In addition to the MMDA mentioned in footnote 1, they were given the authority to offer a so-called Super NOW account to individuals and nonprofit institutions. The Super NOW has no interest rate or transfer restrictions, however, there is a minimum balance requirement of $2500.

loan and securities portfolios, it also greatly reduces the margin between the cost of bank funds and the return on investment. Banks who practice liability management cannot afford to offer financial services such as collections, disbursements and consulting at less than cost. As liability management becomes the norm for banks, financial managers can expect to see major changes in the prices of bank services.

Competition from Non-Bank Financial Intermediaries

High interest rates also encourage non-bank financial institutions to introduce new products designed to attract deposits away from banks. Two such products are the money market mutual funds introduced by some of the large investment companies and the NOW account introduced by mutual savings banks in New England. These products allow customers to earn interest on transactions balances that might otherwise be held in bank demand deposit accounts. They help to explain why non-bank financial intermediaries have grown at a more rapid rate than banks in recent years.

Money market mutual funds are open-end investment companies that invest entirely in money market instruments such as Treasury bills, federal agency securities, commercial paper and CD's. Small savers can participate in the higher yields on these instruments by purchasing one or more shares in the fund. Shares may be redeemed at any time by writing a check, although frequently the amount of the check must be over a fixed minimum. Since money market mutual funds offer most of the advantages of an ordinary checking account, while paying high interest, it is not surprising that by the end of 1983 investments in U.S. money market mutual funds totalled approximately $160 billion.

In 1972 mutual savings banks in Massachusetts introduced an innovative product called the NOW (negotiable order of withdrawal) account. Since the NOW account was a savings account on which individuals could write checks, it allowed customers to earn interest on transaction balances. For some period of time, NOW accounts were only allowed in Massachusetts and New Hampshire, but were later extended (in DIDMCA) to the rest of the Northeast and eventually throughout the nation.

Because they provide other financial institutions with the ability to offer checking services, NOW accounts help to blur the distinction between commercial banks and other financial institutions. In the decade of the 1980s, the financial manager will very likely deal with these financial institutions on equal footing with banks.[6]

Increased Importance of Consulting

The efforts on the part of individuals and firms to minimize cash balances have led banks to expand their consulting activities. Because they play an integral part in the nation's check clearing system, banks are experts on efficient movement of funds. As noted in Chapter 1, they have developed many sophisticated products to help firms and individuals manage their cash resources more effectively.

---

[6]This is even more true now that financial institutions are allowed to offer Money Market Deposit Accounts and Super NOW Accounts. See footnotes 1 and 2. However, it should be noted that these accounts are not available to corporations at the present time.

Banks who have recruited cash management consulting staffs and developed valuable client contacts find it natural to offer and develop other consulting services to the same client set. Today, many banks offer a wide range of corporate consulting services including cash management, financial forecasting, investment advisory services, international finance, and tax planning.

Electronic Banking

The banking industry has been greatly affected by the rapid pace of technological change in computer technology. The term electronic banking refers to a group of technologies and products that allow customers to transfer funds and conduct banking business more economically. The three forms of electronic banking described below provide some insight into the way changing technology has affected the banking business.

Automated Clearing House   The Automated Clearing House (ACH) allows funds to be transferred from one bank account to another without the costly movement of paper that characterizes our traditional check payment system. The ACH is similar in many ways to the local clearing house where banks trade checks and make appropriate debits or credits to clearing house accounts for the net inflow and outflow from each bank. The major difference is that, in the case of the ACH, the bank sends an electronic tape to the clearing house instead of a bundle of checks. The ACH computer reads the tape, and records the amounts on the accounts of all member banks. The ACH has an advantage over the local clearing house in that it interacts with banks over a much wider region of the country. Because many of the ACH's around the country are interconnected, the ACH system allows transfers of funds among different regions of the country. Ultimately, it is conceivable that there could be computer-to-computer linkages between individual banks and one large ACH system that would allow the complete electronic transfer of check information.

Cash Management Information Systems   Banks now offer computerized cash management information systems that permit the financial manager to obtain timely financial information through a computer terminal that accesses a national time-sharing network. Many systems allow the financial manager to wire transfer money from one bank account to another as well.

Customer-Bank Interaction Devices
Banks have introduced a number of customer-bank interaction devices that allow customers to conduct banking business from a remote location and by direct interaction with the bank's computer system. This is less expensive for the bank as it saves teller labor and more convenient for the customer as it may be done at any hour. Three particular such devices are noteworthy.

1. A point-of-sale terminal is a device located on a merchant's premises that facilitates a direct transfer of funds from the customer's account to the merchant's.
2. Automatic teller machines are computer-controlled devices that permit the customer

to make a number of typical banking transactions 24-hours a day at convenient locations. The customer inserts an encoded card into the machine, pushes a series of buttons to convey the desired instructions to the computer, and receives her receipt for the transaction.
3. Telephone instructed transactions are possible from a push-button telephone to a computer for account transfers, and for bill paying instructions from the customer at his home or office to his bank.

Bank Holding Companies

To offset declining profit margins in their traditional business, banks have sought to enter related markets where profit opportunities appear to be more favorable. Under the Bank Holding Company Act of 1970, banks may enter an array of closely related financial service industries by forming a bank holding company that owns separate subsidaries in each industry. Interestingly, the traditional limitation on branching across state boundaries does not apply to the non-bank subsidiary of the holding company. Thus, in addition to entering desirable new lines of business, banks are able to establish offices throughout the country that may someday serve as a base for a national banking network. (Legislation permitting interstate branching has been widely rumored for years.)

Internationalization of Banking

In response to the increased interdependence of the world economy and changing conditions in the financial markets, many banks have opened offices and branches overseas, and expanded the international services offered by their U.S. offices. The internationalization of banking raises a whole new set of issues for banks to face. For the first time, they have to assess the risks of lending to firms in foreign markets and dealing in a multi-currency world. Today, some large U.S. banks receive a substantial portion of their net income from overseas operations.

DEPOSITORY INSTITUTIONS DEREGULATION AND MONETARY CONTROL ACT OF 1980

The Depository Institutions Deregulation and Monetary Control Act of 1980 is the most significant piece of legislation to affect the banking industry in the last 40 years. It contains the following provisions.

1. Uniform reserve requirements are to be set by the Board of Governors of the Federal Reserve System for all financial institutions that offer transactions accounts. The requirements are set at 3% of the first $25 million in transaction deposits and 12% of all transaction balances exceeding $25 million. This provision will be phased in over a 4-year period for Federal Reserve member banks, and an 8-year period for all non-member depository institutions.
2. Interest ceilings on savings deposits are to be phased out by the end of a 6-year

period, with timing of the intermediate adjustments to be worked out by a committee consisting of the Chairman of each of the agencies which regulate banks and the Secretary of the Treasury.

3. The Federal Reserve System is required to set prices for all services rendered to the banking community.
4. All depository financial institutions are authorized to offer NOW accounts as of January 1, 1981. Interest rate ceilings on NOW accounts are to be uniform for all such institutions.
5. Savings and Loan associations are allowed to place up to 20% of their assets in consumer loans, commercial paper and corporate debt securities.
6. Usury laws of the various states are to be inapplicable to all federally insured lenders for a period of 3 years.

Most observers feel that DIDMCA will have a profound impact on the scope of the banking industry and the practice of financial management in the 1980s. In particular, it is felt that DIDMCA will:

1. Increase competition among financial institutions.
2. Encourage financial innovation.
3. Provide incentives for the evolution of electronic funds transfer.
4. Encourage a more efficient allocation of economic resources.
5. Increase the cost of bank services.
6. Reduce the subsidy of the Federal Reserve System to the banking industry.

The financial manager should remain alert to possible future effects of the legislative changes included in the Depository Institutions Deregulation and Monetary Control Act of 1980.

SUMMARY

The financial manager needs to understand commercial banking to perform his job more effectively. Commercial banks provide many financial management services, including cash management consulting, lockbox and disbursement services, money market trading, check reconciliation, and balance reporting. Since they are the primary vehicle for the conduct of monetary policy, commercial banks also have a significant effect on the level of interest rates and the supply of credit. Recent changes in technology and regulation have an important impact on the quality and prices of financial management services. Since commercial banks play such an important role in the financial manager's life, she must monitor these changes to see how they affect her job.

DISCUSSION QUESTIONS

1. What are the major differences between money center, regional, and local banks?
2. How is the Federal Reserve System organized?
3. How does the Federal Reserve System promote the economic goals of the country?

4. How does the Federal Reserve System insure the health of the nation's banking system?

5. Why is the financial community interested in the meetings of the Federal Open Market Committee of the Federal Reserve System?

6. What is the purpose of the 12 district Federal Reserve Banks?

7. Describe the role of the FDIC when a bank becomes insolvent?

8. Describe the advantages of being a state rather than nationally chartered bank.

9. What is the purpose of bank reserves? What was the original purpose?

10. What funds are included by the Federal Reserve towards meeting a particular bank's reserve requirements?

11. How would the presence of "excess" reserves of commercial banks affect economic activity? Why doesn't the Federal Reserve constantly change reserve requirements in order to control economic activity?

12. Do you think the discount window policy of the Federal Reserve is an effective tool of monetary policy? Why or why not?

13. Why do commercial banks hold demand deposit balances in other commercial banks?

14. Describe the meaning of the term "Cash Items in the Process of Collection."

15. When a commercial bank has a demand deposit account with its correspondent bank, is the account subject to reserve requirements for both banks?

16. If the after-tax yield on state and local government securities is substantially greater than U.S. Treasury securities, and the risk is nearly the same, why don't most banks invest more of their assets in these tax-exempt instruments?

17. As a practical matter, a repurchase agreement is a short-term loan secured by one or more Treasury bills. Why would a bank borrow funds using T-bills as collateral, rather than merely selling the T-bills?

18. What are Federal Funds? Explain why Federal Funds usually appear as assets of rural banks.

19. Why are repurchase agreements an attractive financing source?

20. Describe the typical terms of a bank line of credit.

21. Why do some banks prefer to be compensated with balances rather than fees?

22. What do you think would be the interest rate relationships between the following loan types?
    - Term loan
    - Line of credit
    - Real estate loan
    - Mortgage loan

23. Explain the statement that liability management "reduces the margin between the cost of bank funds and the return on investment."

24. What prevents banks from vastly expanding their asset bases through the purchase of federal funds on an ever-increasing scale?

25. What is the rationale for not allowing corporate demand deposit accounts to participate in the "NOW" program offered by most banks and Savings & Loans?

26. How much effect will electronic banking have on the daily float in the banking system, and what effects will be felt by the firm's financial manager?

27. What are the issues (pro and con) surrounding interstate branch banking?

28. What kind of impact will the DIDMC Act have on borrowers?

ADDITIONAL READINGS

1. Robert O. Edmister, *Financial Institutions: Markets and Management,* McGraw-Hill, New York, 1980.

2. J. O. Light and William L. White, *The Financial System,* Richard D. Irwin, Homewood, 1979.

3. John M. Mason *Financial Management of Commercial Banks,* Warren, Gorham & Lamont, New York, 1979.

4. Neil B. Murphy, "Commercial Banking," Chapter 6 in *Financial Handbook,* 5th ed., Edward I Altman (ed.), Wiley, New York, 1981.

5. Edward W. Reed, Richard V. Cotter, Edward K. Gill, and Richard K. Smith, *Commercial Banking,* Prentice-Hall, Englewood Cliffs, N.J., 1980.

6. Peter S. Rose and Donald R. Fraser, *Financial Institutions,* Business Publications, Inc., Dallas, 1980.

SECTION II

CASH MANAGEMENT

CHAPTER 3

Designing Check Collection Systems: The Lockbox Location Problem

U.S. firms receive payment from their customers in a variety of ways, including cash, check, pre-authorized draft, and electronic funds transfer. Among these, cash and check are still the most widely used. Cash is used predominantly in the retail trades, while checks are the primary means of payment in the manufacturing and service sectors of the economy.

When the firm receives payment in cash, the transfer of value from the customer to the firm is immediate. Thus, in designing a cash collection system, the financial manager need not concern herself with delays in the transfer of value. Instead, she is concerned with designing an information system that accurately reports the amounts collected at each field office and deposited in the field office bank, and designing a cash concentration system that efficiently transfers funds from field office accounts to the firm's centralized cash concentration account. The issues involved in the design of these systems will be discussed in Chapter 5.

When the firm receives payment by check, however, the transfer of value from the customer to the firm is delayed, sometimes by as much as 5 to 6 days. In designing a check collection system, therefore, the financial manager is primarily concerned with reducing the delay in the transfer of value. Since this is frequently accomplished through the use of lockboxes, the issues involved in designing a lockbox collection system are discussed here.

LOCKBOXES

A lockbox is a postal address, maintained by the firm's bank, that is used solely for the purpose of collecting checks. As checks arrive at the lockbox, the bank deposits them into the check clearing system and sends a photocopy of the remittance document to the

41

firm for internal processing. Ever since it was first introduced by RCA in 1947 with the help of the First National Bank of Chicago and Bankers Trust, the lockbox has proven to be an effective tool for reducing collection float.

Initially, lockboxes were used only for low volume, high dollar receipts coming from corporate customers. With the development of machine-readable return documents, the cost of lockbox processing was reduced to the point where it became profitable to use them also for high volume, low dollar receipts from individual households. Lockboxes for high volume, low dollar receipts are called retail lockboxes; examples include department store credit cards, utility bills, and insurance premium collection.

Lockbox processing can differ widely from one user to another. In the simplest form, the envelope is opened by the bank, the check removed and photocopied, the original check deposited, and the photocopy, together with the other contents of the envelope, returned to the corporation for further processing. In a variation on this form, the bank records all information contained on the check and other documents in machine-readable form, and transmits this information for direct input into the company's receivable processing system. In many cases, this latter system results in significant savings in receivable processing costs.

With the lockbox, the firm may have its customers mail remittances to almost any city in the country. The firm does not require, and in many cases does not have, a processing center or office in a lockbox city. Thus, a company that formerly had all its customers remit their payments to its home office in Cincinnati, could through the use of lockbox processing have its west coast customers remit their payments to a San Francisco lockbox, its midwest customers remit to a Chicago lockbox, and its east coast customers remit to a Philadelphia lockbox. A firm could *not* establish such a diversified collection system itself, without high expense and much procedural difficulty.

COLLECTION FLOAT

The goal of lockbox system design is to reduce collection float, measured as the sum of mail float, internal processing float, and availability float.

Mail Float

Mail time is the difference between the time an item is postmarked and the time it is received at the company's processing center or office. For the purposes of designing check collection systems, however, mail *float* is more important than mail *time*. Mail float is defined as the product of mail time and the total dollars collected. For example, a firm that collects $1 million a day, and experiences 1.5 days in mail time, has $1.5 million in mail float.

Mail float is an important element in collection float. Mail times for firms that do not use accelerated collection techniques fall in the range 3–5 days on average. Firms that use collection acceleration techniques can reduce mail times by one day or more. The value of reducing mail time by one day on a $1 million check is $274, assuming an interest rate of 10% (i.e., $1 million × 0.10 ÷ 365). For a firm with $100 million in annual credit sales, this amounts to a savings of $27,400, an amount that very likely exceeds the cost of the acceleration techniques themselves.

Processing Float

If a firm does not use a lockbox, its processing float can frequently be significant. After a check arrives at the firm's office, the firm begins the process of updating its accounts receivable records. First, the envelope containing the check is opened, and the amount of the check is compared with the outstanding invoices for this customer. At this time, the firm determines whether the customer took a discount for prompt payment, faulty merchandise, or inaccurate billing. The check is then separated from whatever other documents are contained in the payment envelope, combined with other payments received by the company and taken to the company's bank for deposit.

To be consistent with our treatment of mail float, we need to measure the effect of internal processing delays in terms of the additional *float* generated. This float is calculated as the product of the dollars received and the internal processing delay in days. One of the primary advantages of a lockbox collection system is that it reduces internal processing float to a negligible level. Again, although it is difficult to make industry generalities, the firm that does its own processing usually takes about one day on average to complete the processing work—if it is efficient—and perhaps as long as three days—if it is inefficient. If the firm receives $1 million per day, this delay can result in from $1 million to $3 million processing float.

Availability Float

The firm completes its part in the check collection cycle when it makes a bank deposit. Many individuals assume that such a deposit results in immediate use of the funds. Except when the checks are drawn on the bank at which they are deposited, this is not true. For most large banks, each check is granted an availability based on the bank's availability schedule and time of deposit. The availability schedule indicates whether the firm will have use of the check value in 0, 1, or 2 days. The availability granted depends on the distance between the drawee bank and the deposit bank, as well as several other factors.

If the check is drawn on a bank located in the same city or region as the deposit bank, the deposit bank is generally able to "collect" the item overnight and therefore grants the depositor one-day availability. If the check is drawn on a bank in a distant part of the country, however, it must either be turned over to the Federal Reserve or cleared through a correspondent banking relationship referred to as a "direct send." Since the check cannot be cleared overnight, the bank will generally grant two-day availability for such an item.

Availability times for most firms average between 1.0 and 1.5 calendar days. If the firm is dealing with a distant branch of a bank network, or makes its deposits late in the banking day, it may experience availabilities as long as 2.5 days.

LOCKBOX BENEFITS

Lockboxes are designed to attack all three collection float components. Because they are located close to the firm's customers and are emptied many times each day, lockboxes can considerably reduce the time the average check is in the mail. Further reductions in mail time are obtained through the use of weekend pickup and unique five-digit ZIP codes (i.e., Zip codes that are assigned to only one mail recipient, usually a bank). The unique ZIP code allows the post office to process lockbox mail more rapidly.

Lockboxes also lead to a substantial reduction in internal processing float. Most banks complete the entire lockbox processing cycle—that is, from the time the item is picked up at the post office until it is physically deposited—in two to three hours. Furthermore, since the lockbox processing area is located in the bank itself, the bank is "open" for receipt of lockbox deposits 24 hours a day. In contrast, a firm without a lockbox system can only deposit its items during normal banking hours. Since the majority of lockbox processing is done in the hours from midnight until about 8 A.M., a substantial portion of lockbox items are deposited prior to the opening of the bank. For most companies, lockbox processing saves almost a full day in processing float.

The final element of savings in lockbox processing comes from a reduction in availability time. Although lockbox processing does not change the bank's availability schedule, it does increase the percentage of locally drawn items. Moreover, since processing takes place primarily in the morning hours, the deposits are more likely to make the bank's availability cutoffs.[1]

The Value of Float Reduction

A reduction in collection float is valuable to the firm because it increases the amount of funds available for investment. The interest earned on the additional investment balances is the best measure of the value of float reduction.

Consider a firm that has credit sales of $365 million per year. Assuming there are no bad debts, this firm obviously collects an average of $1 million per day. Suppose the firm is able to reduce its average collection time from 5 to 3 days. This results in a float reduction of $2 million (2 days × $1 million per day). If the firm's cost of capital is 10%, then the value of the float reduction is $200,000 a year.

In designing check collection systems, the financial manager compares the value of float reduction to the cost of enhanced collection methods. If the enhanced collection mechanisms cost $10,000 per month, then it is certainly worthwhile for the firm to use these mechanisms to reduce its collection float by $2 million.

Summary

In measuring the effectiveness of a potential collection system improvement, we need to calculate its impact on the three components of collection float: mail float, processing float, and availability float. By comparing the value of the float improvement to the

---

[1]The bank normally publishes a schedule indicating the availability time it will assign to a check item that is deposited before a prespecified "cutoff" time during the day. Items deposited after this "cutoff" time are assigned an availability time of one additional day.

cost incurred in making the change in collection procedures, the firm can assess the value of a particular collection system change.

THE LOCKBOX LOCATION PROBLEM

Although lockboxes lead to a considerable reduction in collection float, they also increase collection system cost. In designing a lockbox collection system, the financial manager wants to find a set of lockbox sites that maximize the return on dollar float savings minus the fixed and variable costs of the lockbox system. The financial manager's decision problem is formulated in mathematical terms in Appendix A. The mathematical formulation is called the Lockbox Location Problem. A discussion of several aspects of this problem follows.

Data Requirements

To solve the Lockbox Location Problem, the financial manager[2] must obtain data on:

1. The mail and availability times relating group i and lockbox j, and the mail and availability times for the current system.
2. The total amount of incoming funds from each group i.
3. The variable costs associated with the firm's present system.
4. The firm's opportunity cost of capital.
5. The variable and fixed costs for processing group $i's$ checks through lockbox j.

Unfortunately, while reliable estimates of data requirements 1 through 4 can often be obtained at only a modest cost, reliable estimates of data requirement 5 are both costly and difficult to obtain.

Fixed and Variable Costs

The mathematical formulation requires the financial manager to obtain information on the fixed and variable costs associated with each lockbox site. Since there are about 50 relevant lockbox cities, with perhaps two or three banks in each city offering lockbox services, the manager must obtain cost information from more than 150 banks. In gathering these costs, the manager must recognize that bank charges for ''good'' customers may be significantly less than charges quoted to the general public; the charges may change frequently in response to market pressures; and the charges may depend on the volume of checks processed through the box.

Given the high cost of obtaining the data on fixed and variable lockbox charges, the analyst must decide whether to obtain this information or not. Most analysts have decided not to obtain fixed and variable cost information, partly based on their experience that float benefits between cities are frequently greater than cost differences between banks.

---

[2]In practice, the financial manager would rarely solve this problem himself. Instead, she would go to the cash management consulting group at a large commercial bank. This group would have the necessary databases and algorithms necessary to solve this problem for the financial manager. In return for this lockbox study service, the bank will normally receive a fee.

A Practical Reformulation

In light of the above difficulties in obtaining fixed and variable cost information, the financial manager usually employs a simple three-stage solution procedure for the Lockbox Location Problem. In the first stage, the financial manager attempts to determine a functional relationship between the maximum float reduction benefits from the customer's lockbox system and the number of lockboxes in the system. This can be accomplished by solving the Revised Lockbox Location Problem (see Appendix B).

The objective to the Revised Lockbox Location Problem is simply to maximize the return on the funds made available by the float reduction. Since the costs of the lockbox system are not included in this objective, the optimal solution to the Revised Lockbox Location Problem, were it not for a constraint on the number of lockboxes that may be included in the system, would be to locate a lockbox at every available site and then assign checks to the nearest lockbox. When the constraint on the number of lockboxes in the system is included, however, and the Revised Lockbox Location Problem is solved for all values of the number of lockboxes in the system, the financial manager obtains the desired relationship between the maximum float benefits and the number of lockboxes in the firm's lockbox system. Although the solution to this problem is not trivial, algorithms do exist that can solve fairly large-scale problems in a reasonable amount of time. The result of this stage of the solution procedure would then be a curve that may resemble the Net Float Benefit (NFB) curve in Figure 3.1. (Note that although the NFB and TC curves in this figure are really only defined for integer values of r, we have drawn them as continuous curves for the sake of the exposition.) With the best lockbox regions for each value of r (the number of lockboxes in the system) in hand, the financial manager attempts to determine a functional relationship between the total costs of the lockbox system and the number of boxes in the system. She does this by negotiating the "best" lockbox deal that she can obtain from a bank in the relevant regions, and then adding to this price figure her search, negotiation, and administration costs for each value of r. The result of this second stage of the procedure would perhaps be a curve shaped like the Total Cost (TC) curve in Figure 3.1.

The final stage of the solution procedure now obviously involves making a comparison of the benefits and costs of the firm's lockbox system. If the curves are shaped

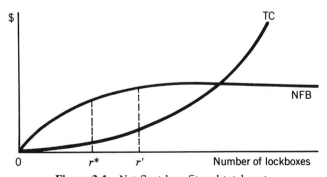

Figure 3.1 Net float benefit and total cost.

West (W)	$300,000/day
North (N)	$100,000/day
South (S)	$200,000/day
East (E)	$500,000/day

Figure 3.2   Customer concentrations.

like those in Figure 3.1, the optimal number of lockboxes is determined by that point, $r*$, on the abscissa where the vertical distance between the NFB and TC curves is greatest. The optimal distribution of lockboxes is then given by the solution to Problem II for $r=r*$.

The three-stage solution procedure just described has several advantages. First, there is likely to be a large reduction in the number of lockbox prices that must be determined in order to solve a particular lockbox problem. Recall that in our approach lockbox prices need not be determined at all until after the NFB curve is known. If this curve becomes nearly horizontal for optimal lockbox combinations beyond some number r', then the TC curve, which is almost certainly increasing in r, need not be computed beyond r'. A considerable savings could result when r' is relatively small. Second, when computing the total cost curve, TC, the firm can include search, negotiation, and administration costs not included in the model. In addition, the firm can more easily account for the dependence of lockbox charges on the other bank services it is purchasing. The true costs of the firm's lockbox system are thus more closely approximated when our approach is used. Finally, when lockbox prices change, as they frequently do, the solution does not have to be recomputed from scratch. Instead, only the relatively inexpensive steps two and three need to be reconsidered. This last advantage could represent a considerable savings in both time and money.

Example   Consider a firm that wants to design a lockbox system for the customer regions and dollar amounts shown in Figure 3.2. Because of existing bank relationships, it will select from the set of cities: San Francisco (SF), Chicago (C), Dallas (D), and New York (NY). The mail times and availability times from each customer region to each lockbox site are shown in Figure 3.3. (For simplicity, we assume that

Customer	Mail Times Lockbox Cities				Customer	Availability Times Lockbox Cities			
Group	SF	C	D	NY	Group	SF	C	D	NY
W	1.0	2.0	3.0	3.0	W	1.0	2.0	2.0	3.0
N	3.0	1.0	1.0	3.0	N	2.0	1.0	2.0	2.0
S	3.0	1.0	1.0	3.0	S	2.0	2.0	1.0	2.0
E	3.0	3.0	2.0	1.0	E	3.0	2.0	2.0	1.0

Figure 3.3   Mail and availability times.

internal processing time in the new system is zero.) The firm believes that it will cost $1000 per month to run a 1-lockbox site system and $1800 per month to run a 2-lockbox system. Finally, the firm currently experiences daily float of $4.5 million. This number represents the sum of its mail, processing, and availability float.

To analyze this problem, we construct a float matrix by first summing the mail and availability times between each customer area and potential lockbox site, and then multiplying by the average daily collections. For example, the first element in the float matrix is found by adding the mail time from the West to San Francisco of 1.0 day to the availability time from the West to San Francisco of 1.0 day and then multiplying the sum by the $300,000 per day received from the West; for example, $(1.0 + 1.0) \times 300,000 = \$600,000$ daily float. The result of these calculations is shown in Figure 3.4 below:

The next step is to determine a single lockbox site that produces minimum float. There are four candidates for this lockbox site. To determine the float associated with each potential site, we add the elements in each column. For example, the daily float for San Francisco is $600 + 500 + 1000 + 3000 = 5100$. This corresponds to the assumption that all customer regions are assigned to the San Francisco lockbox.

Performing this analysis for each of the four possible sites, we find that Dallas produces the lowest float value of $4.2 million. Using this site, the firm will save $300,000 in float compared to the current system. If the firm is in the 50% marginal tax bracket and its after tax cost of capital is 10%, we can calculate the net after tax benefit of a 1-lockbox system as follows:

$$\left(\begin{array}{c} \text{float value} \\ \text{per day} \end{array} \times \begin{array}{c} \text{after tax cost} \\ \text{of capital} \end{array} \right) - \left(12 \times \begin{array}{c} \text{monthly operating} \\ \text{cost} \end{array} \right) \times \left(1 - \begin{array}{c} \text{marginal} \\ \text{tax rate} \end{array} \right)$$

which works out to:

$$(\$300,000 \times 0.10) - (12 \times 1000 \times 0.5) = \$24,000 \text{ per year.}$$

In this instance the firm is better off with a 1-lockbox system by some $24,000 per year on an after tax basis.

Is the firm even better off with a 2-lockbox system? To answer this question, we

| Customer | Lockbox Cities | | | |
Group	SF	C	D	NY
W	600	1,200	1,500	1,800
N	500	200	300	500
S	1,000	600	400	1,000
E	3,000	2,500	2,000	1,000
Total	5,100	4,500	4,200	4,300

Figure 3.4   Float Matrix in Thousands of Dollars per Day

evaluate all six possible two-site combinations.[3] Suppose the firm is considering the use of New York and San Francisco as a 2-lockbox system. Each of the four customer regions must be assigned to either San Francisco or New York. A logical rule is to assign each customer region to the site with the minimum float. Using this rule, the float values for each customer region are:

Customer Region	Lockbox Assignment	Float
West	San Francisco	$ 600,000
North	San Francisco	500,000
South	New York	1,000,000
East	New York	1,000,000
		$3,100,000 per day

Performing a similar analysis for each of the remaining five possible two-site combinations, we get the following float values:

San Francisco/New York	$3,100,000
San Francisco/Chicago	3,900,000
San Francisco/Dallas	3,300,000
Chicago/Dallas	3,800,000
Chicago/New York	3,000,000
Dallas/New York	3,200,000

The best two-site combination is Chicago and New York, which reduces the total float to $3 million, for a float savings of $1.5 million. The net after tax benefit of this two-site lockbox system is:

$$(\$1,500,000 \times 0.10) - (12 \times 1800 \times 0.5) = \$139,200 \text{ per year.}$$

Several features of this example are worth highlighting, because they frequently characterize real-world problems as well:

1. The city that was found to be optimal in the 1-lockbox system, Dallas, is not included in the set of cities, Chicago and New York, that are optimal in the 2-lockbox system. Intuitively, this occurs because the best city in a 1-lockbox system needs to be a relatively good collection site for all customer groups, while the best cities in a 2-lockbox system need only be good collection sites for some customer groups. The cities in an optimal 2-lockbox system are good "in combination," but not necessarily good individually.
2. In regard to the analysis of a 2-lockbox system, the float for the second best combination, San Francisco and New York, is almost the same as the float for the

---

[3]For instructional purposes, we evaluate each site one at a time, a method that might be called Complete Enumeration. In practice, one might want to use either an optimization or heuristic algorithm to find the best sites. These are discussed below.

best combination, Chicago and New York. There are many factors not included in the analysis, which may dictate that the firm choose the "second best" combination. These include the existence of credit relationships, the quality of services, and the ability of banks in the different cities to interface with the firm's accounts receivable system.

3. Differences in float savings between lockbox cities or city-pairs may not be as large as the numbers in the example indicate. Most analysts argue that a float difference of ±0.1 days is not statistically significant, because of uncertainty in the mail times and other measurement problems. In this example, with $1 million received each day, a float difference of $30,000 is not significant. Since the Chicago/New York combination shows only $30,000 better float than San Francisco/New York, the two city-pairs are actually equivalent from a statistical point of view.

HEURISTIC SOLUTION PROCEDURES

Because the number of lockbox combinations can be very large in practice (in a system with n lockbox sites, there are $2^n - 1$ possible lockbox combinations), a complete enumeration of all possible lockbox combinations may be infeasible. For this reason, many banks use heuristic algorithms that evaluate only a subset of the total possible lockbox combinations. Because the heuristic algorithms make use of a common sense rule of thumb to decide which lockbox combinations to evaluate, they frequently produce optimal or near-optimal solutions without incurring the expense of searching every possible combination. The two most commonly used heuristic algorithms for evaluating lockbox systems are called the Greedy Algorithm and the Interchange Algorithm. Anyone interested in lockbox analysis should have some insight into how these algorithms work.

The Greedy Algorithm

The Greedy Algorithm was first proposed by Ferdinand K. Levy in 1965.[4] For the problem of finding the best 2-lockbox system, it can be described as follows:

1. Find the best 1-lockbox system by assigning all customers to each lockbox sequentially and calculating the resulting float. The lockbox with the minimum float is the best.
2. Determine whether any of the customer regions should be assigned to the best lockbox. A customer region should be assigned to this lockbox if the float for that customer region cannot be reduced by assigning it to any other lockbox.
3. Remove those customer regions assigned to the best lockbox from further analysis.
4. Find the best lockbox to add to the best 1-lockbox system.
5. The best 2-lockbox system includes the best 1-lockbox and the best lockbox to add to the best 1-lockbox.

---

[4]See Ferdinand K. Levy, "An Application of Heuristic Problem Solving to Accounts Receivable Management," *Management Science,* February, 1966, B236-B244.

Example   For the example discussed above, the float matrix is shown in Figure 3.4. To find the best 1-lockbox system, we proceed as before to add the numbers in each column of the float matrix. We find that Dallas is the best lockbox to have if we can only have one, and the South should be assigned to Dallas because all other assignments for the South have higher float. After assigning the South to Dallas, the new float matrix is:

	SF	C	D*	NY
W	600	1,200	1,500	1,800
N	500	200	300	500
E	3,000	2,500	2,000	1,000

To find the best lockbox to add to Dallas, we evaluate the three possible pairs: San Francisco/Dallas, Chicago/Dallas, and New York/Dallas. Taking the lowest float value from each region and summing, the float associated with these are:

Lockbox Combination	Float/Day
San Francisco/Dallas	$2,900
Chicago/Dallas	3,400
New York/Dallas	2,800

Of these combinations, New York and Dallas have the lowest total float, so they are considered to be the best 2-lockbox system.

Discussion   The principle advantage of the Greedy Algorithm over Complete Enumeration is that it considerably reduces the number of lockbox combinations that have to be evaluated. Using this algorithm, we only have to evaluate three combinations of 2-lockbox systems, whereas using Complete Enumeration we evaluate six. The principle disadvantage is that it may not find the optimal solution. For this example, the optimal 2-lockbox system is Chicago/New York. The Greedy Algorithm never evaluates this optimal combination because, once the first step has been completed, it only evaluates systems including Dallas.

The Interchange Algorithm

Interchange algorithms are heuristic procedures that seek to improve any initial solution through substitution of lockboxes not in the initial solution for those that are in the initial solution. The most commonly used interchange algorithms include both 1-for-1 substitutions and 2-for-2 substitutions. For the problem of finding the best 2-lockbox system, the 1-for-1 interchange algorithm can be described as follows.

1. Start with a randomly selected 2-lockbox solution. Call this the initial solution.
2. Substitute one lockbox not in the solution for each lockbox in the initial solution to

see if float reduction is possible. If the substitution of this lockbox for any of the lockboxes in the initial solution reduces float, make that substitution. Call this new solution the current solution. If no float improvement is found, try substituting one of the other lockboxes not in the current solution for each lockbox in the current solution to see if float reduction is possible. If float reduction is possible, make the substitution and call this the new current solution.
3. Terminate the process when all 1-for-1 substitutions of lockboxes not in the current solution for those in the current solution produce no float reduction.

Example   To find the best 2-lockbox system for the above example, we need a randomly chosen initial solution. Suppose the initial 2-lockbox system is San Francisco and Chicago. We then try to substitute Dallas into the initial solution by substituting it for San Francisco and Chicago one at a time. The results are:

Lockbox Combination	Float/Day
San Francisco/Chicago	$3,900,000
Dallas/Chicago	3,800,000
San Francisco/Dallas	3,300,000

Since the substitution of Dallas for Chicago produces the largest float reduction, we make this substitution. San Francisco and Dallas is now the current solution.

Next we try to substitute New York into the current solution with the result:

Lockbox Combination	Float/Day
San Francisco/Dallas	$3,300,000
New York/Dallas	3,200,000
San Francisco/New York	3,100,000

Since substituting New York for Dallas produces a float reduction, we make this substitution. The current solution is now San Francisco/New York.

Although the two lockbox sites not in the current solution were in previous solutions, we should still try to substitute them into the current solution. This is because they may not have been tried in combination with those now in the current solution. The results of substituting Chicago into the current solution are:

Lockbox Combination	Float/Day
San Francisco/New York	$3,100,000
Chicago/New York	3,000,000
San Francisco/Chicago	3,900,000

This too leads to a float reduction, and so the new current solution is Chicago/New York.

From the results of our complete enumeration, we know that Chicago/New York is indeed the optimal solution. However, the interchange algorithm does not know this, and so it continues to try new substitutions. The reader can easily verify that substituting either San Francisco or Dallas into this current solution produces no further float reduction. The algorithm terminates at this point.

Discussion   For this example, the Interchange Algorithm actually evaluates all six possible 2-lockbox systems. Thus, in this instance, there is no computational savings compared to Complete Enumeration. This result is not typical. In general, the Interchange Algorithm performs exceedingly well both in terms of computational savings and in terms of quality of solution. Its major drawback is that it cannot guarantee that an optimal solution will be found in every case.

Evaluation of Solution Procedures

Since heuristic algorithms cannot guarantee an optimal solution to the Lockbox Location Problem, it is worth investigating how well they work in practice. In their award-winning paper,[5] Corneujols, Fisher, and Nemhauser analyze various exact and approximate algorithms to the Lockbox Location Problem. Their results may be summarized as follows:

1. It is difficult to find an algorithm that always produces an optimal solution to the Lockbox Location Problem in a reasonable amount of computer time. In fact, since the Lockbox Location Problem is NP-complete, there is no known algorithm to the problem with an upper bound on running time that is polynomial in the problem parameters.[6]
2. A theoretical analysis of the worst possible case indicates that heuristic algorithms are capable of producing poor solutions.
3. However, experience with some reasonably realistic data sets indicates that heuristic algorithms produce very close-to-optimal solutions in practice. For instance, the 1-for-1 interchange heuristic achieves the optimal solution in two-thirds of the sample problems, and is never more than 3% away from the optimal solution in the remaining sample problems.

The Corneujols, Fisher, and Nemhauser conclusions on the value of heuristic procedures versus optimization algorithms are further supported by test results obtained by Baker, Maier, and Vander Weide.[7] These authors test a sequential heuristic procedure that obtains an initial solution from a dynamic programming algorithm, and improves

[5]G. Corneujols, M. L. Fisher, and G. L. Nemhauser, "Location of Bank Accounts to Optimize Float: An Analytic Study of Exact and Approximate Algorithms," *Management Science,* April 1977, 789–810.
[6]In essence, this means that it is generally not possible to put an upper limit on the amount of computer time it will take to solve this problem.
[7]K. R. Baker, S. F. Maier, and J. H. VanderWeide, "Heuristic Methods for Solving the Lockbox Location Problem and Related Location-Allocation Problems," Working Paper, Fuqua School of Business Administration, Duke University, September 1975.

this initial solution with 1-for-1 and 2-for-2 interchanges of lockboxes not in the solution with those currently in the solution. In no case did this heuristic procedure fail to obtain the optimal solution.

Given the above results, the analyst can be assured that existing algorithms, both heuristic and optimization, will find the set of lockbox sites that minimize total system costs. As we shall see below, the problems of data accuracy are far more severe than those associated with the quality of algorithms.

ADDITIONAL ISSUES

The above discussion glossed over a number of important issues in solving the Lockbox Location Problem. These involve the choice of homogeneous customer groups, the measurement of mail and availability times, and the estimate of the amount of incoming funds from each group i.

Homogeneous Customer Groups

Since the mathematical formulation does not address the issue of how to form homogeneous customer groups, the analyst must employ his judgement to design groups that are homogeneous relative to mail and availability times, and, at the same time, are not so refined or complex to substantially increase the cost of analysis.

At one extreme, the analyst can simply group customers by states or, possibly, two-digit zip code areas. Simple groupings such as these significantly reduce the cost of collecting mail times and availability times, and by keeping the number of customer groups to a minimum, are both easy to analyze and implement.

The primary disadvantage of grouping customers by states or two-digit zip codes is that it ignores the sometimes substantial differences between customers within the group. Such differences are especially pronounced when some of the firm's customers draw checks on banks outside of the area where they reside. Whereas a lockbox located in Los Angeles would no doubt best serve the customer who both mails and draws his checks from this city, a Chicago lockbox could very well be superior for a California customer who draws checks on a North Carolina bank. Differences caused by the use of controlled disbursing cannot be ignored, since recent surveys have shown that more than 70% of the Fortune 500 firms use this practice.[8]

At the other extreme, the analyst can treat each individual customer as a separate customer group. Although this choice has some merit in theory, it is prohibitively expensive because it requires extensive data collection and complex implementation instructions for the firm's accounts receivable department.

A middle ground is to treat some of the firm's largest customers as single-member customer groups and to group all the remaining customers by two- or three-digit zip code areas. This alternative recognizes some of the more significant differences be-

[8]See M. B. Brandon, "Contemporary Disbursement Practices and Products: A Survey," *Journal of Cash Management*, Vol. 2, No. 1, March 1982, 26–39.

tween customers in a state or zip code area, and yet is relatively easy to implement. This alternative also requires a great deal of analyst's judgement.

The analyst's choice of homogeneous customer groups can also have a significant effect in the design of lockbox systems for firms with many divisions. For such firms, it is both economically and administratively expensive to have each division instruct its customers to send remittances to, say, ten lockbox sites. Accordingly, multidivision firms often instruct all customers of smaller divisions to remit to only one of the sites selected. By assigning all customers of this division to a separate customer group, it is possible to consider this practice within the framework of the overall optimization process.

Mail and Availability Times

Mail and availability times play a key role in the analysis of lockbox systems. With regard to these times, the analyst faces several important issues.

1. In comparing the firm's current collection system to the "optimal" lockbox system, the analyst needs to decide whether to use Phoenix-Hecht Surveyed Mail Times or a sample of actual mail times to measure the mail float in the current system. (There is universal agreement that the mail times surveyed by Phoenix-Hecht, Inc., a subsidiary of University Analytics, Inc., are the best and most comprehensive times to use in finding the optimal system.) If the analyst chooses to use actual mail times, he must recognize that there are a great many measurement errors caused by the unscientific nature of the sampling process; for example, the date may have been incorrectly stamped on the envelope, the date may have been stamped on the envelope at a late stage in the mail process, and so on. If he chooses to use Phoenix-Hecht mail times, the analyst must recognize that these were collected under certain ideal circumstances that may not characterize the firm's actual experience. Phoenix-Hecht mail times, for instance, are measured from a central location within each customer region, whereas his customers may not remit from that central location.

2. With regard to availability times, the analyst must first decide whether to use availability times at all. Early implementations of the lockbox model ignored availability times on the grounds that availability differences from city to city were small, since the Federal Reserve guarantees a maximum of two-day availability no matter where a check is deposited. If the analyst decides he wants to include availability times in the analysis, he must choose whether to measure them by quoted Federal Reserve availabilities, city average bank availabilities, or individual bank availabilities. Since 1979, most analysts have relied on individual bank availabilities, a transition that caused significant changes in the solutions found. Individual bank availabilities tend to reduce the optimal number of lockboxes and to change their locations.

3. If the analyst decides to use both mail and availability times, he must also decide how to combine these times into a total collection time. The problem arises because of differences in the units by which mail and availability times are measured.[9]

[9]For an insightful discussion of this issue see R. M. Nauss and R. E. Markland, "Theory and Application of an Optimizing Procedure for Lockbox Location Analysis," *Management Science*, August 1981, 855–865.

Amount of Incoming Funds from Region

To estimate the amount of incoming funds from customer region i, the analyst typically collects a sample of the firm's incoming checks covering a one month period. For the purposes of analysis, the analyst wants to make sure that the sample is representative of the firm's long-run collection experience. Since most firms experience considerable seasonality and frequent changes in customer collection patterns, this is no simple matter.

SUMMARY

The problem of finding the number and location of lockboxes that maximizes the difference between the funds made available by float reduction and the fixed and variable costs of the lockbox system, is called the Lockbox Location Problem. This problem can be formulated in mathematical terms and solved with both heuristic and optimization algorithms. The mathematical formulation, however, ignores several very important problems in data collection. The decisions the analyst makes regarding the design of the data collection process can have a significant impact on the quality of the solutions obtained. Recent improvements in data collection and a better understanding of the consequences of alternative data choices have greatly improved the quality of lockbox system design. The financial manager should be aware of both the economic and judgemental issues in lockbox system design if he wants to improve his firm's collection system.

DISCUSSION QUESTIONS

1. Float is a key concept in our discussion of collection techniques. If a company could somehow eliminate all its float, what would happen? What changes would occur to the balance sheet?
2. What is the difference between how a bank treats an individual and a corporation with respect to availability?
3. Besides float reduction, what advantages might a company get from a lockbox?
4. Why is processing float likely to be much lower in a lockbox processing system than for in-house processing?
5. Why are lockbox cost considerations usually not part of the actual lockbox site selection process?
6. Why is the after-tax cost of capital used in valuing float reduction?
7. Discuss the key assumptions used in formulating the Lockbox Location Problem in mathematical terms.
8. How does the practical reformulation of the Lockbox Location Problem differ from the original problem?
9. What are the major advantages of this reformulation?
10. What is a heuristic solution procedure?

11. What are the advantages of heuristic solution procedures over complete enumeration?
12. What are the major differences between the Interchange Algorithm and the Greedy Algorithm?
13. How well do heuristic procedures work in practice?
14. What are the major choices the analyst can make in designing homogeneous customer groups?
15. Discuss the issues involved in measuring mail and availability time.
16. Discuss the issues involved in estimating the amount of incoming funds from region i.

PROBLEMS

1. What is the value of reducing the mail time by four days on a $10 million check when the cost of capital is 12%?
2. Consider a firm that has credit sales of $542 million per year. Suppose this firm is able to reduce its average collection time from six to three days. If the firm's cost of capital is 15%, what is the annual value of the float reduction?
3. Consider a firm that has credit sales of $425 million per year. Suppose this firm is considering the implementation of a lockbox collection system. It has determined that it can save 1.5 days of collection time through the use of 1 lockbox, 2.0 days of collection time through the use of 2 lockboxes, 2.5 days of collection time through the use of 3 lockboxes, and 2.7 days of collection time through the use of 4 lockboxes. If the firm's cost of capital is 12%, what is the value of implementing a 1-lockbox system, a 2-lockbox system, 3-lockbox system, and a 4-lockbox system.
4. Consider again the firm discussed in Problem 3. Suppose that each lockbox costs $9000 per month to maintain. How many lockboxes should the firm use?
5. Consider a firm that wants to design a lockbox system for the customer regions and dollar amounts shown below.

Amounts Due	
Customer Group	Dollars/Day
1	$300,000
2	100,000
3	200,000
4	500,000

Because of existing bank relationships, it will limit its search for lockbox sites to the following four cities: Los Angeles (L), Chicago (C), Houston (H), and Atlanta (A). The mail times and availability times from each customer region to each lockbox site are:

Customer Group	Mail Times Lockbox Cities				Customer Group	Availability Times Lockbox Cities			
	L	C	H	A		L	C	H	A
W	1.0	2.0	3.0	3.0	W	1.0	2.0	2.0	3.0
N	3.0	1.0	1.0	3.0	N	2.0	1.0	2.0	2.0
S	3.0	1.0	1.0	3.0	S	2.0	2.0	1.0	2.0
E	3.0	3.0	2.0	1.0	E	3.0	2.0	2.0	1.0

The firm's after tax cost of capital is 10%.

(a) Construct a float matrix that the firm could use to determine the optimal set of lockbox cities and the correct customer assignments.

(b) Using the Greedy Algorithm and the above data, determine which are the best two lockbox sites.

(c) Using the 1-for-1 Interchange Algorithm and the above data, determine which are the best two lockbox sites.

(d) What is the value of the float associated with the optimal set of two lockbox sites?

6. Using the above data, write a mathematical expression for the objective of the Revised Lockbox Location Problem. *Hint:* Study Appendix B and assume (1) that the firm currently has no collections—that is, all times associated with the current system are zero—and (2) the goal is to *minimize* total collection float.

7. Using the above data, write a mathematical expression for the constraint that all customer groups must be assigned to at least one lockbox site.

8. Using the above data, write a mathematical expression for the constraint that customer groups cannot be assigned to a "closed" lockbox site.

9. Explain why you did or did not use the cost of capital in the mathematical formulation of the objective of the Revised Lockbox Location Problem.

ADDITIONAL READINGS

1. K. R. Baker, S. F. Maier, and J. H. Vander Weide, "Heuristic Methods for Solving the Lock-Box Location Problem and Related Location-Allocation Problems," Working Paper, Graduate School of Business Administration, Duke University, September 1975.

2. B. M. Brandon, "Contemporary Disbursing Practices and Products: A Survey," *Journal of Cash Management,* Vol. 2, No. 1, March 1982, 26–39.

3. R. L. Bulfin and V. E. Unger, "Computational Experience with an Algorithm for the Lock Box Problem," Proceedings of the National Association of Computing Machinery, 28th National Conference, Atlanta, August, 1973, 16–19.

4. R. F. Calman, *Linear Programming and Cash Management/Cash Alpha,* The MIT Press, Cambridge, Mass., 1968.

5. F. F. Ciochetto, H. S. Swanson, J. R. Lee, and R. E. D. Woosley, "The Lock Box Problem and Some Startling But True Computational Results for Large Scale Systems," Working Paper presented at the National Meeting of the Operations Research Society, April 1972.

6. G. Cornuejols, M. L. Fisher, and G. L. Nemhauser, "Location of Bank Accounts to Optimize Float: An Analytic Study of Exact and Approximate Algorithms," *Management Science*, Vol. 23, No. 8, April 1977, 789–810.

7. D. M. Ferguson and S. F. Maier, "Finding the Real Float-A New Standard for Lockbox Studies," *CASHFLOW*, September/October, 1980, 55–59.

8. B. D. Fielitz and D. L. White, "A Two-Stage Solution Procedure for the Lock Box Location Problem," *Management Science*, Vol. 27, No. 8, August 1981, 881–886.

9. N. C. Hill, W. Sartoris, and D. M. Ferguson, "Corporate Credit Policies and Corporate Payable Policies: Results of Two Surveys," forthcoming in the *Journal of Cash Management*.

10. R. L. Kramer, "Analysis of Lock-Box Locations," *Bankers Monthly Magazine*, Vol. 83, May 1966, 36–40.

11. R. L. Kramer, "Feedback: The Lock Box Location Problem," *Journal of Bank Research*, Vol. 2, Spring 1971.

12. A. Kraus, C. Janssen, and A. K. McAdams, "The Lock-Box Location Problem," *Journal of Bank Research*, Vol. 1, Autumn 1970, 51–58.

13. F. K. Levy, "An Application of Heuristic Problem Solving to Accounts Receivable Management," *Management Science*, Vol. 12, February, 1966, B236–B244.

14. A. K. McAdams, "Critique of: A Lock-Box Model," *Management Science*, Vol. 15, October 1968, B88–90.

15. S. F. Maier and J. H. Vander Weide, "The Lock-Box Location Problem: A Practical Reformulation," *Journal of Bank Research*, Vol. 5, Summer 1974, 92–95.

16. L. P. Mavrides, "An Indirect Method for the Generalized k-Median Problem Applied to Lock-Box Location," *Management Science*, October 1979, 990–996.

17. R. M. Nauss and R. E. Markland, "Real World Experience with an Optimal Lock-Box Location Algorithm," Working Paper presented at the TIMX/ORSA Joint National Meeting, San Francisco, May 1977.

18. R. M. Nauss and R. E. Markland, "Theory and Application of an Optimizing Procedure for Lock-Box Location Analysis," *Management Science*, Vol. 27, August 1981, 855–865.

19. R. J. Shanker and A. A. Zoltners, "An Extension of the Lock-Box Location Problem," *Journal of Bank Research*, Winter, 1972, 62.

20. J. M. Stancill, "A Decision Rule Model for the Establishment of a Lock-Box," *Management Science*, October 1968, 884–887.

21. B. K. Stone, "Lock-Box Selection and Collection System Design: Objective Function Validity," *Journal of Bank Research*, Vol. 10, Winter 1980, 251–254.

22. B. K. Stone, "Break-Even Receivable Size and the Allocation of Receivables to Lock Boxes," Working Paper No. MS-78-1, College of Industrial Management, Georgia Institute of Technology.

23. B. K. Stone, "Zero Balance Banking and Collection System Design in a Divisionalized Firm," Working Paper No. MS-79-10, College of Industrial Management, Georgia Institute of Technology, January 1979.

24. B. K. Stone, "Design of a Receivable Collection System," *Management Science,* Vol. 27, August 1981, 886–880.

APPENDIX A

Mathematical Formulation of the Lockbox Location Problem

The Lockbox Location Problem can be described mathematically as follows:

PROBLEM I

$$\text{Maximize } G = \sum_{i=1}^{m} \sum_{j=1}^{n} A_{ij}x_{ij} - \sum_{j=1}^{n} F_j z_j \tag{3.1}$$

$$\text{subject to } \sum_{j=1}^{n} x_{ij} = 1 \qquad \text{for } i = 1, \ldots, m \tag{3.2}$$

$$x_{ij} \leq z_j \qquad \text{for } i = 1, \ldots, m; j = 1, \ldots, n \tag{3.3}$$

$$x_{ij} \geq 0 \qquad \text{for } i = 1, \ldots, m; j = 1, \ldots, n \tag{3.4}$$

$$z_j = 0 \text{ or } 1 \qquad \text{for } j = 1, \ldots, n \tag{3.5}$$

where

$A_{ij} = \alpha(T_i^* - T_{ij})D_i - C_{ij} = $ the variable net benefits stated in dollars per day obtained from clearing customer group i's checks through lockbox j[10]

α = the firm's opportunity cost of capital

T_{ij} = average mail time in days from group i to lockbox j + average availability time in days from lockbox j to group i's bank

T_i^* = average mail time in days from group i to the firm's main office + average availability time in days from the main office to group i's bank[11]

D_i = total incoming funds from group i

C_{ij} = differential cost of clearing group i's checks through bank j instead of the main office

x_{ij} = one if group i's checks are sent to lockbox j, zero otherwise

---

[10]For the purposes of lockbox analysis, a customer group is any set of customers having reasonably similar mail and availability times, usually this will be all customers in the same state or two-digit zip code area.
[11]At this point, we are assuming that internal processing time is zero.

F_j = the fixed charge per period for maintaining lockbox j

z_j = one if lockbox j is used, zero otherwise

Constraint set (3.2) is used in this formulation to ensure that all checks are assigned to a lockbox, while constraint set (3.3), along with (3.5), is needed to ensure that no check is sent to a "closed" lockbox. (A "closed" lockbox is one that is not in the solution, i.e., $z_j = 0$ for that j.)

APPENDIX B

Mathematical Formulation of The Revised Lockbox Location Problem

The Revised Lockbox Location Problem may be described mathematically as follows:

PROBLEM II

Maximize $G = \sum_i \sum_j A_{ij} x_{ij}$ (3.6)

subject to $\sum_j x_{ij} = 1$ for $i = 1, 2, \ldots, m$ (3.7)

$\sum_i x_{ij} \leq m z_j$ for $j = 1, 2, \ldots, n$ (3.8)

$\sum_j z_j = r$ (3.9)

$x_{ij} \geq 0$ for $i = 1, 2, \ldots, m; j = 1, 2, \ldots, n$ (3.10)

$z_j = 0$ or 1 for $j = 1, 2, \ldots, n$ (3.11)

where

$A_{ij} = \alpha(T_i^* - T_{ij})D_i$ = the benefits stated in dollars per day obtained from clearing group i's checks through lockbox j

r = the number of lockboxes currently being considered from the pool of potential lockbox sites

APPENDIX C

Designing Check Collection Systems: Lockbox Studies

The process of gathering the data, doing the analysis, and making the judgements required to design a lockbox collection system is called a lockbox study. Since the costs of acquiring the requisite data bases and computer software is prohibitively high for a firm doing a single study of its own lockbox needs, lockbox studies are frequently performed by banks for their corporate customers. The corporate financial manager should understand the study process, however, so that she can evaluate the bank's approach and feel comfortable with the results.

STEPS IN THE STUDY PROCESS

A lockbox study includes the following steps:

1. Initial discussion.
2. Data collection and encoding.
3. Current system analysis.
4. First-stage optimization.
5. Refined optimization.
6. Presentation of results.

We shall discuss each of these steps below.

INITIAL DISCUSSION

Before the lockbox study begins, the bank analyst and corporate client should agree on several important issues. First, they should be confident that the study benefits are likely to exceed the study costs. If the average size of the firm's checks is small, its customers are located in a small geographical region surrounding the firm's headquarters, or the firm's collection system was studied within the last year, there is reason to believe that the benefits of a new lockbox study will not justify the costs. The analyst and corporate client should be able to determine this in their initial conversation.

Second, the analyst should find out from the corporate client if there are any restrictions on the firm's potential lockbox sites. Many firms prefer to locate lockboxes at major credit banks. These banks allow them to earn credits on compensating balances held under a loan agreement that may be used to cover some of the costs of the lockbox service. In addition, some firms feel "comfortable" with certain of their current banking relationships and would be reluctant to abandon these relationships without significant offsetting benefits. Firms falling in either of these two categories may want to restrict the set of potential lockbox sites to a subset of all possible sites— that subset which includes the "favored" bank relationships.

Third, the bank analyst and corporate client should agree on how to collect a check sample that is representative of the firm's collection experiences. In making this decision they should consider the following factors:

1. *Seasonality.* If the firm experiences pronounced seasonal patterns in its collections, a sample of checks from any one month may be unrepresentative. Consider a recreational equipment firm that sells rifles and other equipment to hunters during the winter months and fishing/camping equipment during the summer months. Since the geographic distribution of this firm's receivables is likely to change with the season,

the analyst and client should collect a sample that includes checks from several seasons of the year.

2. *Encoding costs.* The cost to the company for encoding the relevant information into computer-readable form and verifying that it is correct is between $.25 and $.50 per check. It is therefore quite possible that an unwarranted proportion of the study cost will come from this source. If 90% of the dollars remitted come from only 10% of the items, the company may be better off encoding just 10% of the total monthly checks.

3. *Outliers.* Mail and availability times may be affected by certain events (e.g., a winter blizzard) that occur only infrequently. The check sample should be collected from a period in which such unusual events did not occur.

4. *Corporate divisions.* Firms that have divisions in different lines of business must decide whether they want the lockbox study to be done on a corporatewide or division-by-division basis. If they decide to do the study on a corporatewide basis, they should take care to collect a sample representative of corporatewide collection patterns. Such a sample would, very likely, contain checks from all of the firm's divisions. If they decide to do the study on a division-by-division basis, they must take care to segregate the sample by division and identify each subsample appropriately.

5. *Large customers.* If the firm has a small number of large customers, whose mail and availability times are significantly different from the average for their geographic region (perhaps because they use remote disbursing), it may be reasonable to treat these large customers as distinct customer groups during the optimization stage of the lockbox study. If so, the collected information has to include the customer names as well as the dollar amounts of each check.

The decisions that the bank analyst and corporate client make during the initial discussion period can have a significant effect on the quality of lockbox system design. Since banks offering lockbox studies differ greatly in the care they give to the initial discussion, the financial manager can frequently choose the best bank to do the study on the basis of initial discussions with several banks.

DATA COLLECTION AND ENCODING

The second step in a lockbox study is to collect a representative sample of remittances and encode the desired data in machine-readable form. If the firm and its bank have taken due care in the initial discussion stage to set the criteria for a representative sample, the actual collection of remittances should be straightforward. Encoding the appropriate data is another matter. It can be a major source of both cost and error in lockbox studies.

The remittance information that needs to be encoded depends on the agreements reached in the initial discussion. At a minimum, the bank should encode information on the firm's customer locations by three-digit zip code and the dollar amount of checks received from each location. For some types of analysis, it is necessary to encode information on the drawee bank, the mail, and receipt dates of each item and the customer name as well.

Cash management consulting firms have developed two interactive computer software programs that significantly reduce the cost of encoding and verifying customer remittance information.[12] The first, called the Input Prompter, has two purposes: it creates a set of control records that specify such parameters as the cost of capital and number of days in the sample period, and tells the program which optimization runs are to be performed and which reports are to be printed. It also checks for many common types of error that occur in these records. The Input Prompter produces a report indicating each item containing an error together with its sequence number in the check sample. The analyst can then correct errors through an on-line text editor.

The second program, called the Parser, produces a listing of the firm's customers in dollar-descending order and assigns customer numbers, subsequently used to control the lockbox model's individual customer optimization features, to each customer in the remittance sample. The Parser can be accessed through a computer terminal by a program called the Parser Prompter, which allows the analyst to check the accuracy of the names and to correct for any inconsistencies in the name field.

CURRENT SYSTEM ANALYSIS

The next step in a lockbox study is called Current System Analysis. The purpose of this step is threefold: to verify that the check sample is indeed representative of the firm's collection experience, to measure the float in the current system, and to determine if the customers in state or zip code areas have reasonably similar mail and availability times.

Profile of Check Sample

To verify that the check sample is representative of the firm's collection experience, the analyst needs to obtain a profile of the data contained in the sample. The typical lockbox analysis program provides this profile in the form of a series of frequency distributions, including the distribution of remittances by day and date, the geographic distribution of remittances by mail point, the geographic distribution of remittances by drawee bank location, and the distribution of receivables by dollar amounts. The analyst should review the information summarized by these frequency distributions with the corporate client to verify its consistency with the client's knowledge of the current system. If the client feels that the sample is not representative of the firm's current system, it may not be worthwhile to continue to the optimization stage in the analysis. Instead, the analyst should attempt to collect a new sample that *is* representative of the firm's current collection experience.

Current System Float

The second purpose of the current system analysis is to estimate current system float. Since current system float serves as the benchmark for evaluating the benefits of a

[12]The lockbox analysis model developed by University Analytics, Inc., is our reference point throughout this chapter. The Input Prompter and the Parser are part of the University Analytics lockbox model. The University Analytics model is used by most major commercial banks nationwide.

redesigned collection system, it is important that the analyst attempt to measure current system float as accurately as possible. The lockbox analysis model offers three alternatives: Current System-Actual, Current System-Scheduled, and Current System-Optimal. Although all three of these current system float measures may be used as a benchmark for measuring the benefits of a new lockbox system, most banks make the comparison on the basis of Current System-Scheduled, since this treats mail times in the same way they are treated in the optimization stage.

Current System–Actual The Current System—Actual reports calculate the mail time based upon the actual receivable data sample. The difference between the receipt date and the mail date is used to compute the number of days for each item. This is converted to the float dimension by multiplying by the dollar amount of each check and then dividing by the number of days in the sample period. The clearing time is taken from the lockbox program data base and the processing float is user specified.

Although the Current System-Actual float calculations are intuitively appealing, they have several serious drawbacks. First, the mail time in the receivable data sample is keyed off the mail date on the customer's remittance envelope and the deposit date stamped on the back of the check. This date may be a faulty measure of when the item was actually mailed, since the postal system does not always cancel envelopes at the first mail station. In addition, it is well known that customers frequently predate meter envelopes so that they can be eligible for discounts.

Current System—Scheduled The Current System-Scheduled uses the Phoenix-Hecht mail time study to measure the mail time between the sending and receiving sites. Processing float and clearing float are calculated the same way as in the Actual System.

Current System—Optimal The Optimal System uses the same mail times, processing float, and clearing times used in the Scheduled System. The only difference is that customer areas are reassigned to the existing lockbox sites that minimize float. Because it is frequently less costly to simply reassign customers to existing lockbox sites than to negotiate agreements at new lockbox banks, the analyst is frequently interested in comparing the float in the Current System-Optimal to the Current System-Scheduled.

Homogeneous Customer Group

The third purpose of current system analysis is to examine if there are any dissimilarities in mail and availability times within the usual state or two-digit zip code customer areas that may be of sufficient magnitude to affect the optimization. The analyst does this in two ways. First, by matching mail point and drawee bank locations, he examines whether there is a significant amount of remote disbursing being done by the firm's customers. If there is, the analyst will realize that the optimization program may produce anamolous results that need to be explained to the corporate client. One such result is the assignment of a customer region to other than the closest lockbox. Second, the analyst can examine the activities of the firm's largest customers to see if there is anything unique about their mail and clearing times. If there is, he may want to treat the customers as separate customer regions in the optimization stage.

INITIAL OPTIMIZATION

The initial optimization is the next stage in the lockbox study process. As noted in this chapter, the usual approach is to find the optimal set of lockboxes sequentially beginning with 1 open, then 2 open, and so on. The float values for the optimal set of lockboxes are then compared to the float in the current system to determine the float savings associated with different numbers of lockboxes in the collection system. Finally, the value of the float savings is compared to the cost of the lockbox system to determine the recommended solution.

In addition to producing solution values for the optimal 1 open system, the optimal 2 open system, and so on, the initial optimization should produce information on alternative 1 or 2 open lockbox systems that are very close to the optimal system in terms of float savings, but may be more satisfactory to the customer on the basis of nonquantifiable factors such as the maintenance of a current bank relationship or availability of credit lines.

REFINED OPTIMIZATION

After the initial optimization is completed, the analyst may want to perform additional runs of the lockbox program in which the search is restricted to less than the full complement of available sites or certain sites are blocked into the solution. For example, he may want to instruct the program to select the best 3-site system from a subset of 15 (where the 15 sites are preselected from a universe of as many as 107 sites) and also specify that a particular city (say New York) be one of the 3 sites selected. These additional runs allow the analyst to implicitly consider certain cost factors that are not included in the lockbox model.

An important part of the refined optimization is an analysis of whether the firm's large customers should be treated separately for purposes of optimization. The model should produce a set of reports that compare the float that can be gained or lost from various treatments of the large customer set. For example, a company might originally be assigned, along with other firms in its area, to a lockbox in Chicago, producing a float value for them of 3.35 days. If the same company were assigned on an individual basis, however, it might be assigned to Charlotte, producing a float value of 2.83 days. Thus, there is some benefit to treating this company on an individual company basis.

PRESENTATION OF RESULTS

For the purpose of presenting the results to the corporate customer, it is helpful to have a simple summary of the various optimization runs that were tried and a comparison of each optimization to the current system.

SUMMARY

Since the cost of doing a lockbox study are prohibitively high for a single firm studying its own collection system, most financial managers obtain studies from banks who specialize in this activity. To help the financial manager understand and evaluate the bank's approach, we have outlined the steps a lockbox study bank might follow in the study process. The discussion highlights the importance of good data, knowledge of the firm's current banking relationships, and analyst judgement in designing a lockbox collection system.

DISCUSSION QUESTIONS

1. What is the purpose of the initial discussion stage of the lockbox study?
2. Why would a firm place any restrictions on the lockbox sites it was willing to use?
3. Under what conditions is it misleading to take a check sample from just one month in doing a lockbox study?
4. What special issues arise in lockbox studies for firms with many divisions?
5. Under what conditions is it appropriate to sample only a fraction of the firm's remittances?
6. What effect do large customers have on a design of a lockbox study?
7. What kind of data does the analyst need to collect in doing a lockbox study?
8. Describe the Input Prompter and its role in performing studies.
9. Describe the Parser and its role in performing studies.
10. Why does the analyst want to study the firm's current lockbox system when the goal is to find the best lockbox system?
11. What is the difference between the Current System-Actual, Current System-Scheduled, and Current System-Optimal measures of current system float?
12. How can the analyst determine whether the firm's customers are practicing remote disbursing?
13. Discuss how homogeneous customer groups are chosen.
14. Why would the analyst want to perform more than one optimization run of the lockbox program?
15. Discuss what factors the analyst should consider in making a final recommendation in a lockbox study.

CHAPTER 4

Disbursement Site Selection

Financial managers have found that they can increase the amount of funds available for investment by selecting disbursement sites that extend the delay between the time the firm mails the check and the time the check is presented for payment. Although this practice is discouraged by the Federal Reserve System, it can yield significant benefits. This chapter discusses the many factors that affect the financial manager's choice of disbursement sites, and presents a number of models that help him choose the "best" sites.

DISBURSEMENT FLOAT

The delay between the time the financial manager places the check in the mail and the time the check is presented to the firm's bank is composed of three elements: mail time, internal processing time, and presentation time. Mail time is the time it takes for the check to reach the recipient; internal processing time is the time it takes the recipient to deposit the check; and presentation time is the time it takes (from the time of deposit) for the check to be presented to the drawee bank for collection. For later reference, we note that presentation time can itself be broken into two elements: availability time and clearing system slippage. The latter distinction recognizes that the deposit bank's availability schedule may not correspond to the time it actually takes to present the check to the drawee bank.

With these delays in mind, we present three definitions of disbursement float. The set of actions the financial manager takes to increase the amount of funds available for investment depends on which definition he adopts. (Since the amount of dollars being disbursed is constant, it is convenient to express these definitions in units of days rather than dollar days.)

Mail Plus Presentation Time   Disbursement float may be defined as the sum of mail and presentation time. This definition recognizes that the financial manager can extend *both* the mail time and the presentation time of her check. Mail time can be extended by sending the check from a distant office, while presentation time can be extended by writing the check on a distant bank.

In practice most financial managers feel uncomfortable with this definition of disbursement float. First, it makes sense only if the vendor uses the mail date to determine when an item is paid. This is by no means universal practice. Second, extending mail time is such a blatant form of float extension that most vendors will not accept this practice for long. They will either raise the price of the product or change the terms of payment. Thus, the benefits of extending mail time cannot be expected to last for long.

Presentation Time   Disbursement float is most commonly defined as the presentation time on the check. This definition recognizes that the financial manager can disburse from distant banks. It is at the heart of most disbursement studies performed by major banks.

Availability time   Disbursement float may also be defined as the availability time granted to the firm's vendor. This definition recognizes that clearing system slippage is an unstable component of disbursement float, and that financial managers may want to choose disbursement banks that maximize availability time, rather than the sum of availability time and clearing system slippage. The financial manager should be aware, however, that extending availability time may lead to a deterioration in vendor relations.

OBTAINING VALUE FROM DISBURSEMENT FLOAT

The financial manager can only obtain value from disbursement float if he is able to earn interest on the additional funds released by float extension. Since the financial manager does not want to risk having checks returned for "insufficient funds," obtaining value is not as easy as it may at first seem. In practice, it is obtained in one of two ways: forecasting and use of a zero balance account.

Zero Balance Account   To allow firms to obtain value from disbursement float, some banks offer a service known as the externally funded zero balance account (ZBA). The bank offering this service agrees to notify the firm by a certain time each day of the total checks it has received for presentation. It agrees to honor these checks as long as the firm can fund the account with immediately available funds—that is, by wire transfer of funds from another bank or by a simple transfer of funds from an "interest earning" account in the same bank.

For this service to work effectively, the firm's bank must receive a large proportion of presentments early in the morning. This is most likely for banks that receive presentments only from the Federal Reserve, since the Federal Reserve usually makes its check presentments (called "cash letters") before 6:00 A.M. For banks that receive checks directly from other banks (i.e., accept "direct sends") this is rarely true, because these directly sent checks are timed to meet late in the day availability cut offs. If the firm's bank does not receive a large proportion of presentments early in the morning, the firm will have to maintain a buffer stock of cash in the disbursement account to cover checks presented later in the day. The higher this buffer stock is the lower are the benefits from disbursement float extension.

DISBURSEMENT SITE SELECTION PROBLEM

Our discussion of the Disbursement Site Selection Problem begins with an analysis of a simple "pure case" firm that desires to select sites that maximize presentation time. Assume that this firm has vendors in the North (N), South (S), East (E) and West (W), and that the following payments are owed to vendors in each of these areas:

Region	Dollars/Day
N	$200,000
S	100,000
E	175,000
W	150,000

Suppose that our firm has three choices of drawee bank locations: Missoula, Montana; Lubbock, Texas; and Chapel Hill, North Carolina. The presentation times from each vendor region to these three drawee banks are:

	Drawee Bank		
	M	**L**	**C**
N	2.3	2.5	3.8
S	3.2	2.0	2.3
E	4.4	3.7	1.6
W	1.9	2.2	4.9

Multiplying these presentation times by the amounts owed to vendors in each region produces the disbursement float matrix shown below:

Disbursement Float Matrix in Dollars Per Day

	Drawee Bank		
	M	**L**	**C**
N	460,000	500,000	760,000
S	320,000	200,000	230,000
E	770,000	647,500	280,000
W	285,000	330,000	735,000

What is the best set of disbursement sites for this firm? To answer this question, we proceed as we did in Chapter 3 to find the one best site, the two best sites, and the three best sites sequentially.

To find the 1-best disbursement site, we calculate the disbursement float associated with each site under the assumption that it is the only one used. The results are:

Analysis of 1-Best Disbursement Site

Drawee Bank	**Float**
M	1,835,000
L	1,677,500
C	2,005,000

where the $1,835,000 disbursement float associated with Missoula is the sum of the float figures shown in the first column of the disbursement float matrix above, the $1,677,500 float figure for Lubbock is the sum of the second column and the $2,005,000 float figure for Chapel Hill is the sum of the third column. Clearly, Chapel Hill is the best disbursement site to use, if the firm can use only one.

To determine the 2-best disbursement sites, we calculate the float associated with all three combinations of two sites: Missoula/Lubbock, Missoula/Chapel Hill, and Lubbock/Chapel Hill. In performing these calculations, we assign vendor regions to that disbursement site in each pair with the largest disbursement float. The results are:

Analysis of 2-Best Disbursement Sites

Sites	**Float**	**Assignments**
M,L	$1,920,000	N,W–L; S,E–M
M,C	2,585,000	N,W–C; S,E–M
L,C	2,372,500	N,S,W–C; E–L

Evidently, Missoula/Chapel Hill is the best 2-site combination.

The analysis of the 3-best disbursement system is relatively simple, since there is only one such system. In calculating the float of this system, we have to be sure to assign vendor regions to those disbursement sites with the largest float. The results are:

Analysis of 3-Best Disbursement Sites

Sites	Float	Assignments
M,L,C	$2,585,000	N,W–C; S,E–M

From this analysis we reach the following conclusions.

1. A three-site disbursement system is certainly nonoptimal, since it yields no additional float benefits over a two-site disbursement system.
2. The decision to use either a one- or two-site disbursement system depends on both the opportunity cost of capital and the fixed costs of using the second site. (Unlike in the lockbox problem, the option of using a zero-site system is infeasible.) If the firm's opportunity cost of capital is 10%, then the value of the additional float obtained in a two-site system is $58,000. As long as the fixed cost of opening the second site is less than this value, the firm should employ a two-site disbursement system consisting of Missoula and Chapel Hill.

MATHEMATICAL FORMULATION

The Disbursement Site Selection Problem of our ''pure case'' firm was solved by enumerating all of the possible site combinations and evaluating the float associated with each. This alternative is not available for disbursement site selection problems of realistic size, so the financial manager will have to employ either heuristic methods or an optimization algorithm. In the latter case, the mathematical formulation of the Disbursement Site Selection Problem found in Appendix A is useful.[1]

PROBLEMS WITH THIS FORMULATION

There are several problems with the mathematical formulation of The Disbursement Site Selection Problem shown in Appendix A that make it impractical for implementation purposes.[2] These problems are discussed below:

---

[1]The reader should compare this formulation to that for the Lockbox Location Problem found in Appendix A of Chapter 3.

[2]Even though the formulation is impractical in our opinion, we present it here because it is still used by some banks and it is the original formulation found in the academic literature. (See R. J. Shanker and A. A. Zoltners, ''The Corporate Payments Problem,'' *Journal of Bank Research.* Spring 1972, 47–53.)

Quality of Data

Many of the same data issues that arise in the Lockbox Location Problem arise in the Disbursement Site Selection Problem as well. First, the fixed and variable costs of setting up disbursement systems are hard to measure and the value of control and float extension far overshadows small cost differences that exist between banks. Moreover, as long as the payment system remains primarily paper based, the firm must write its checks on at least one bank. The elective feature of a lockbox is not a consideration when setting up a disbursement system.

Second, clearing time surveys are not as accurate as the mail and availability time surveys used in the Lockbox Location Problem. This basic fuzziness of the database has discouraged analysis, and made much of the existing analysis suspect. The major banks that do disbursing analysis report two to four times as many lockbox studies performed as disbursement studies. This fact is surprising when one considers that all firms make disbursements, while only some firms use lockboxes.

Finally, it should be noted that the same problems in defining homogeneous vendor groups exist here as they did in the lockbox problem. Consequently, studies are performed in which vendors are grouped by states, zip codes and individually isolated. In addition, there is greater sophistication in handling individual vendors than in handling individual customers; some of the more advanced disbursement control systems assign individual vendors on a check-by-check basis.

Federal Reserve Policies

The solutions to the original formulation of the Disbursement Site Selection Problem frequently produce an increase in "clearing system slippage." Clearing system slippage is defined as the difference between the clearing time experienced by the check issuer and the availability time granted to the check depositor. The greater is this number, the greater the difficulty the clearing agent, principally the Federal Reserve, is having in moving checks through the system. It is argued that the Federal Reserve will concentrate on the points that have large slippage in its efforts to discourage remote disbursing and to reduce its own Federal Reserve float. Its activity in reducing Federal Reserve float has been very well publicized. In 1979 Fed float stood at 6.7 billion dollars on an average daily basis, while in 1982 it averaged less than 2 billion dollars per day.

An attempt to include in the analysis the risk that the Federal Reserve will further reduce clearing system slippage is described in Ferguson and Maier [10]. This paper suggests that the concept of the Efficient Frontier from Portfolio Theory can be applied to measure the risk/return trade-off faced by the corporate financial manager as he designs his disbursement system. Nine of the nation's leading cash management consulting banks have adopted this technology as their consulting approach.

Credit Problems

Remote cities such as Helena, Montana, Reno, Nevada, and Midland, Texas frequently appear in the solution to the Disbursement Site Selection Problem. Unfortunately, these cities are not always well suited as banking locations. For example, a firm will normally want its disbursing bank to be part of its credit group. This is because if for any reason there is a failure to fund the disbursing account, the disbursement bank can use its already preauthorized credit lines to extend credit to the firm and not have to return the items marked "insufficient funds," a situation most companies would consider unacceptable. However, banks are restricted by the Federal Reserve to lend no more than 25% of their equity capital to any one customer. Since banks in cities such as Helena and Reno have a small equity base, they cannot extend sufficient credit to fund the disbursements of large firms.

Vendor Ill Will

Attempts to implement the solutions to the Disbursement Site Selection Problem may lead to deteriorating relationships with the firm's vendors or creditors. More than one firm has found that its vendors refuse to grant a discount for prompt payment when it uses a remote disbursement location. In one celebrated case, Merrill Lynch was sued by customers who were unable to get prompt refunds from security transactions. (Merrill Lynch had a practice of paying East Coast customers with checks drawn on West Coast banks and West Coast customers with checks drawn on East Coast banks.)

THE EFFICIENT FRONTIER APPROACH

The Efficient Frontier Approach allows the analyst to deal directly with the above problems in disbursement site selection modeling. It recognizes the risks in establishing a disbursement bank system whose benefits stem primarily from clearing system slippage, at a time when the Federal Reserve is dedicated to eliminating clearing system slippage; it recognizes the potential problems of "criss-cross" vendor assignments (remember Merrill Lynch); and it recognizes the credit problems of some banks offering remote disbursing services.

In the Efficient Frontier Approach, the disbursement site selection problem is reformulated as shown in Appendix B. The primary difference between this and the formulation shown in Appendix A is the presence of a parameter λ that allows the financial manager to obtain alternative solutions, depending on the weight given to the objective of maximizing presentation time and the weight given to the objective of simply maximizing availability time. With $\lambda = 1$, the problem becomes just the presentation time maximization problem described above. With $\lambda = 0$, the problem is reduced to the maximization of availability time. This corresponds to the position that the risk associated with clearing system slippage is such that it should be ignored in the design of disbursing systems. An even more radical position occurs when $\lambda = -\infty$, a case where the objective becomes minimize clearing system slippage at all costs. In practice, most firms would place positive value on clearing system slippage, since it still provides possible float benefit, albeit at greater risk than availability float. Therefore, we would expect most firms to choose an optimal availability—slippage tradeoff corresponding to a value of λ between 0 and 1.

Vendor Assignment Rules

In the original formulation of the Disbursement Site Selection Problem, vendors are assigned to the disbursing site with the largest presentation time float. As noted earlier, this approach frequently produces unacceptable solutions. The Efficient Frontier Approach to the Disbursement Site Selection Problem allows the analyst to choose one of several alternative vendor assignment rules. These are noted briefly below.

1. *Closest disbursement site:* Vendors are assigned to the geographically closest disbursement site.
2. *Minimum clearing system slippage.* Vendors are assigned to the disbursement site with minimum clearing system slippage.
3. *Specified distance.* Vendors are assigned to the disbursing site that maximizes presentation time without exceeding a specified distance.
4. *Maximization of presentation time subject to restrictions.* Vendors are assigned to the disbursing site that maximizes presentation time subject to a user specified restriction. Such restrictions might include banks located in the same federal reserve district or a specially designated set of banks.
5. *Presentation target.* Vendors are assigned to the disbursing site that is closest to a user specified presentation time target.

These restrictions tend to reduce the risk of unacceptable disbursement site solutions by reducing both clearing system slippage and the likelihood of criss-cross vendor assignments.

CASE STUDY

The case study described in this section is based upon an actual disbursement site location problem faced by a major corporation. The company disburses on average $20 million per month and currently disburses all of its checks against a bank account located in Kansas City, Missouri. Using Kansas City, the company has average presentation time of 1.38 days and has clearing system slippage of .18 days.

After discussions with the company, it was determined that the firm only wished to consider disbursing from banks with whom it had current relationships. In order to achieve the control aspect of disbursing, however, the firm would permit the use of affiliates of its credit banks and/or remote branches. Cities selected as appropriate for consideration as disbursing sites for this company were: Rochester, New York; Waukesha, Wisconsin; Knoxville, Tennessee; San Francisco, California; Lukfin, Texas; and Philadelphia, Pennsylvania. The Rochester, New York site is an upstate branch of a major New York bank, while the Lufkin, Texas site is an affiliate of a major Houston bank. Using this set of cities, the model mapped the efficient frontier for one-site systems. This is shown in Figure 4.1. (For illustrative purposes, we have mapped the efficient frontier using a vertical dimension that is the sum of presentation time and mail time. Note, however, that mail time was held constant at 2.93 days.) The efficient frontier is composed of Lufkin, Knoxville, Waukesha, and Rochester. Also

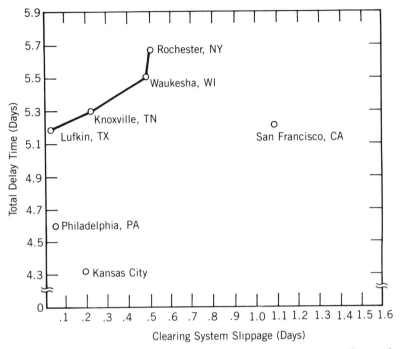

Figure 4.1 Efficient frontier total delay time versus check clearing system slippage for alternative drawee banks.

note that Lufkin, Texas is superior to the current Kansas City disbursing site in that it has both higher presentation time and lower clearing system slippage.

In Figure 4.2, we show the efficient frontier for a two-site system. This figure also illustrates the use of the vendor assignment rule of minimizing geographic distance. The efficient frontier created by the use of these two-site systems is for some points inferior to that created by using only a single disbursing site. This reflects the inherent disadvantage of using minimization of geographic distance as the vendor assignment rule.

In Figure 4.3, we illustrate the efficient frontier for two-site systems when the vendor assignment rule is maximization of presentation time. As might be anticipated, this efficient frontier shows somewhat higher presentation time than the efficient frontier using minimization of geographic distance. A particularly interesting point to examine for comparison is the two-site system composed of Lufkin, Texas and Rochester, New York. In Figure 4.2, Lufkin, Texas and Rochester, New York have a total delay time of 5.18 days and a clearing system slippage of 0.07 days. In Figure 4.3, Lufkin–Rochester shows a total delay time of 5.71 days and a 0.49 days clearing system slippage. This difference is solely attributable to the use of different vendor assignment rules.

It is interesting to examine what would occur if, instead of using the set of six selected sites, one examined the entire universe of sites surveyed in the Phoenix–Hecht

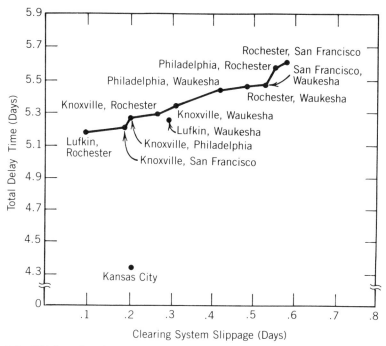

Figure 4.2 Efficient frontier total delay time versus check clearing system slippage for alternative drawee banks.

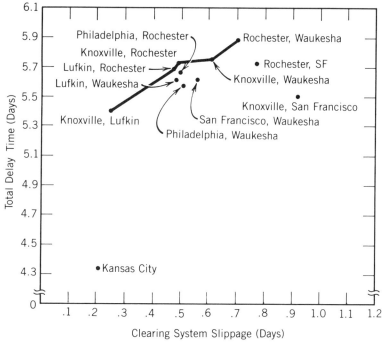

Figure 4.3 Efficient frontier total delay time versus check clearing system slippage for alternative drawee banks.

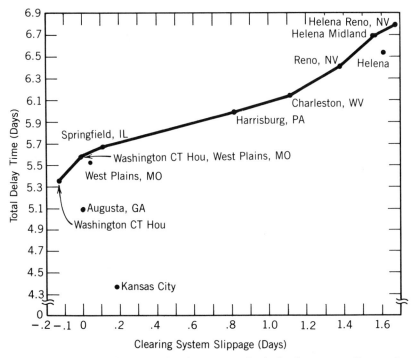

Figure 4.4 Efficient frontier total delay time versus check clearing system slippage for alternative drawee banks.

clearing study. The efficient frontier plotted in this case is shown in Figure 4.4. In this figure, the combination site of Helena, Montana and Reno, Nevada achieves the highest presentation time for a two-site system, and Helena achieved the highest presentation time for a one-site system. If the company's disbursement system had been analyzed under the old approach of purely maximizing presentation time, then sites such as Helena or Helena–Reno might very well have been selected. Notice, however, the extremely high level of clearing system slippage and risk that such a combination would have entailed.

SUMMARY

The original formulation of the Disbursement Site Selection Problem ignores recent changes in Federal Reserve policy toward remote disbursing, vendor ill-will, and the credit problems of some banks offering remote disbursing services. In addition to discussing these problems, this chapter presents an alternative approach to disbursement site selection that allows the manager to trade-off the risks and benefits of various disbursement systems. A case study is used to illustrate how this approach can be applied in practice.

DISCUSSION QUESTIONS

1. Discuss the various delays that occur from the time the financial manager places the check in the mail to the time the check is presented to the firm's bank for payment.
2. Discuss three alternatives for defining disbursement float.
3. How can the firm take advantage of disbursement float?
4. How does the disbursement site selection problem differ from the lockbox location problem?
5. Discuss several rules that may be used to assign vendor regions to disbursement sites and discuss the advantages and disadvantages of each.
6. Under what conditions would a 2-best disbursement site solution produce worse float than a 1-best site solution?
7. Discuss the problems associated with the initial formulation of the disbursement site selection problem.
8. What is the current status of Federal Reserve attempts to eliminate Federal Reserve float?
9. Why is it sometimes infeasible to disburse from a remote bank that produces optimal float characteristics?
10. Describe the Efficient Frontier Approach to the disbursement site selection problem.
11. Describe the vendor assignment rules used in the efficient frontier approach.
12. Discuss what factors the analyst should consider in making a final recommendation in a disbursement study.

PROBLEMS

1. Suppose that the Sun Flower Seeds Corporation (SFS) has vendors in the North (N), South (S), East (E), and West (W), and that the following payments are owed to vendors in each of these areas:

Region	Dollars/Day
N	$125,000
S	250,000
E	200,000
W	175,000

Suppose also that SFS has three choices of drawee bank locations: Boise (B), El Paso (E) and Rochester (R). The presentation times and clearing system slippages from each vendor region to these three drawee banks are:

	Presentation Times				Clearing System Slippage		
	Drawee Bank				Drawee Bank		
	B	E	R		B	E	R
N	2.4	2.7	2.3	N	.4	1.7	1.3
S	3.7	2.2	2.9	S	1.7	1.2	1.9
E	4.3	3.8	1.7	E	2.3	1.8	.7
W	1.8	2.5	3.6	W	.8	.5	1.6

If SFS's goal is to maximize presentation time and it has no constraints on vendor assignments, what is the best set of two disbursement sites?

2. How does the solution to Problem 1 change if SFS's goal is to maximize availability time rather than presentation time?

3. How does the solution to Problem 1 change if SFS has a policy of only using drawee banks that are in the same region of the country as the vendor?

ADDITIONAL READINGS

1. M. B. Brandon, "Contemporary Disbursing Practices and Products: A Survey," *Journal of Cash Management*, Vol. 2., No. 1, March 1982, 26–39.

2. P. Coldwell, "Remarks," Bank Administration Institute Conference on Contemporary Issues in Cash Management, New Orleans, September 13, 1979.

3. D. M. Ferguson and S. F. Maier, "By Any Other Name . . . Controlled Disbursing in the New Environment," *CASHFLOW*, May 1981, 31–35.

4. D. M. Ferguson and S. F. Maier, "Disbursement System Design for the 1980s," *Journal of Cash Management*, Vol. 2, No. 4, November 1982, 56–69.

5. L. J. Gitman, D. K. Forrester, and J. R. Forrester, Jr., "Maximizing Cash Disbursement Float," *Financial Management*, Summer 1976, 15–24.

6. T. O. Johnson, "Operations Research Techniques in Corporate Cash Management—Cash Disbursement Analysis," paper presented at the Tenth American Meeting, The Institute of Management Sciences, Atlanta, Georgia, October 1969.

7. S. F. Maier and J. H. Vander Weide, "A Unified Location Model for Cash Disbursements and Lock-Box Collections," *Journal of Bank Research*, Summer 1976, 166–172.

8. R. J. Shanker and A. A. Zoltners, "The Corporate Payments Problem." *Journal of Bank Research*, Spring 1972, 47–53.

9. *Wall Street Journal*, December 18, 1978, 14.

APPENDIX A

Mathematical Formulation of The Disbursement Site Selection Problem

The Disbursement Site Selection Problem may be described mathematically as follows:

$$\text{Maximize} \sum_{i=1}^{m} \sum_{j=1}^{n} \alpha \, A_{ij} x_{ij} - \sum_{j=1}^{n} F_j z_j - \sum_{i=1}^{m} \sum_{j=1}^{n} C_{ij} x_{ij}$$

$$\text{subject to} \sum_{j=1}^{n} x_{ij} = 1 \qquad \text{for all } i \tag{4.1}$$

$$\sum_{i=1}^{m} x_{ij} \le M z_j \qquad \text{for all } j \tag{4.2}$$

$$\sum_{j=1}^{n} z_j \le p \tag{4.3}$$

$$0 \le x_{ij} \le 1 \qquad \text{for all } i \text{ and } j \tag{4.4}$$

$$z_j = 0 \text{ or } 1 \qquad \text{for all } j \tag{4.5}$$

where

A_{ij} = the presentation time (measured in units of dollar days) when checks to vendor group i are disbursed from bank j

C_{ij} = the variable cost of processing group i's checks through bank j

α = the firm's opportunity cost of capital

F_j = the fixed cost of disbursing from bank j

x_{ij} = 1 if vendor group i is assigned to bank j, 0 if otherwise

z_j = 1 if disbursement bank j is used; 0 if otherwise

m = the number of vendor groups

n = the number of disbursement banks

p = the number of disbursement banks allowed to be open

In this formulation the objective is to maximize the interest earned on the dollar float minus the fixed and variable costs of the disbursement system. Constraint set (4.1) is needed to ensure that all checks owed to creditor group j are processed, while constraint sets (4.2) and (4.5) are needed to ensure that all disbursement activities occur at "open" banks. The constraint set (4.3) places an upper bound on the number of disbursement sites that may be open. The parameter p would normally be varied from one to the maximum number of sites the firm was willing to use.

APPENDIX B

Mathematical Formulation of The Efficient Frontier Approach

The Efficient Frontier Approach may be described mathematically as follows:

$$\text{Maximize } \sum_i \sum_j \alpha[A_{ij} + \lambda S_{ij})x_{ij} - \Sigma_j F_j z_j$$

$$\text{subject to } \sum_j x_{ij} = 1 \qquad \text{for all } i$$

$$\sum_i x_{ij} \leq Mz_j \qquad \text{for all } j$$

$$\sum_j z_j \leq p$$

$$0 \leq x_{ij} \leq 1 \qquad \text{for all } i \text{ and } j$$

$$z_j = 0 \text{ or } 1 \qquad \text{for all } j$$

where

A_{ij} = the availability granted to vendor group i (measured in dollar-days) if the check is disbursed from bank j

S_{ij} = the clearing system slippage (measured in dollar-days) associated with a deposit by vendor group i when check is disbursed from bank j

λ = the efficient frontier mapping parameter which is systematically varied between $-\infty$ and 1

F_j = the fixed cost of using disbursement bank j

z_j = 1 if disbursement bank j is used in the solution; otherwise 0

x_{ij} = 1 if vendor group i is assigned to disbursing bank j, otherwise 0

M = the number of vendor groups

P = the maximum number of disbursing banks permitted in the solution

α = the firm's cost of capital

CHAPTER 5

Designing Cash Concentration Systems

Under current corporate practice many of the balances kept at the bank of first deposit have little value to the corporation.[1] This is because these balances reside in demand deposit accounts earning no interest.[2] Since the corporation cannot earn a money market rate, companies move such funds through the banking system to what is commonly called a concentration account. Concentration accounts exist primarily at money center banks or banks that are part of the corporation's credit line consortium.

The corporation gains several significant benefits from this process of concentrating funds. First, by accumulating funds at one central location the corporation has significantly larger amounts of money to invest in a single transaction in the money markets. For example, a fast food franchise chain might make deposits on the order of $2000 per day and have collected balances of $5000 on average in its depository accounts. Such a small amount would not be viable for money market investing, especially if the firm only intended to make such an investment on an overnight basis. On the other hand, if the fast food franchise concentrated its 400 depository accounts (one per store) at a single bank it could, assuming it moved all its collected balances, have a pool of funds available for investing of $2,000,000. This total would be sufficient to provide access

---

[1]The bank of first deposit or simply the depository bank is the bank at which the corporation makes its first deposit of funds as part of the collection process. Such funds may be generated by field units such as a local outlet for a fast food chain, department store, or gas station. They may also come about as a deposit made to a lockbox processing bank.

[2]Until recently, corporations did not have access to full service interest bearing checking accounts. Regulatory changes in January of 1983 permitted corporate access to demand deposit accounts that did earn interest, but were limited in terms of the number of checks or electronic transfers that could be initiated against such accounts. Moreover, these accounts generally paid a lower interest rate than could be obtained by the company through other money market investments.

to many money market instruments, including repurchase agreements and commercial paper.

A second benefit to be gained from concentration is an increase in the "visibility" or control of the funds. Most depository accounts of less than $100,000 would be too small to tie into a balance reporting system. Without such a system, a corporation would have no information on a day-to-day basis of the exact amount of the collected balances in its depository bank network. Thus, even though a corporation would know that it had $2 million in collected balances in its bank network, it would not know at which banks the balances were located, and would therefore be unable to effectively use the funds. On the other hand, money that has been concentrated at a major money center bank can be monitored on a day-to-day basis, or even on an intra-day basis, using a balance reporting system.

There is actually a third possible benefit to corporations from moving funds to concentration banks. This benefit arises because in the process of moving the money, especially with paper-based systems (checks), there is a possibility that balances may exist in two of the firm's bank accounts simultaneously. These dual balances are created by "slippage" in the clearing system resulting from availability being granted to the firm before the funds are removed from the drawee bank.

There are, however, problems with slippage created in a concentration system that are not of concern in a disbursing system. When slippage arises in the process of concentration it generates additional balances at the banks of first deposit. This, however, does not necessarily lead to any additional value or benefit to the concentrating corporation. If the depository banks are already being adequately compensated for services, then balance creation through slippage at these depository banks has no value to the corporation. Slippage is, therefore, a twofold issue for a company doing concentration. First, it must determine that slippage is occurring. Second, it must be able to make use of the phenomena by mobilizing funds even more rapidly so as to cause whatever balances are created through slippage at the depository banks to be moved to the concentration bank.

Figure 5.1 illustrates a typical corporate concentration system. Deposits are initially made at the depository banks and moved to regional concentration banks. From the regional concentration banks funds are then further moved to a central concentration bank. Investments or borrowing is then transacted through this central concentration bank as required in order to maintain adequate corporate liquidity. Finally, the central concentration bank becomes the conduit through which disbursements move to various vendors, employees, taxing authorities and shareholders.

The rationale for having a "tiered" concentration system as shown in Figure 5.1[3] is usually twofold. First, by locating a regional concentration bank in each Federal Reserve District in which the corporation does a significant amount of business, it will be able to obtain the best availability on the fund transfer instruments. If the funds are transferred using the wire transfer system between the regional concentration bank and

---

[3]This is a modified version of a figure that appeared in Bernell K. Stone, "Cash Management," in Edward I. Altman (ed.), *Financial Handbook*, Wiley, New York, 1981.

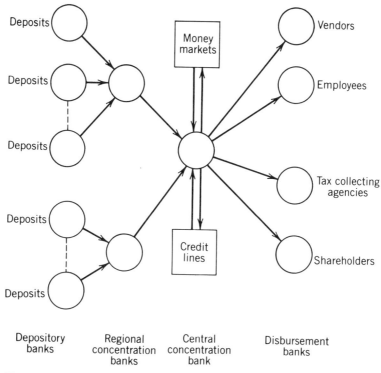

Figure 5.1 A typical corporate concentration and funds movement system.

the central concentration bank, the effect will be a more rapid transfer of funds than would be possible if a single transfer were made between the bank of first deposit and the central concentration bank.

A second reason for using a tiered concentration system is that it may provide for additional slippage opportunity, since two separate transfer instruments are now created. Moreover, the transfer between the central concentration bank and the regional concentration banks creates slippage that is easier to monitor, and therefore easier to take advantage of. This results because both the regional concentration banks and the central concentration bank are likely to have balance reporting system linkages to the corporate headquarters.

TRANSFER MECHANISMS

In moving funds between depository banks, regional concentration banks, and the central concentration bank, the corporation usually has a choice of three different transfer mechanisms. Each has its advantages. Moreover, the three transfer mechanisms have uses in other funds movement situations, such as drafting customer accounts. We discuss each in turn, including their other nontransfer uses.

Depository Transfer Checks

Perhaps the most widely used transfer mechanism in concentration systems is the depository transfer check (DTC). A DTC differs from an ordinary check in that it does not carry a signature. Instead, the corporation authorizes its banks both to initiate and to receive unsigned DTC transfers. The bank to which the funds will be transferred originates the DTC by depositing it in the corporation's account. The bank then obtains availability from a check collecting agent, such as the Federal Reserve, usually resulting in the use of the funds in either one or two business days.

The corporation's account at the depository institution will then be debited by the collecting agent presenting the check to that institution. Usually the presentation time will be the same as the availability granted by the concentration bank. Of course, the check may also be delayed. In such instances, the corporation observes slippage and has use of its funds simultaneously at two locations: the depository institution and the concentration bank.

In many situations, the DTC has advantages over other means of collecting funds. For example, it may be an effective mechanism of collection in a dealer network or for retail collection. The following example illustrates these advantages.

Example A major national oil company sells gasoline through a dealer network. The company's standard credit policy is to provide 15-day terms on gasoline sales. Assuming the dealer pays on the last possible day, the firm usually receives the check at its lockbox processing center 18 days after shipment and receives value after 20 days. The dealer has 20 days from receipt of the gasoline shipment until he needs to have the necessary funds in his checking account. Of course, the dealer does not know that it would take 5 days from the day he mailed the check until the funds are withdrawn from his checking account. This uncertainty usually causes him to place the money in his checking account perhaps after 18 days. The oil company similarly does not know when it will receive payment from its dealers, although its problem is somewhat easier in that it deals with many dealers, and can forecast average collections. Because it is to their mutual advantage, the dealer and the oil company come to an agreement to let the oil company initiate DTC's for payment. The system works by the oil company creating the DTC so that the dealer's account is drafted 18 days after the gasoline shipment arrives. Procedurally, the oil company actually prepares the DTC, and deposits it in the banking system after 17 days, with the oil company being granted availability, and the dealer debited, one business day later.

This example illustrates several advantages of the DTC over other forms of payment. First, the collecting corporation can determine precisely when it will receive the payment value. This is generally not true if the payor initiates payment. Second, the payee-initiated payment usually results in both prompter payment and less delinquency problems. There is less possibility that the payor will make payment late, involving additional collection expense for the payee. Finally, there is usually reduced expense both to the payor and the payee, because of the automated nature in which the DTC's are created.

ACH Transfers

Several years ago, the banking system recognized the inherent inefficiencies involved in paper item payments. To collect a check, one must physically present the check to the bank on which it is drawn. This requires a tremendous amount of paper handling equipment and the transporting of high volumes of checks throughout the banking system. In the early 1970s, there was a feeling within the industry that banks would eventually die in an avalanche of paper, unless they came up with a paperless payment system. From this idea was created the Automated Clearing House (ACH). The ACH system is today run, with the exception of the New York ACH, by the Federal Reserve. The basis of the system is computer-to-computer data transmission of payment instructions. Usually, a payment can be made and collected through the ACH system without a paper item ever being created.

The most direct use of the ACH system in the collection of funds is as a potential replacement for the DTC. The process of funds transfer is very similar to that for the DTC. The corporation receiving the funds initiates the transfer. The transfer itself is called either an ACH debit or an electronic DTC. The initiator of the transfer does so by sending a computer tape containing information on the customer, or depository accounts, it wants drafted to its local bank, which in turn passes the computer tape on to the local ACH. The ACH then transmits the computer images to the computers of the ACH's located in the geographic areas of the customer or depository accounts. These local ACH's then transmit the payment request to the bank.

The process works as described above in most cases. However, not all commercial banks are members of the ACH system. If a bank is not a member of the ACH, then the DTC must be used. This problem has led to significant difficulties in implementation, because most corporations using an ACH concentration system have in place as well a DTC concentration system in order to transfer funds from those banks that are not members of the ACH. It should be noted, however, that most banks are members of the ACH system; all large banks are members without exception.

The ACH is not a mechanism for immediate transfer of funds. Usually the transfer request must be given to the ACH one business day prior to the funds transfer. Thus, the same delay inherent in the paper-based DTC is also present in the electronic ACH. However, the problem of slippage is usually not present in the ACH system.

An interesting use of the ACH system was pioneered by Amway Corporation. Amway sells consumer products through a network of individuals acting as dealers. Dealers take orders for Amway products from their customers and send the orders to Amway headquarters. Amway then ships the product to its dealers, who in turn deliver the product and simultaneously collect payment from their customers. Amway uses the ACH system to collect payment from its dealers. After allowing for shipping time and a few days for the dealer to collect the payment, Amway drafts its dealer's accounts using the ACH. Amway uses the ACH system because it is cheaper than using DTC drafting. See Figure 5.2[4] for a comparison of the costs of various transfer mechanisms.

---

[4]This figure appeared in Bernell K. Stone and Ned C. Hill, "Alternative Cash Transfer Mechanisms and Methods: Evaluation Frameworks," *Journal of Bank Research,* Volume 3, No. 1, 9.

Transfer Methods	Delay (days)	Typical Cost Range[a]	Cost Components
Wire	0	$6.00–$20.00	1. Outgoing wire 2. Wire receipt
DTC: Third-party assisted	1–2	$.60–$1.00	1. Third-party charge 2. Deposit charge 3. DTC preparation charge 4. Check charge
DTC: Centralized company initiation	1–2	$.05–$.40 plus the cost of bank and/or company preparation of either the DTCs and/or the DTC tape image and any communication costs.	1. Deposit charge 2. Check charge 3. Bank processing charge 4. Company processing cost 5. Communication cost
DTC: Mail based	2–7	$.30–$.55	1. Deposit charge lockbox 2. Check charge 3. Postage/envelope
EDTC: Third-party assisted	1	$.24–$.36 plus any bank preparation charge	1. Third-party charge 2. Electronic transfer charge 3. Bank preparation charge
EDTC: Centralized company initiation	1	$.03–$.06 plus any bank preparation charges and/or the cost of company preparation of the EDTC tape and any communication costs.	1. Electronic transfer charge 2. Bank preparation charge 3. Company processing cost 4. Communication cost

[a]Cost ranges reflect variation in charges across banks and third-party information gathering services.

Figure 5.2 Transfer methods: key attributes.

Since Amway has over 500,000 distributors, a few pennies saved on each draft can produce significant savings.

The ACH system is not without its detractors. As Amway found out, when a mistake occurs it can be a big one. Several thousand of its distributors were drafted twice for the same payment because a computer tape containing the payment information was labelled defective and duplicated. Unfortunately, the original tape was not destroyed and it, together with the duplicate, was transmitted through the system!

The cost advantage currently enjoyed by ACH transfers may not be a permanent phenomenon. In an effort to stimulate the use of the ACH system, currently the Federal Reserve operates the system at a significant deficit. However, the Monetary Control Act of 1980 mandates that the Fed set its ACH prices so as to fully recover its costs, and even make a profit on its investment. The Federal Reserve has indicated that it will comply with this Act by slowly moving up the prices of the ACH system over the next several years. This issue of cost may prove quite significant. The Federal Reserve currently sets ACH prices based on a full volume utilization, yet current volume is less than 10% of this level.

Wire Transfers

In some cases, the amount of transfer may be so large that payment will be affected by wire transfer. Wire transfer is, however, a very expensive transfer mechanism. The individual making payment by wire and the individual receiving the wire each incur approximately a $6.00 cost. (See Figure 5.2.) The advantage of the wire transfer over the DTC and ACH is that funds are immediately available. However, it has none of the slippage associated with the DTC.

Wire transfers are many times utilized between regional concentration banks and the central concentration bank. Here, the amounts of the transfers are large enough to warrant the more costly wire transfer. Moreover, the number of transfers are small since there are no more than a dozen regional concentration banks in most corporate systems.

INFORMATION TRANSFER

The DTC, ACH, and wire transfer are mechanisms for the actual movement of funds. A corporation must, however, have sufficient information to determine the amount of funds that need to be moved. Usually, a separate parallel system exists for providing this information to the corporation. Four means are most often used to get information to the corporate headquarters.

Mail A popular system used in the 1960s was deposit notification using the postal system. In some instances, this was accomplished by actually mailing a check drawn on the depository institution to a lockbox bank. This mail DTC was then deposited by the lockbox bank and transfer was made as a normal DTC. The disadvantage of this mail DTC system was the added delay of mail delivery to the corporate headquarters or lockbox bank.

Information Vendors In the early 1970s, a number of companies went into the business of providing an information gathering network for corporate transfers. Two of the largest of these companies are National Data Corporation (NDC) and Automated Data Process (ADP). The service works as follows. The depositor of the funds (the regional manager of the store) makes a phone call to a telephone number answered by a NDC operator. The manager then indicates the date of the deposit, her special identification number, and the amount of the deposit to the operator. This information is then gathered from all field locations and ultimately transmitted to a concentration bank for preparation of either DTC's or ACH debits. If a touch-tone phone is available, the information may be transmitted digitally by the manager to a computer. Of course, the advantage of this mechanism over the mail DTC is the elimination of both the mail time delay and the manual preparation of the DTC or other documents.

Point-of-Sale Terminals In some service outlets, such as grocery stores or fast food franchisers, computerized point-of-sale terminals are used to transfer deposit information to the headquarters or the headquarters' bank. The Hardee's fast food chain is a good example. The managers of each of the Hardee's outlets make deposits in the local banks equal to the daily receipts. Each evening, a central computer polls each of the stores' point-of-sale terminals for the total daily receipts. It then automatically creates a computer tape containing ACH transfer amounts that will be given to its concentration bank. One advantage of this system is its ability to detect theft by employees, since the direct computer link provides a check on the deposits that are being made by the employees.

Balance Reporting Systems   In instances where the deposits are made in rather large amounts, it may pay for the corporation to have these deposits reported through its balance reporting system. A good example of the use of such a system would be for lockbox deposits or for deposits made by a processing center. In this instance, the corporation receives, through a computer link-up with its concentration bank, a daily report on the amount of the deposits being made. Some balance reporting systems provide intra-day information on balance levels, which can be particularly useful if the corporation is active in money market investments, since it must then have a precise balance level by 11 a.m. to make its daily money market purchases. The greater expense of a balance reporting system generally precludes their use for small dollar deposits.

RUNNING A CONCENTRATION SYSTEM

The process of running a concentration system is very complex, both because the number of bank accounts that must be monitored is large, and because there are many cost trade-offs the corporation must consider. In this section, we describe some of the issues inherent in running a concentration system.

Cost Considerations

A company instituting a concentration system has a number of cost components it must trade off. These costs are divisible into four categories.

Excess Balances   The mere process of making deposits at a depository account creates collected balances. In the example cited at the beginning of this chapter, a fast food outlet making daily deposits averaging $2000 a day could easily create $5000 or more in average collected balances. In many instances, these balance levels will be greater than what is required to compensate the depository bank for its services. Balances greater than those required to compensate for services are called excess balances; they are a cost to the corporation. One of the firm's four cost objectives is to minimize the level of excess balances at its depository banks.

Transfer Fees   Depending upon the transfer mechanism chosen (DTC, ACH, or Wire), the corporation will incur certain transfer costs. Usually, there will be costs at both the concentration bank for initiating the transfer and at the depository bank for paying the transfer.

Reporting Network Fees   This is the fee associated with a third-party vendor, such as NDC, or a balance reporting system for providing the information to the corporation or concentration bank of the daily deposit amount.

Dual Balances   If slippage occurs in the transfer process, usually applicable only to a paper-based DTC transfer system, this must be taken into account in costing out the concentration system. It should be noted that dual balances created through slippage actually tend to *reduce* the cost of operating the concentration system. This is because dual balances create an opportunity for generating higher balances on which interest can be earned.

Costing Out a Concentration System

Figure 5.3 is an illustration of a cost analysis for a concentration system. In this example, the corporation currently has $622,500 in excess balances located at depository banks. This amount does not include any balances the corporation has at its concentration banks. Assuming that the corporation could invest funds on a short term basis at 14%, and that there is some small good will value created at the depository banks for maintaining excess balance levels, estimated at 2%, the net cost of maintaining these excess balances to the company is 12%. This yields an annual cost (lost opportunity value) of $74,700.

The corporation also makes daily transfers from 300 depository accounts that cost an average $.50 each or $125.00 per year for each account, or $37,500 on an annual basis.

The corporation also pays a third-party network a fee of $.40 per day per account for information gathering, amounting to $30,000 per year.

Finally, the corporation experiences an average level of slippage equal to 0.1 calendar days on average daily deposits of $365,000. This results in dual balances of $36,500, which valued at 14% produces a negative cost (profit) of $5110. The net cost of operating the system is therefore $137,090 on an annual basis.

Each of the cost components provides opportunities for savings. For example, lowering the excess balances could possibly eliminate more than $70,000 in cost. One

Average Depository Account Balances	$1,057,500	
Less Compensating Balances	435,000	
	$ 622,500	
Value of Excess Balances at 12%		$ 74,700
Transfer Fees (300 accounts @ $125)		37,500
Reporting Network Fees (300 reporting points @ $100)		30,000
Dual Balances		$ 36,500
(0.10 days slippage × average $365,000 daily deposits)		
Value of dual Balances at 14%		(5,110)
		$137,090

Figure 5.3   XYZ Corporation—annual concentration system cost analysis.

method often suggested for doing this is to initiate a one-time transfer of the average excess balance from each of the depository banks. Unfortunately, unless great care is taken, this many times will result in periodic overdrafts of the depository accounts.

As illustrated in Figure 5.4, the operation of a depository account is much like a water container that receives liquid through the top in the form of deposits and disposes of liquid through the bottom in the form of withdrawals. On Monday, the system begins the day with $12,000 in funds. A cash deposit is made of $17,000, while a transfer is paid of $11,000. This leaves a balance in the account equal to $18,000 at the end of Monday, which becomes the initial balance level for Tuesday. On Tuesday, a cash deposit is made of $7000 and a transfer is paid of $17,000 leaving a balance of $8000 at the end of the day. Notice that the transfer paid on Tuesday is exactly the same as Monday's deposit. This is fairly typical because the $17,000 deposit is reported on Monday and a DTC or ACH is presented to the depository bank the following day.

Figure 5.4 shows this account over a full one-week's cycle. Notice that the account reaches a level of only $3000 on Wednesday. On the other hand, the average over the week is $11,000. [Computed as follows: (18,000 + 8,000 + 3,000 + 6,000 + 14,000 × 3)/7 = $11,000 per day average. Notice that Friday counts as three days since it is held over the weekend.] Assuming it actually took only $2000 in balances to compensate the depository bank for its services, this would leave $9000 in average excess balances.

However, if an attempt were made to transfer out the excess $9000 in balances, the system would then look like Figure 5.5. Here overdrafts have occurred on Tuesday, Wednesday, and Thursday. These overdrafts may result in either transfers failing, that is being returned for insufficient funds, or a phone call being received from an irate banker. In this illustration. the maximum amount that could be transferred out without causing an overdraft would be $3000. Given the uncertainties in the amounts of future

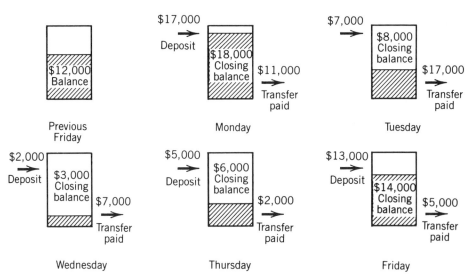

Figure 5.4   The weekly balance cycle of a depository account.

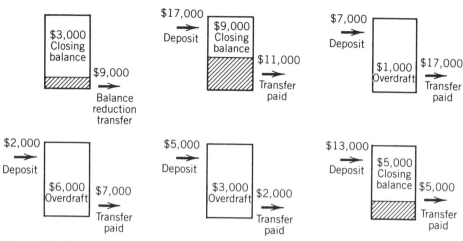

Figure 5.5   The weekly balance cycle with an initial deposit reduction.

deposits, perhaps not even this amount can be safely removed without incurring at least some probability of an overdraft.

One way to improve this system—that is, to reduce excess balances—is to better synchronize the transfers and the deposits. Ideally, one would like to transfer out exactly the amount being deposited. Unfortunately, this is usually impossible because of the information delays incurred in determining the actual deposit amounts and the presentation time associated with either DTC's or ACH transfers.

A second way of reducing cost is to use a less expensive transfer mechanism. Because of the cost savings inherent in the ACH system, many corporations have adopted the use of this system over their former paper-based DTC system. Of course, if the company uses wire transfers, significant cost savings can be achieved by switching to either an ACH- or DTC-based system. Keep in mind, however, that a wire system, since it does not have the one-day delay associated with the ACH or DTC, can provide better synchronization between deposit and transfer amounts. This in turn can provide an opportunity to reduce excess depository account balances.

There is sometimes also a cost advantage to transferring less than every day. Unfortunately, there is also a disadvantage. A corporation that transfers only once each week loses its ability to detect theft on the part of its employees, since the employees will have been able to remove more than a week's deposits before a transfer instrument might fail and indicate a problem has arisen.

Since reporting networks charge primarily on the basis of the number of phone calls they receive, it is possible to reduce costs by having the field location report less frequently. However, this again, raises the issue of theft and most companies would prefer to have these deposit reports on a daily basis.

Finally, when analyzing the potential value of dual balances created by slippage, there is a natural tendency to prefer transfers on Thursday over other days of the week. This occurs because a normal one-day DTC transfer that slips and is initiated on Thursday will be presented against the depository bank the following Monday, turning a one-business-day delay into a three-calendar-day delay. Usually, however, the largest transfers occur earlier in the week. This is because weekend sales are deposited on Monday, resulting in the initiation of a large DTC on either Monday or Tuesday.

DESIGNING A CONCENTRATION SYSTEM

Recent articles have been written in the finance literature on the use of optimization methods for designing concentration systems.[5] These tend to focus on what is called the transfer scheduling problem. This problem is concerned with the determination of which days of the week transfers should be made and the amounts of these transfers. The optimization process attempts to synchronize transfers with deposits so as to permit the maximum amount of excess balances to be withdrawn from the depository institutions. The optimization models also attempt to simultaneously reduce the number of transfers and maximize any slippage benefits that might exist.

A second optimization problem arises in concentration system design. The concentration design problem is concerned with the selection of the central concentration bank and regional concentration banks in a tiered system. The problem may also involve the selection of an appropriate concentration mechanism. Usually the concentration mechanism issue boils down to either the ACH or DTC. As mentioned previously, the ACH is preferred on the basis of cost, but the DTC provides some potential for slippage.

The selection of concentration banks usually depends on a tradeoff between the availability the banks grant various transfer instruments, costs, and bank slippage characteristics. Although the analysis can be reduced to a simple cost comparison, the issues usually go a good deal deeper. If a bank can be selected as a concentration bank by a corporation, it is likely to obtain more than simply the corporation's concentration transfer business. It is almost certain to be selected as part of the corporation's credit line bank group, and has some likelihood of being active in money market transactions for that corporation. Since providing credit lines tends to be a very profitable service, banks compete actively in trying to become concentration points. The flip side of this issue is that most corporations would not select a concentration bank purely for cost considerations. Instead, a corporation will usually only consider banks it would also wish to use for credit and/or money market transactions. Thus, concentration accounts tend to be located in money center or major regional banking centers.

SUMMARY

The firm's concentration system is the third part of the trilogy of float management systems. As was the case with the lockbox and disbursement areas, the manager of a concentration system has as a primary objective the maximization of investable funds for his company. Concentration systems tend to be of particular interest to companies

---

[5]See Bernell K. Stone, and Ned C. Hill, ''Cash Transfer Scheduling for Efficient Cash Concentration,'' *Financial Management*, Autumn 1980, 35–43.

with many retail outlets such as fast food franchises or department stores. For very large corporations, there is also the issue of concentrating funds from lockbox networks.

Over the past dozen years, there has been a remarkable transformation of industry practice in the area of concentration. In the late 60's, systems were almost entirely mail-based DTC transfers. The creation of National Data Corporation, and other information gathering companies, has almost completely eliminated the use of mail based DTCs. Currently, many corporations are examining tradeoffs between DTCs and ACH concentration systems, with the tendency being to adopt the more cost effective ACH alternative.

In the future, one would anticipate a continued movement to electronic concentration systems, with ACH transfers perhaps one day entirely replacing DTC-based systems. In addition, direct computer linkage through point-of-sales terminals may eliminate the need for many third-party information gathering services.

DISCUSSION QUESTIONS

1. What is the purpose of concentrating funds in one account?
2. Describe the mechanisms firms use to transfer funds to the concentration bank.
3. What are the advantages of a 2-tiered system of concentration banks?
4. What are the advantages of using an ACH system of cash concentration?
5. Describe how the financial manager may obtain information on the amounts that have been deposited in regional bank accounts.
6. Describe how dual balances may be created during the cash concentration process.
7. Discuss the different costs associated with different cash transfers.
8. How can the firm prevent having excess balances in field office accounts?
9. Under what conditions would one tend to schedule transfers near the end of the week?
10. Under what conditions would one tend to schedule transfers near the beginning of the week?
11. Given the cost of transferring funds to the concentration bank, why would the financial manager ever want to make transfers on a daily rather than periodic basis?
12. What should be the objective of cash concentration system design?
13. What are the typical constraints on the design of cash concentration systems?

PROBLEMS

1. Gregory's Hamburgers is a fast food chain with approximately 1000 retail outlets scattered throughout the country. Ms. Gregory, President of Gregory's Hamburgers, has asked you to evaluate several alternatives for transferring funds from deposit accounts in its system of regional banks to a central concentration account

in New York. She has given you the following information on deposit patterns and cost components for a typical retail outlet:

Beginning Balance = $10,000 = Minimum Required Balance
Deposits: Monday—$22,000, Tuesday—$6,000, Wednesday—$9,000, Thursday—$8,000, Friday—$4,000
Interest Rate (annualized) = 12%; Cost per Transfer = $.50

After reviewing these data, you have decided to evaluate three alternative transfer strategies:

Strategy I: Initiate a transfer whenever the balance level in the regional account exceeds $20,000.
Strategy II: Transfer each day's deposits on the following business day.
Strategy III: Every Thursday, transfer deposit balances in excess of $10,000. (Assume that Thursday transfers provide dual balances for two days.)

Which of these three strategies is most cost effective?

2. Suppose now that the $10,000 minimum balance requirement does not have to be met everyday; instead, the firm must keep an average balance of $10,000 over the course of the week. Can you suggest a variant of any of the above strategies that takes advantage of this information?

3. Consider once again the information provided in Problem 1. Suppose now that the deposit figures for Monday to Friday are only expected (i.e., forecasted) values. The actual deposits are normally distributed about these expected values with a standard deviation of 10% of the expected value. How can the firm use this forecast information to improve its transfer schedule policy?

ADDITIONAL READINGS

1. Bernell K. Stone, "Cash Management," Chapter 27 in *Financial Handbook*, Edward I. Altman (ed.), Wiley, N. Y., 1981.

2. Bernell K. Stone, Daniel M. Ferguson, and Ned C. Hill, "Cash Transfer Scheduling and Overview," *The Cash Manager*, March 1980, 3–8.

3. Bernell K. Stone and Ned C. Hill, "Cash Transfer Scheduling for Efficient Cash Concentration," *Financial Management*, Autumn 1980, 35–43.

4. Bernell K. Stone and Ned C. Hill, "Alternative Cash Transfer Mechanisms and Methods: Evaluation Frameworks," *Journal of Bank Research*, Spring 1982, 7–16.

5. Bernell K. Stone and Ned C. Hill, "Cash Concentration Design," *Journal of Financial and Quantitative Analysis*, June 1979.

SECTION III

CASH FORECASTING AND FINANCIAL PLANNING

CHAPTER 6

An Introduction to Cash Forecasting

The purpose of cash forecasting is to identify the amount and timing of the firm's near-term cash requirements. Knowledge of the firm's cash requirements is helpful in negotiating lines of credit, scheduling cash transfers into a concentration bank, and planning the maturity structure of a short-term investment/borrowing portfolio. In times of stress, the cash forecast alerts the manager to pending financial problems. It allows him time to solve these problems before they become serious.

Because forecasting goals and environments differ among firms significantly, no single technique is best for all firms. Many firms feel most comfortable with forecasting methods that rely on the structure provided by the firm's financial statements. Examples are the cash budget and *pro forma* financial statement analysis. These methods are based on a sales forecast together with assumptions concerning inventory and receivables policy, work force levels, and changes in plant capacity.

Other firms use statistically based forecasting methods, such as regression and time series analysis, to supplement the information obtained from the cash budget and *pro forma* financial statements. The statistical methods are designed to discover patterns and relationships that are not apparent from casual observation. By quantifying the uncertainty inherent in the cash forecast, they also help the financial manager to choose an appropriate buffer stock of liquidity.

The two most widely used statistical approaches to cash forecasting are the Payments Pattern Approach and the Distribution Approach. The Payments Pattern Approach relates a component of the cash stream, such as cash collections, back to the source that generates it, such as customer bills. It then estimates the distribution of the time delay between the mailing of the bill and the receipt of payment. If it were estimated, for example, that the firm typically collects 80% of a given month's sales generated receivables in one month and the remaining 20% the following month, then the forecast of cash collections for the current month is the sum of 80% of last month's sales and 20% of the sales made two months ago. Although the Payments Pattern Approach is usually applied to the preparation of monthly cash forecasts, there is no reason why it cannot be applied to time periods less than a month, including the problem of daily cash forecasting.

The Distribution Approach to cash forecasting is especially designed to forecast the firm's daily cash position. This approach uses a dummy-variable regression equation to estimate the typical pattern of cash flows over the days of the week and the days of the month. The resulting pattern is then used to "distribute" the firm's monthly cash budget over the days within the month.

This chapter discusses the two most widely used approaches to cash forecasting: the cash budget and *pro forma* financial statement analysis. The following two chapters are devoted to a discussion of statistically based approaches to cash forecasting. After finishing these three chapters the reader should be able to choose the best approach for his or her situation.

CASH BUDGET

The cash budget is a simple projection of the firm's cash receipts and disbursements over some future time period. The various components of cash receipts and disbursements are obtained from a sales forecast along with assumptions about how the firm's operating activities relate to sales. Cash budgets may be prepared for any time frame including months, weeks, and days. They are generally most effective for relatively short time horizons, because the underlying assumptions frequently do not hold over a longer period.

Example   The mechanics of preparing a cash budget are best explained by an example.

The marketing department of Precision Products, Inc. (PPI) has estimated sales for the last two months of 1983 and the first eight months of 1984 to be those shown in Table 6.1. From previous experience, the firm estimates that 10% of sales in a given month are for cash, 60% are collected the following month, and 30% are collected the second month after the sale. (No allowance is made for bad debt expense because uncollectable accounts are neglible.) From this information, the financial manager has prepared the schedule of cash receipts for the first half of 1984 (see Table 6.2).

The $1480 of cash receipts in January is equal to 30% of the $1400 estimated sales for November plus 60% of the $1500 estimated sales for December plus 10% of the

Table 6.1   Estimated Sales of PPI (in 000's)

Nov.	Dec.	Jan.	Feb.	March	April	May	June	July	Aug.
1,400	1,500	1,600	1,600	2,000	2,500	2,400	1,800	1,400	1,400

Table 6.2 PPI Cash Receipts for January–
June 1984 (in 000's)

Jan.	Feb.	March	April	May	June
1,480	1,570	1,640	1,930	2,340	2,370

$1600 estimated sales for January, and the remaining cash receipts are estimated similarly.

The financial manager realizes that the raw materials and labor required to produce a given month's sales must be purchased two months in advance and that the cost of goods sold averages 75% of the sales price. (Thus, for March's sales of $2 million, $1.5 million in materials and labor expenses are incurred in January.) Material purchases are made on account and, like labor expense, are paid in the month after they are incurred.

The financial manager also knows that:

1. PPI has monthly outlays for general administrative and selling expenses of $250,000.
2. Tax payments of $150,000 will be made in March and June.
3. There will be no change in fixed assets other than depreciation of $200,000 per year, realized for accounting purposes as $100,000 in June and $100,000 in December.
4. Dividends of $50,000 are paid in June.
5. The firm currently has a cash balance of $250,000. It desires to maintain its cash position at least at this level throughout the year to protect itself against all contingencies.

With this knowledge, the financial manager has prepared the schedule of cash disbursements (see Table 6.3).

The information from Tables 6.2 and 6.3 can be used to estimate the change in the firm's cash position for the first half of 1984. Table 6.4 shows that the firm is expected to have net inflows of cash in January, May, and June and net outflows of cash in February, March, and April.

The cash budget shows that the firm is expected to have a cumulative financial requirement of over $900,000 in the first four months of 1984. Since most financing

Table 6.3 PPI Disbursements for January–June 1984 (in 000's)

	Jan.	Feb.	March	April	May	June
Materials and labor	1,200	1,500	1,875	1,800	1,350	1,050
General selling and administrative expenses	250	250	250	250	250	250
Tax payments			150			150
Dividends						50
Total disbursements	1,450	1,750	2,275	2,050	1,600	1,500

Depreciation expense is not included in this table because it is not a cash outlay.

Table 6.4 PPI Cash Budget January–June 1984 (in 000's)

	Jan.	Feb.	March	April	May	June	Total Cash Flow
Receipts	1,480	1,570	1,640	1,930	2,340	2,370	
Disbursements							
Materials and labor	1,200	1,500	1,875	1,800	1,350	1,050	
General selling and administrative expenses	250	250	250	250	250	250	
Tax payments			150			150	
Dividends						50	
Total disbursements	1,450	1,750	2,275	2,050	1,600	1,500	
Net cash flow	30	(180)	(635)	(120)	740	870	705
Minimum cash balance	250	250	250	250	250	250	
Forecasted cash balance	280	100	(535)	(655)	85	955	
Financial requirement	(30)[a]	150	785	905	165	(705)	

[a]Parentheses in this row indicate a surplus.

arrangements take some time to negotiate, the firm would be wise to begin its search for sources of financing before the beginning of the year. The cash budget is a useful document for explaining the firm's cash requirements to potential lenders.

Sensitivity Analysis

The cash budget shown in Table 6.4 was prepared using a point estimate of sales for the first eight months of 1984 and a set of specific assumptions about the firm's receivables' collections, purchasing policy, and tax payments. The financial manager, of course, recognizes that actual economic conditions may vary considerably from those that were assumed. For this reason, he may want to examine what his financial requirements would be under several alternative economic scenarios. For example, he may want to ask such questions as:

1. What if sales exceed the expected level by 20%? We would expect this to increase the amount of financing required, because materials and labor payments will now be higher. As shown in Table 6.5, the maximum projected financial requirement is now $1,210,000.
2. What if sales are 20% below expectations? This will decrease our projected financial requirement to a maximum of $600,000, as shown in Table 6.6.
3. What if sales remain constant, but collections slow to 5% cash, 50% collected in one month, and 45% in two months? Table 6.7 shows that this would increase the amount of financing required to $1,330,000.
4. What if sales decrease by 20% and collections slow to 5% cash, 50% collected in one month, and 45% in two months. In this case there are two offsetting impacts on our cash requirements. Cash requirements increase due to the slowing in collections, but this is offset somewhat by the lower materials and labor costs. Table 6.8 shows financial needs at $940,000.

Uses of Cash Budget

The cash budget is used to make the following kinds of decisions:

1. *Maximum line of credit.* By examining Tables 6.4–6.8, the financial manager at PPI can determine that his maximum cash requirement is likely to be no greater than $1.4 million. He may want to negotiate a line of credit for an amount slightly larger than this to protect against the worst possible case. (Another reason it may be larger is that the firm may need to maintain a minimum level of compensating balances.) Most firms would want to negotiate this line of credit well in advance of their borrowing need.
2. *Maturity of short-term borrowing/investment portfolio.* The cash budget helps the financial manager determine the appropriate maturities for his short-term investments and borrowings. In the most likely scenario (Table 6.4), the financial manager will have a surplus of cash in January. He may be tempted to invest this surplus cash in securities of 90–120 days maturity to take advantage of their higher yields. However, the cash budget alerts him to the expected shortfall of funds in February,

Table 6.5 PPI Cash Budget January–June 1984 (in 000's) (sales 20% above expected)

	Jan.	Feb.	March	April	May	June	Total Cash Flow
Receipts	1,512	1,794	1,968	2,316	2,808	2,844	862
Disbursements							
Materials and labor	1,440	1,800	2,250	2,160	1,620	1,260	
General selling and administrative expenses	250	250	250	250	250	250	
Tax payments			150			150	
Dividends						50	
Total disbursements	1,690	2,050	2,650	2,410	1,870	1,710	
Net cash flow	(178)	(256)	(682)	(94)	938	1,134	
Minimum cash balance	250	250	250	250	250	250	
Forecasted cash balance	72	(184)	(866)	(960)	(22)	1,122	
Financial requirement	178	434	1,116	1,210	(272)	(862)[a]	

[a]Parentheses in this row indicate a cash surplus that can be invested.

Table 6.6 PPI Cash Budget January–June 1984 (in 000's) (sales 20% below expected)

	Jan.	Feb.	March	April	May	June	Total Cash Flow
Receipts	1,448	1,346	1,312	1,544	1,872	1,896	
Disbursements							
Materials and labor	960	1,200	1,500	1,440	1,080	840	
General selling and administrative expenses	250	250	250	250	250	250	
Tax payments			150			150	
Dividends						50	
Total disbursements	1,210	1,450	1,900	1,690	1,330	1,290	
Net cash flow	238	(104)	(588)	(146)	542	606	548
Minimum cash balance	250	250	250	250	250	250	
Forecasted cash balance	488	384	(204)	(350)	192	798	
Financial requirement	(238)[a]	(134)	454	600	58	(548)	

[a]Parentheses in this row indicate a cash surplus that can be invested.

Table 6.7 PPI Cash Budget January–June 1984 (in 000's)
(collections slow to 5% cash, 50% in one month, 45% in two months)

	Jan.	Feb.	March	April	May	June	Total Cash Flow
Receipts	1,400	1,330	1,620	1,845	2,270	2,415	
Disbursements							
Materials and labor	1,200	1,500	1,875	1,800	1,350	1,050	
General sales and administrative expenses	250	250	250	250	250	250	
Tax payments			150			150	
Dividends						50	
Total disbursements	1,450	1,750	2,275	2,050	1,600	1,500	
Net cash flow	(50)	(420)	(655)	(205)	670	915	255
Minimum cash balance	250	250	250	250	250	250	
Forecasted cash balance	200	(220)	(875)	(1,080)	(410)	505	
Financial requirement	50	470	1,125	1,330	660	(255)[a]	

[a]Parentheses in this row indicate a cash surplus that can be invested.

Table 6.8 PPI Cash Budget January–June 1984 (in 000's) (collections slow and sales down)

	Jan.	Feb.	March	April	May	June	Total Cash Flow
Receipts	1,384	1,154	1,296	1,476	1,816	1,932	
Disbursements							
Materials and labor	960	1,200	1,500	1,440	1,080	840	
General sales and administrative expenses	250	250	250	250	250	250	
Tax payments			150			150	
Dividends						50	
Total disbursements	1,210	1,450	1,900	1,690	1,330	1,290	
Net cash flow	174	(296)	(604)	(214)	486	642	188
Minimum cash balance	250	250	250	250	250	250	
Forecasted cash balance	424	128	(476)	(690)	(204)	438	
Financial requirement	(174)[a]	122	726	940	454	(188)	

[a]Parentheses in this row indicate a cash surplus that can be invested.

March, and April. Thus, it would be unwise to invest the January surplus in maturities greater than 30 days.

3. *Dividend policy.* The cash budget can also be used to assess the financial implications of the firm's dividend policy. The current policy of paying $50,000 in dividends in June does not cause any undue financial hardships for PPI. If the dividend were to be paid in March or April, however, it would add to the total financing required. The firm would then have to decide whether it preferred to change the payment date.

4. *Receivables policy.* In our example, a slowing in receivables collection can have significant consequences for the firm's financial requirements. The financial manager can use this information to assess whether or not he should tighten the firm's credit policies.

5. *Accounts payable policy.* In this example, it is assumed that the firm pays for materials purchased in the month following the purchase, so that it can take advantage of the trade discount for timely payment. If the firm decided, instead, to forego the discount, and pay in the second month following purchase, the firm's total financial requirements would be reduced. The cash budget can be used to measure the resulting reduction in borrowing and to assess the cost of borrowing versus delaying payment.

PRO FORMA FINANCIAL STATEMENTS

Pro forma financial statements are projections of the firm's income statement and balance sheet for various future periods. Like the cash budget, *pro forma* financial statements depend on a sales forecast and assumptions about the relationship of sales to receivables, inventories, and labor. However, *pro forma* financial statements provide information on the firm's profitability and financial condition that is not available from the cash budget. For this reason, the two should be used in conjunction with each other to provide better information on the financial implications of the firm's strategic and operating plans.

Long-Run Versus Short-Run Analysis

Pro forma financial statements are used in analyzing both long- and short-run financial decisions. Decisions regarding the firm's capital investment program, mix between debt and equity, and long-term dividend payout policy can be assessed with yearly *pro forma* financial statements covering a 5- or 10-year period. Decisions regarding the maturity of the firm's short-term investment/borrowing portfolio, the limit on its line of credit, and its receivable and payable policies are best evaluated with *pro formas* for monthly or quarterly periods.

The distinction between short- and long-run decision categories is important because it affects the manner in which information necessary for preparing the *pro formas* is obtained. If the *pro formas* are being used to analyze short-run financial decisions, as we assume in this book, then information on balance sheet items such as property, plant, and equipment, long-term debt, common equity other than retained earnings, and interest due on long-term debt may be taken as given from a prior stage of analysis. That is to say, they may be treated as known, once the long-term financial plan has been established.

Information For Pro Forma Analysis

Some information required for preparing short-run *pro forma* financial statements is obtained from knowledge of the firm's long-run financial plan. The remaining information is obtained in one of two ways.

1. *Percent of sales method.*   The easiest way to obtain information on items such as receivables, inventories, materials purchases, and labor is to assume that they vary in a constant proportion to sales. Thus, if receivables turn over every 30 days on average, we might assume that they are equal to 1/12th of annual sales.
2. *Budgeted expense method.*   The information may also be obtained from the firm's operating plan, which contains detailed purchasing schedules, work schedules, and so on. This second method is usually more costly, but also more accurate.

Interrelationship of Pro Forma Statements

To forecast the firm's financial requirements, the financial manager must prepare both a *pro forma* balance sheet and a *pro forma* income sheet. These two statements are interrelated in the sense that information from the *pro forma* income statement is required to determine the level of retained earnings on the *pro forma* balance sheet. On the other hand, the information on the *pro forma* balance sheet is used to determine the firm's total new borrowings, and the interest on these new borrowings is an important item on the *pro forma* income statement.

The financial manager may address this interrelationship in one of two ways: (1) she may ignore interest payments on new debt in the initial stage of *pro forma* preparation, as in the above cash budget example; and (2) she may use a computer model that "solves" for the *pro forma* balance sheet and income statement items simultaneously.

Relationship of Pro Formas to Cash Budgets

The estimate of the firm's total financial requirements obtained from *pro forma* financial statements should be identical to that obtained from the cash budget. However, the truth of this statement depends on the use of consistent assumptions in performing both types of analysis. If the financial manager assumes in preparing the cash budget that (1) 90% of sales are for credit and (2) 50% of receivables are collected in one month and the remainder the following month, she should use this same assumption in preparing her *pro forma* financial statements. If, instead, she uses the percent-of-sales method and assumes that receivables are 25% of sales, she should not be surprised when the results of her *pro forma* analysis differ from those of her cash budget.

The main advantages of the *pro forma* financial statements are that they may be easier to prepare (especially if the percent of sales method is used), they are readily adapted to the firm's existing accounting systems, and they provide important information not in the cash budget. In particular, they provide valuable information on the profitability of the firm's operations and the relationships between balance sheet and income statement accounts. This information is helpful in deciding whether to satisfy the financial requirements with debt or equity, and in deciding whether to make additions to the firm's plant and equipment. It is also helpful to a bank loan officer who is trying to determine whether the firm can repay a term loan. For long-run decisions of these types, the *pro forma* statements are clearly superior to the cash budget.

The principal advantage of the cash budget is that it highlights those factors that directly impact the firm's cash position. Since it is based on direct estimates of all cash receipt and disbursement items, the cash budget often provides a more accurate estimate of short-run changes in financial requirements. This is especially true when interest calculations are ignored and the percent of sales method is used in preparing *pro forma* financial statements.

Because the cash budget and *pro forma* financial statements each has its own direct advantages, it is common to see firms using these statements in ways that take advantage of the benefits of each. One approach is to prepare the cash budget from detailed information on the firm's collection of receivables, operating plan, and purchasing schedule, and then use the same detailed information to estimate balance sheet items such as cash, receivables, inventories, and payables in the *pro forma* financial statements. Thus, the cash budget and *pro forma* statements would be prepared in sequence for the same time period. Another approach is to prepare detailed cash budget information for a series of short time periods, such as days or weeks, and then prepare *pro forma* financial statements for longer time periods, such as quarters, from rather crude assumptions about the relationships of various items of sales. Obviously, the best approach to take depends on the purpose for which the analysis is performed.

Table 6.9 PPI *Pro forma* Balance Sheet January–June 1984

	Jan.	**Feb.**	**March**	**April**	**May**	**June**
Assets						
Cash	280	250	250	250	250	955
Accounts receivable	1,890	1,920	2,280	2,850	2,910	2,340
Inventory	1,500	2,175	2,475	1,950	1,200	900
Total current assets	3,670	4,345	5,005	5,050	4,360	4,195
Fixed assets	4,000	4,000	4,000	4,000	4,000	4,000
(less acc. depreciation)	(1,200)	(1,200)	(1,200)	(1,200)	(1,200)	(1,300)
Total assets	6,470	7,145	7,805	7,850	7,160	6,895
Liabilities and equity						
Notes payable	0	150	785	905	165	0
Taxes payable	260	320	270	420	560	450
Accounts payable	1,500	1,875	1,800	1,350	1,050	1,050
Equity and L-T debt	4710	4,800	4,950	5,175	5,385	5,395
Total liabilities and equity	6,470	7,145	7,805	7,850	7,160	6,895

Table 6.10   PPI *Pro forma* Income Statements January–June 1984

	Jan.	**Feb.**	**March**	**April**	**May**	**June**
Sales	1,600	1,600	2,000	2,500	2,400	1,800
Cost of goods sold	1,200	1,200	1,500	1,875	1,800	1,350
Gross margin	400	400	500	625	600	450
General selling and administrative expenses	250	250	250	250	250	250
Depreciation						100
Earnings before interest and tax	150	150	250	375	350	100
Taxes at 40%	60	60	100	150	140	40
Net income	90	90	150	225	210	60
Dividends						50
To retained earnings	90	90	150	225	210	10

Example   A *pro forma* balance sheet and income statement for Precision Products, Inc. in the months January to June, 1984 are shown in Tables 6.9 and 6.10.

These statements were prepared under the same assumptions used in preparing the cash budget. The accounts receivable in each month are determined from the sales forecast and the assumptions regarding the collection of receivables. For instance, the $1.89 million in receivables in January is equal to 90% of the January sales of $1.6 million plus 30% of December's sales of $1.5 million. Inventories in each month are equal to beginning inventories, plus purchases, minus cost of goods sold. Accounts payable are equal to accounts payable at the beginning of the period, plus purchases, minus payments during the period. The notes payable category in the *pro forma* balance sheet shown in Table 6.9 is the balancing item; that is, it measures the firm's cumulative financial requirement.

Tables 6.9 and 6.10 show that the firm is operating on a profitable basis throughout the first six months of 1984, even though it is short of cash for much of this period. Analysis of the *pro forma* balance sheet reveals that the cash shortage arises primarily from increases in the level of accounts receivable and inventory, which result from increases in sales.

COMPUTER-BASED FINANCIAL PLANNING MODELS

In recent years, many firms have either developed or purchased computer-based financial planning models to help reduce the time and effort required to forecast and plan effectively. Computer-based financial planning models represent the firm's financial statements in terms of a set of mathematical equations that are programmed into a computer. Once the manager has developed a database and formulated a set of relationships that fairly represent the firm's financial activities, she may use the model to generate a cash budget and *pro forma* financial statements, and to explore the financial implications of alternative corporate policies and economic scenarios.

Benefits of Financial Modeling

According to a survey conducted by Naylor and Schauland,[1] managers obtain at least seven benefits from the use of computer-based financial planning models: (1) ability to explore more alternatives, (2) better quality decision making, (3) more effective planning, (4) better understanding of the business, (5) faster decision making, (6) more timely information, and (7) more accurate forecasts. The primary shortcomings cited were: (1) lack of flexibility, (2) poor documentation, and (3) excessive input data requirements. The overwhelming majority of the managers surveyed expressed favorable experiences with these models.

Financial Model of PPI

The characteristics of a typical financial planning model may be illustrated with the help of the equations shown in Tables 6.11–6.13. These equations were used to generate the cash budget and *pro forma* financial statements described above for Precision Products, Inc. Together they constitute a financial planning model for PPI.

Several aspects of the PPI financial model are noteworthy. First, the PPI model contains four different kinds of variables:

1. *Exogenous variables.*   Some variables—for example, sales—are determined external to the financial planning environment. They may be forecast by means of a separate marketing model, or simply determined by subjective judgement. In either case, they are taken as given for the purpose of financial planning, and are referred to as exogenous variables.
2. *Predetermined variables.*   Variables such as long-term debt, equity, dividends, and beginning inventories are determined either at a prior stage of planning or by the firm's history. They, too, are treated as constants in the financial planning model.
3. *Policy variables.*   The coefficients describing the firm's collection and purchasing patterns are partly determined by firm policies regarding receivables and payables, and partly from the past history of the firm. Like the values of the exogenous and predetermined variables, they are treated as constants in the first stage of the financial planning analysis.
4. *Endogenous variables.*   The values of the remaining variables are determined by solving the system of equations comprising the model. They are said to be endogenous variables, because they are determined by the model rather than accepted as given from the outside. The major balance sheet and income statement line items are the major endogenous variables in most financial planning models.

As part of the forecasting and planning exercise, the manager must make certain assumptions about the variables falling in categories 1, 2. and 3. These assumptions are in many cases mere guesses, and the financial manager will want to see how sensitive the values of the endogenous variables are to changes in these assumptions.

---

[1]Thomas H. Naylor and Horst Schauland, ''A Survey of Users of Corporate Simulation Models,'' *Management Science,* May 1976.

Table 6.11 Financial Model for Generating PPI Cash Budget

1. Sales (in 000's) are given from a forecast external to model (Table 6.1):

Sales (1)[a] = 1,400	Sales (5) = 2,000	Sales (9) = 1,400
Sales (2) = 1,500	Sales (6) = 2,500	Sales (10) = 1,400
Sales (3) = 1,600	Sales (7) = 2,400	
Sales (4) = 1,600	Sales (8) = 1,800	

2. Cash collections from credit sales are 10% in the month of the sale, 60% one month later and 30% two months later:
   $$CCS(t) = .1Sales(t) + .6Sales(t - 1) + .3Sales(t - 2)$$

3. Materials and labor are purchased two months in advance of sales, disbursements for materials and labor are made one month after purchase and cost of goods sold equals 75% of sales:
   $$DMS(t) = .75Sales(t + 1)$$

4. Outlays for general administrative and selling expenses are $250,000/month:
   $$DGSA(t) = 250$$

5. Tax payments of $150,000 will be made in March and June:
   $$DTP(t) = 150 \quad \text{for } t = 5 \text{ and } 8$$
   $$\qquad\quad\ = 0 \qquad \text{otherwise}$$

6. Dividends of $50,000 are paid in June:
   $$DDIV(t) = 50 \quad \text{for } t = 8$$
   $$\qquad\qquad = 0 \qquad \text{otherwise}$$

7. Total receipts equals cash collections from credit sales:
   $$TREC(t) = CCS(t)$$

8. Total disbursement equals the sum of disbursements for material and labor, general selling and administrative expenses, tax payments, and dividends:
   $$TDISB(t) = DML(t) + DGSA(t) + DTP(t) + DDIV(t)$$

9. Net cash flow generated in each month equals the difference between total cash receipts and total cash disbursements:
   $$NCF(t) = TREC(t) - TDISB(t)$$

10. The minimum cash balance is $250,000:
   $$MCB(t) = 250$$

11. The forecasted cash balance equals the beginning cash balance plus the sum of all net cash flows generated to date:
   $$FCB(t) = 250 + \sum_{s=1}^{t} NCF(s)$$

12. The funds requirement equals the difference between the minimum balance of $250,000 and the forecasted cash balance:
   $$FREQ(t) = 250 - FCB(t)$$

[a]The number in parentheses indicates the month in the model: $t = 1$ refers to November, $t = 2$ refers to December, $t = 3$ refers to January, and so on.

One benefit of the financial planning model is that sensitivities of this kind may be evaluated very rapidly.

Second, the equations in the PPI financial model may be solved recursively. This means it is possible to arrange the equations in such a way that we could solve them one at a time. In a more general representation of PPI's financial statements this would

Table 6.12   Financial Model for Generating PPI Balance Sheet

1. Accounts receivable equal 90% of sales this period plus 30% of sales last period:
    $$AR(t) = .9Sales(t) + .3Sales(t - 1)$$
2. Inventories equal beginning inventories plus new purchases minus cost of goods sold:
    $$INV(t) = INV(t - 1) + PUR(t) - CGS(t)$$
    $$= INV(t - 1) + .75Sales(t + 2) - .75Sales(t)$$
3. Cash balance equals forecasted cash balance if the forecasted cash balance exceeds $250,000. It is set equal to $250,000 if the forecasted cash balance is less than $250,000:
    $$CASH(t) = FDB(t) \quad \text{if } FCB(t) > 250$$
    $$= 250 \qquad \text{if } FCB(t) \leq 250$$
4. Total current assets are the sum of cash assets, accounts receivable, and inventories:
    $$TCA(t) = CASH(t) + AR(t) + INV(t)$$
5. Fixed assets remain constant at $4,000,000:
    $$FA(t) = 4,000$$
6. Accumulated depreciation is $1,200,000, except that an additional $100,000 is realized in June:
    $$ADEP(t) = 1,200 \text{ for } t < 8$$
    $$= 1,300 \text{ for } t \geq 8$$
7. Total assets equals total current assets plus fixed assets minus accumulated depreciation:
    $$TA(t) = TCA(t) + FA(t) - ADEP(t)$$
8. Taxes payable are equal to beginning taxes payable plus 40% of net income minus tax payments:
    $$TP(t) = TP(t - 1) + .4NI(t) - DTP(t)$$
9. Accounts payable equal beginning accounts payable plus new purchases minus disbursements for material and labor:
    $$AP(t) = AP(t - 1) + PUR(t) - DML(t)$$
    $$= AP(t - 1) + .75Sales(t + 2) - .75Sales(t + 1)$$
10. Total equity and long-term debt equals beginning total equity and long-term debt plus retained earnings:
    $$ELTD(t) = ELTD(t - 1) + RE(t)$$
11. Notes payable are the balancing item; that is, they equal total assets minus the sum of taxes payable, accounts payable and equity and long-term debt:
    $$NP(t) = RA(t) - TP(t) - AP(t) - ELTD(t)$$
12. Total liabilities plus equity equals the sum of notes payable, taxes payable, accounts payable, and equity and long-term debt:
    $$TLE(t) = NP(t) + TP(t) + AP(t) + ELTD(t)$$

not be possible. If, for instance, we had included an equation in the income-statement part of the model expressing interest as a function of the amount of notes payable, it would have been necessary to solve them simultaneously. This is easy to do on a computer.

Third, the financial requirements shown in the income statement section of the model will equal the notes payable in the balance sheet segment of the model in all cases where the financial requirements are positive. This is because the assumptions about the firm's receivables and purchasing policies are consistent in both segments of the model.

Table 6.13   Financial Model for Generating PPI Income Statement

1. Sales: See Equation 1 of Table 6.11
2. Cost of goods sold equals 75% of sales:
    $CGS(t) = .75Sales(t)$
3. Gross margin equals sales minus cost of goods sold:
    $GM(t) = Sales(t) - CGS(t)$
4. General selling and administrative expense equals \$250,000/month:
    $GSA(t) = 250$
5. Depreciation of \$100,00 is recorded in June:
    $DEP(t) = 100$ for $t = 8$
    $\quad\quad = 0$ otherwise
6. Earnings before interest and taxes equals the gross margin minus general selling and administrative expenses minus depreciation:
    $EBIT(t) = GM(t) - GSA(t) - DEP(t)$
7. Taxes are 40% of earnings before interest and taxes:
    $TAX(t) = .4EBIT(t)$
8. Net income equals earnings before interest and taxes minus taxes:
    $NI(t) = EBIT(t) - TAX(t)$
9. Dividends of \$50,000 are paid in June:
    $DIV(t) = 50$ for $t = 8$
    $\quad\quad = 0$ otherwise
10. Retained earnings equal net income minus dividends:
    $RE(t) = NI(t) - DIV(t)$

Risk Analysis

In some financial planning software packages, it is possible to extend the analysis of the firm's financial requirements to allow for the possibility of uncertain sales. To illustrate how this is done, suppose that the Vice President-Marketing at PPI believes that each month's sales are independent, normally distributed random variables with the set of means and standard deviations shown in Table 6.14. The user inputs this information into the computer, and the computer proceeds to make a series of draws from the set of monthly sales distributions. After each draw, the computer calculates the firm's financial requirements, using the assumptions about cash collections and disbursements stated above. It continues to do this for 100 or more draws. At the end, it presents a frequency distribution of the firm's financial requirements in each month.

Table 6.15 displays the means and standard deviations of PPI's monthly financial requirements obtained from a typical risk analysis simulation package. Note that the

Table 6.14   Means and Standard Deviations of Probability Distributions
for PPI's Monthly Sales

	Nov.	Dec.	Jan.	Feb.	March	April	May	June	July	Aug.
Mean	1,400	1,500	1,600	1,600	2,000	2,500	2,400	1,800	1,400	1,400
Standard deviation	70	75	80	80	100	125	120	90	70	70

Table 6.15   Means and Standard Deviations of Frequency Distributions (100 draws) for PPI's Monthly Financial Requirements

	Jan.	Feb.	March	April	May	June
Mean	$27	−158	−793	−907	−166	707
Standard deviation	$59	99	131	158	183	201

means of the financial requirement distributions are reasonably close to the estimated financial requirements shown in Table 6.4. However, the analysis indicates that PPI's peak financial requirement may exceed the $907,000 found above by a substantial margin. In fact, the firm would have to obtain a line of credit of $1,397,000 if it wanted to take no more than 1 chance in 1000 of running out of cash.

FINANCIAL PLANNING

Once the financial manager has prepared her forecast of the firm's financial requirements over the near to medium term future, she must begin to prepare a plan for satisfying these financial requirements in a cost-effective way. In this section, we describe how the financial manager can prepare such a plan and evaluate its effectiveness.

The Nature of the Planning Problem

The nature of the short-run financial planning problem may be illustrated with our earlier example. Recall that the cash requirements of Precision Products, Inc. (PPI) are forecast to be:

PPI Cash Flows January–June 1984 (in 000's)

Jan.	Feb.	March	April	May	June
30	(180)	(635)	(120)	740	870

Suppose that PPI has available three alternative means of financing its projected cash deficits in the first six months of 1984:

1. *Line of credit.*   PPI has a line of credit at the Main Street National Bank that permits it to borrow up to $550,000 at an annual interest rate of 12%. For ease of analysis, we assume that PPI must repay the amount borrowed at the beginning of any month with interest at the beginning of the following month.
2. *Commercial paper.*   PPI can borrow up to $400,000 by issuing 90-day commercial paper at an annual interest rate of 11%. Although commercial paper is normally sold on a discount basis, for the purposes of analysis we assume that interest is payable at maturity.

3. *Term loan.* PPI has an especially attractive offer from the City National Bank that would allow it to borrow up to $400,000 under a term loan arrangement at an interest rate of only 9%. However, the term loan can only be taken out in January and repaid with interest in July.

Furthermore, suppose that PPI can invest any surplus balances in a 30-day CD earning 8%.

Which financing alternative should PPI accept? The answer is not self-evident. The term loan has the most attractive interest rate, but it must be taken out for the entire six-month period, with the result that the firm would be paying 9% interest on money that in some months it was investing in a CD earning only 8%. The line of credit is unattractive from an interest rate point of view, but it gives the firm flexibility to borrow only as much as it needs in each month. Commercial paper is an intermediate alternative that is available at a lower interest rate than the line of credit, but is also more flexible than the term loan.

In deciding which financing alternative to adopt, the financial manager must come up with a number of alternatives that meet all of the firm's financial constraints. The three constraints previously noted are that borrowing under the line of credit can be no greater than $550,000, while borrowing under the commercial paper or term loan alternatives must be no greater than $400,000. Another important constraint is that the firm's sources and uses of funds must be equal in every period. In terms of the borrowing and investment alternatives described above, this means that the amount invested in CD's plus the amount used to repay previous borrowings must equal the amount of new borrowings plus the amount of maturing CD's plus the projected cash flow in each period, that is,

$$\text{Investment} + \frac{\text{Repayment of}}{\text{Borrowing}} = \frac{\text{New}}{\text{Borrowing}} + \frac{\text{Maturing}}{\text{Investments}} + \frac{\text{Projected}}{\text{Cash Flow}}$$

With this information in mind, the financial manager's first task is to prepare a financial plan that satisfies all of the firm's financial constraints. (We call this a feasible financial plan.) To accomplish this task, the financial manager makes use of a table that reflects the important sources and uses of funds constraint:

Strategy

Period	CD Investment	+	Repayment of Borrowing	=	New Borrowing	+	Maturing CD's	+	Projected Cash Flow
1									30
2									(180)
3									(635)
4									(120)
5									740
6									870

Beginning with period 1, the financial manager sees that investing $30,000 in a 30-day CD is certainly feasible. She therefore writes 30 in the first row under the column labeled CD Investment. She simultaneously writes 30 in the second row under the column labeled maturing CD because the first period investment matures in period 2.

Moving to period 2, the financial manager recognizes that she has two alternatives for financing the $150,000 period-2 requirement: the credit line and commercial paper. (Recall that the term loan can only be taken out in period 1.) Since commercial paper has the lower rate of interest, the financial manager decides to use it. Furthermore, she decides to borrow up to the $400,000 limit in commercial paper, because she sees that she will need at least that amount in the next two periods. The decision to issue $400,000 of commercial paper in period 2 requires three entries in the above table: it requires $400 under the new borrowing column for period 2, $250 in the CD investment column in period 2, and $400 under the repayment of borrowing column in period 5.

At this point, the financial manager has no alternative but to satisfy her remaining financial requirements by borrowing under the credit line. The additional entries and the interest cost of this entire strategy is shown in Table 6.16.

Proceeding in a similar manner, the financial manager can identify alternative feasible financial strategies and evaluate their interest cost. Table 6.17 displays a financial strategy whose total interest cost is less than that of strategy 1. The financial manager would obviously prefer this strategy to strategy 1 if she had to choose between them, but if she could, she would prefer finding a strategy with an even lower cost.

Table 6.16   An Evaluation of Financial Strategy 1

Period	Investment +	Repayment of Borrowing =	New Borrowing +	Maturing CD's +	Predicted Cash Flow
1	30				30
2	250		400(CP)	30	(180)
3			385(CL)	250	(635)
4		385	505(CL)		(120)
5		505 CL	165(CL)		740
		400 CP			
6	705	165 CL			870

Cost of Strategy 1

Period	Invest	Borrow	Cost
1	30		−0.2
2	250	400(CP)	−1.67 + 11
3		385(CL)	3.85
4		505(CL)	5.05
5		165(CL)	1.65
6	705		−4.72
			14.96 or $14,960

Table 6.17   An Evaluation of Financial Strategy 2

Period	Investment	+	Repayment of Borrowing	=	New Borrowing	+	Maturing CD's	+	Predicted Cash Flow
1	430				400(TL)				30
2	250						430		(180)
3					385(CL)		250		(635)
4			385		505(CL)				(120)
5	235		505						740
6	1105						235		870
7			400				1015		

Cost of Strategy 2

Period	Invest	Borrow	Cost
1	430	400(TL)	−2.88 + 18
2	250		−1.68
3		385(CL)	3.85
4		505(CL)	5.05
5	165		−1.11
6	1015		−6.80
			14.43 or $14,430

LINEAR PROGRAMMING FORMULATION

The evaluation of alternative financial plans can be an exceedingly difficult task. The financial manager must identify a number of alternative feasible plans and perform the many calculations required to evaluate their cost.[2] Furthermore, there is nothing to assure the financial manager that he has identified the best plan.

To avoid the above difficulties, some firms have either developed or purchased financial software packages that allow them to formulate and solve the short-run financial planning problem as a linear program. The linear programming formulation has, as an objective, the goal of minimizing the net interest cost of the financial plan. It allows for a great variety of financial constraints, including the familiar sources and uses of funds constraint and upper limits on the amounts borrowed from various sources. For the more advanced reader, it may be instructive to examine the linear programming formulation of the above example shown in Appendix A.

SUMMARY

Cash budgets and *pro forma* financial statements are the most widely used techniques for forecasting the firm's financial requirements. These techniques are easy to understand and provide insights into financial relationships that are not obtainable using

[2]The calculations for the above examples are not too bad because we ignore the compounding of interest. This is not desirable in practice.

more sophisticated techniques. By performing a sensitivity analysis, the manager can use these techniques to determine her financial requirements in a variety of economic circumstances.

The most serious drawback of the accounting-based approaches discussed in this chapter is that they provide inadequate information on the likelihood that different cash levels will occur. Although the risk analysis programs available as part of some financial planning packages do provide a small amount of information on the probability distribution of the firm's cash requirements, this information is a direct consequence of the assumed probability distribution of the firm's sales; it was not determined from rigorous statistical analysis. More advanced statistical approaches to cash forecasting are discussed in the next two chapters.

DISCUSSION QUESTIONS

1. What are the major purposes of forecasting a firm's cash requirements?
2. How do accounting-based methods of cash forecasting differ from statistically based methods?
3. What is the one most critical element underlying the cash budget and *pro forma* income statement methods of cash forecasting?
4. Describe how the numbers in Table 6.2 are derived?
5. How can the cash budget be used to determine the size of the firm's line of credit?
6. What decisions is the cash budget used to analyze?
7. When establishing a line of credit based on a cash budget or *pro forma* analysis, the lending bank will generally specify a minimum cash balance that the firm must maintain. Why?
8. How are the *pro forma* income statement and *pro forma* balance sheet interrelated?
9. Describe the two major methods of constructing *pro forma* financial statements.
10. It is certainly conceivable that a firm experiencing steady growth at a rapid rate could consistently show accounting profits, while at same time experience an inability to meet all its obligations on time. In Tables 6.9 and 6.10 consider the effect on the firm's cash position and net borrowings if sales continue to rise above $2500 in June, July, and August.
11. What is the relationship between short- and long-term *pro forma* statements?
12. What advantages do *pro forma* statements have over cash budgets? What are the advantages of the cash budget over *pro formas?*
13. How can sensitivity analysis of cash budgets and *pro formas* be used to improve cash management decision making?
14. What are the limitations of these kinds of sensitivity analyses?

PROBLEMS

1. The marketing department of Flashy Ski Wear (FSW) has estimated the following levels of sales (in 1000's) for the last three months of 1984 and the first five months of 1985:

Actual Sales (July–Sept.)

July	Aug.	Sept.	Oct.	Nov.	Dec.	Jan.	Feb.	March	April	May
600	750	900	1,600	1,700	2,100	1,100	900	500	500	600

From previous experience, the firm's financial manager estimates that 20% of sales in a given month are for cash, 40% are collected the following month, 30% are collected the second month after the sale, and 10% are collected the third month after the sale. The financial manager knows that the raw materials and labor necessary to produce a given month's sales must be purchased two months in advance and paid for one month in advance of the sales. Cost of goods sold averages 70% of the sales price. Finally, the financial manager has determined that:

(a) FSW has monthly outlays for general administrative and selling expenses of $175,000.

(b) Tax payments of $150,000 will be made in September, December, and March.

(c) $50,000 of depreciation expenses are allocated to each quarter; they appear in the quarterly statements for the three months ending September, December, and March.

(d) Dividends of $15,000 are paid at the end of each quarter.

(e) The firm currently has a cash balance of $175,000, which it desires to maintain throughout the year.

(f) FSW's tax rate is 40%.

(g) The following balances exist on September 30, 1984:

Taxes Payable	220
Fixed Assets	3,500
Equity and L-T-D	3,000
Accumulated Depreciation	2,000
Notes Payable	439

From the above information, prepare both a cash budget and a set of *pro forma* financial statements for the period October, 1984 to March, 1985.

2. The financial manager of FSW realizes that sales are uncertain, and that sales for the peak months of October, November and December could easily be 10% above or below his estimates. What is the effect of a 10% increase or decrease in sales for these months on his financial requirements?

3. The financial manager of FSW is considering the possibility of generating his cash budget electronically. He has asked you to write a set of equations that can be used to generate FSW's cash budget. What equations do you propose to use?

4. Christmas Toys Inc. has prepared the following forecast of its cash flows for the next six months (in 000's):

July	Aug.	Sept.	Oct.	Nov.	Dec.
(45)	(120)	(780)	(200)	950	1130

Suppose that CTI has available three financing alternatives:

(a) *Line of credit.* CTI has a line of credit at the First National Bank that permits it to borrow up to $600,000 at an annual interest rate of 14%. (Assume that CTI must repay the amount borrowed at the beginning of any month with interest paid at the beginning of the following month).

(b) *Commercial paper.* CTI can borrow up to $550,000 by issuing 90-day commercial paper at an annual interest rate of 13%. (Assume that interest is payable at maturity and that CTI can never have more than $550,000 outstanding at any one time).

(c) *Term loan.* CTI has an offer from the Second National Bank that would allow it to borrow up to $550,000 under a term loan arrangement at an interest rate of 12%. However, the term loan can only be taken out in July and repaid with interest in January.

In addition, suppose that CTI can invest any surplus balances in a 30-day CD earning 9%.

CTI is considering two different strategies for satisfying its financial requirements. They can be characterized as follows:

Strategy I: Borrow $550,000 under the term loan in period 1; meet the remaining financial requirements with the line of credit.

Strategy II: Sell $550,000 of commercial paper in period 1; meet the remaining financial requirements with the line of credit and additional sales of commercial paper, if necessary.

With regard to CTI's financing problem, please answer the following questions.

(a) Under Strategy I, CTI's December investment in CD's will equal:
   (1) $1,395,000
   (2) $1,435,000
   (3) $1,465,000
   (4) $1,485,000

(b) Under Strategy II, CTI's new borrowings in October will be:
   (1) 595,000—Credit Line
   (2) 550,000—Commercial Paper
       595,000—Credit Line
   (3) 550,000—Commercial Paper
       545,000—Credit Line
   (4) 550,000—Commercial Paper
       495,000—Credit Line

(c) Under Strategy I, CTI's net interest expense through the horizon will be approximately:
   (1) $23,000
   (2) $23,500
   (3) $24,000
   (4) $24,500

(d) Let S_t = the total dollars invested in CD's in period t
   X_t = the total dollars borrowed under the line of credit in period t
   Y_t = the total dollars of commercial paper issued in period t

Z_t = the total dollars borrowed under the term loan in period t

C_t = the projected cash flow in period t.

Using this notation, CTI's sources and uses of funds constraint may be formulated as follows:

(a) $1.0075S_{t-1} - S_t + X_t - 1.0117X_{t-1} + Y_t - 1.0325Y_{t-3} + Z_t = C_t$

(b) $1.0075S_{t-1} - S_t + X_t - 1.0117X_{t-1} + Y_t - 1.0108Y_{t-3} + Z_t = C_t$

(c) $S_t - 1.0075S_{t-1} + X_t - 1.0117X_{t-1} + Y_t - 1.0325Y_{t-3} + Z_t = C_t$

(d) $S_t - 1.0075S_{t-1} + X_t - 1.0117X_{t-1} + Y_t - 1.0108Y_{t-3} + Z_t = C_t$

ADDITIONAL READINGS

1. Francis, Jack C. and Dexter R. Powell, "A Simultaneous Equation Model of the Firm for Financial Analysis and Planning," *Financial Management,* Spring 1978, pp. 29–44.

2. Lerner, Eugene M., "Simulating a Cash Budget," *California Management Review,* Winter 1968, pp. 78–87.

3. Naylor, Thomas H., *Corporate Planning Models,* Addison-Wesley, Reading, Mass., 1979.

4. Naylor, Thomas H. and Horst Schauland, "A Survey of Users of Corporate Simulation Models," *Management Science,* May 1976.

5. Scott, David F., Lawrence J. Moore, Andre Saint-Denis, Edouard Archer, and Bernard W. Taylor, "Implementation of a Cash Budget Simulator at Air Canada," *Financial Management,* Summer 1979, pp. 46–52.

6. Stone, Bernell K., "Cash Planning and Credit-Line Determination with a Financial Statement Simulator: A Case Report on Short-Term Financial Planning," *Journal of Financial and Quantitative Analysis,* December 1973, pp. 711–729.

7. Warren, James M. and John P. Shelton, "A Simultaneous Equation Approach to Financial Planning," *Journal of Finance,* December 1971, pp. 1123–1142.

APPENDIX A

Linear Programming Formulation of PPI's Financial Decision Problem

Let

S_t = the total dollars invested in CD's in period t

X_t = the total dollars borrowed under the line of credit in period t

Y_t = the total dollars of commercial paper issued in period t

Z_t = the total dollars borrowed under the term loan in period t

C_t = the projected cash flow in period t

Using this notation, PPI's short-run financial decision problem may be formulated as follows:

$$\text{Max } 1.0067S_6 - 1.01X_6 - 1.0275Y_4 - 1.045Z_1 \tag{6.1}$$

$$\text{s.t. } 1.0067S_{t-1} - S_t + X_t - 1.01X_t + Y_t$$
$$- 1.0275Y_{t-3} + Z_t = C_t \qquad \text{for } t = 1, \ldots, 6 \tag{6.2}$$

$$X_t \le 550 \qquad \text{for } t = 1, \ldots, 6 \tag{6.3}$$

$$Y_t + Y_{t-1} + Y_{t-2} \le 400 \qquad \text{for } t = 1, \ldots, 6 \tag{6.4}$$

$$Z_t \le 400 \qquad \text{for } t = 1, \ldots, 6 \tag{6.5}$$

$$Y_5 = Y_6 = Z_2 = Z_3 = Z_4 = Z_5 = Z_6 = 0 \tag{6.6}$$

$$X_t = 0, \quad Y_t = 0, \quad Z_t = 0, \quad S_t = 0 \tag{6.7}$$

The following comments help to clarify this formulation.

1. The objective function 6.1 is the horizon value of the firm's short-term financial portfolio. It is measured by the difference between the cash inflows and outflows at the beginning of period 7. ($1.0067S_6$ is the cash inflow from dollars invested in CD's in period 6, $1.0X_6$ is the interest plus principal due on line-of-credit borrowings in period 6, $1.0275Y_4$ is the interest plus principal due on commercial paper borrowings in period 4, and $1.045Z_1$ is the interest plus principal due on the term loan taken out in period 1.)

2. The constraint 6.2 is the firm's sources and uses of funds constraint. It says that the total borrowings in period t plus the principal and interest on investments maturing in period t must equal the predicted cash flow in period t plus the interest and principal on borrowings due in period t plus new investments.

3. Constraints 6.3 to 6.5 are the upper bound constraints on the different borrowing sources.

4. Constraint 6.6 indicates that commercial paper cannot mature beyond the horizon and the term loan cannot be taken out after period 1.

CHAPTER 7

Statistical Approaches to Cash Forecasting

The accounting-based cash forecasting techniques described in Chapter 6 are the most commonly used methods of cash forecasting in U.S. firms. They have the advantage of conforming to the accounting language that financial officers use for reporting and control purposes. They also highlight relationships between various balance sheet accounts so that the financial manager can obtain a complete picture of the firm's financial performance in the near term.

Recently, many firms have begun to recognize that they can enhance their cash forecasting ability through the use of statistical techniques such as regression and time series analysis. The primary advantages of these techniques are:

1. They provide an estimate of the uncertainty associated with the cash forecast. This is helpful in negotiating lines of credit and determining buffer stocks of liquid assets.
2. They can be used to detect "patterns" in the data that are not apparent from examining accounting statements alone.

This chapter describes how statistical models can be used to improve the manager's ability to forecast his cash position. It begins with a description of how a statistical model is developed and what choices one has to make in the development process. It then describes two statistical approaches to cash forecasting that have been successfully used in U.S. industry. These approaches were developed by Bernell K. Stone, a leading scholar in this area.

PROBLEM STRUCTURING

Statistical techniques work on the assumption that history tends to repeat itself. Thus, the past is studied to see if there are any "patterns" or "regularities" that might serve as useful guides to predicting the future. The power of statistical techniques is that they are helpful in discovering historical "patterns" that are not apparent to the casual observer.

When using statistical techniques, one must take great care to structure the data so that the basic assumption of a stable pattern is justified. There are three basic principles of data structuring that can help assure the success of statistical forecasting techniques.[1] It should be recognized that these principles are to be applied well before the model building process begins.

Major versus Non-major Cash Flows

A major part of the firm's cash flows are either known with certainty or are essentially nonrepetitive in nature. Cash flows such as wages, interest payments, rent, taxes, and utility payments are known with a high degree of certainty several months in advance. Cash flows such as the payment for a building or the receipt of money from the sale of a bond may not be known with certainty, but they are nonrepetitive in nature and hence are not proper subjects for statistical forecasting techniques. Both the cash flows that are known with certainty and those that are nonrepetitive will be called major cash flows, because they are usually a large percentage of the firms total cash flow. Major cash flows should be segregated from the firms non-major cash flows before the statistical model-building process begins. Failure to do so is one of the most common reasons why statistical models frequently yield poor results in practice.

Cash Flow Components

The firm's total non-major cash flows frequently can be divided into components that are determined by different statistical forces. Cash inflows should certainly be separated from cash outflows because the statistical determinants of these two components are not the same. Likewise, the factors that affect the cash disbursements of one division of a firm may differ significantly from the factors affecting the disbursements of another division. Combining cash flow components often produces a "confounding" of statistical "patterns" that leads to poor forecasting results. Cash forecasting can be improved if a separate statistical model is developed for each cash flow component.

Time Sequence of Cash Flows

It is important to recognize that the firm's cash flows occur in distinct time sequences. On the collection side, the time sequence might consist of the mailing of bills, the time

---

[1]These three data structuring principles were first described in B. K. Stone and R. A. Wood, "Daily Cash Forecasting: A Simple Method for Implementing the Distribution Approach," *Financial Management* (Fall 1977), pp. 40–50.

lag between receipt of the bill and payment by the customer, the mail time or the time the customer's check is in the mail, and the bank availability time. On the disbursement side, the time sequence might consist of the receipt of an invoice, the payment of the bill, and the delay between the day the check is mailed and the day it is presented to the disbursing firm's bank for payment. Frequently, statistical forecasting techniques are more appropriate for one stage of the time sequence than for another. For instance, most firms can forecast accurately, without statistical techniques, the dollar amount and mailing date of payments it sends in the mail from information on invoices received and the due dates on the invoices. Statistical techniques can then be applied to predict the time delay between the mailing date and the presentment date. Examples of such disbursement float forecasting models will be discussed later in Chapter 8.

BUILDING A STATISTICAL MODEL

Once the data have been properly structured to assure that the stability assumptions of statistical analysis are satisfied, the model builder has to make several important choices regarding the form of the model. These involve the selection of information to use in making the forecast (often called the forecast input), the choice of functional form, the assumptions about the forecast error, and the choice of technique for estimating the coefficients of the model.

Choice of Forecast Input

The choice of what information to use in making the forecast greatly affects the success of the forecasting model. Frequently, the firms total cash flow will be broken into components for forecasting purposes, and different variables will be used to forecast each component. Cash collections, for instance, usually depend on credit sales in previous months, so they are the logical choice for input in a model for forecasting cash collections. On the other hand, cash disbursements depend on invoices received in prior months or purchases of raw materials in prior months, and so these are the more logical choices of forecast input in a model for forecasting disbursements. If cash collections or disbursements exhibit a regular pattern over time, the appropriate forecast input is a variable that indicates the passage of time.

Choice of Functional Form

After he has chosen the forecast input, the model builder must decide how the forecast variable is related to the forecast input. The assumption of a linear relationship is used most often in practice, but the model builder should carefully analyze whether this assumption is reasonable. A scatter diagram of the data is helpful in this regard. Figure 7.1 shows several possible scatter diagrams of the relationship between two variables. The first diagram indicates that a linear relationship is most appropriate, while the others suggest that various nonlinear relationships are more appropriate for describing the relationship between the two variables. It should be clear from these diagrams that any attempt to fit a straight line to data that are related in a nonlinear fashion is likely to

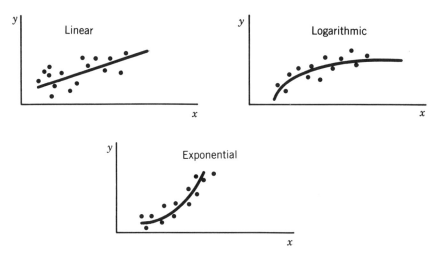

Figure 7.1 Scatter diagrams of relationship between two variables.

produce unsuccessful forecasts. This is unfortunate because the most commonly used statistical models depend on the assumption of linearity.

Assumption About the Error Term

In order to make inferences about the level of uncertainty surrounding the forecast, the model builder must make certain assumptions about the distribution of the forecast error. Three aspects of the error-term distribution are important. These are:

1. Does the error-term distribution fall in the family of normal distributions (i.e., bell-shaped distributions), or is some other family of distributions more appropriate? The assumption of a normal distribution is most convenient because there are only a limited number of parameters to be estimated and the theoretical and computational aspects of this distribution are well known. However, the normal distribution does not apply in all cases. The user may have to perform a post-audit of the errors to check whether they fit this distribution.
2. Are the errors independent of one another? The usual assumption is that they are, but in cash management this is frequently not appropriate. For instance, if more checks are presented to the firm's bank on a given day than was previously forecast, the chances are good that the amount presented the following day will be less than was forecast. After all, the firm sent out a fixed amount of checks. Statistical methods for taking into account the dependence in the error pattern will be discussed later in the chapter.
3. Is the distribution of the errors stable from one time period to the other or does it shift? Almost all statistical techniques require the assumption of a large degree of stability (statisticians use the word "stationarity") in the error-term distribution. When this assumption does not hold, statistical methods are likely to fail.

Summary of Model-Building Principles

Success in statistical forecasting depends on several key decisions that are made at various stages. These decisions may be conveniently summarized by writing the cash forecasting model in a general form. The cash forecast may be expressed in symbols as:

$$CF = f(x,y,z) + e \qquad (7.1)$$

In equation 7.1, CF refers to the component of cash flow that is to be forecast. This may be cash collections for a certain division of the firm, cash disbursements to vendors, or any other component of cash flow for which the assumption of a stable relationship is legitimate. The letter f along with the parentheses indicate that this cash flow component is a function of, or depends on, the values of certain other variables. These variables, denoted for ease of reference by the letters x, y, and z, may be credit sales in previous periods, invoices received from suppliers in previous months, or simply time, depending on the particular application. The letter e in Equation 7.1 is used to indicate that our cash forecast is rarely exact; it is a random variable measuring the forecast error.

The symbolic form of describing a statistical forecasting model, given by Equation 7.1, helps us to understand the various choices that the model builder must make before the actual forecasting begins. In particular he must choose:

1. The information he is going to use to forecast cash—that is, his choices for the independent variables x, y and z.
2. The functional form of the relationship between x, y, and z and the firm's cash flow—that is, a linear or nonlinear relationship.
3. A set of assumptions about the distribution of the error, so that he can estimate the degree of uncertainty in his forecast.

ESTIMATION TECHNIQUES

Under the assumption that the relationship between the forecast variable and the forecast input is linear, we may write the statistical forecasting model 7.1 as

$$CF = ax + by + cz + e, \qquad (7.2)$$

where the letters a, b, and c are coefficients that need to be estimated from the available data. The proper method for estimating these coefficients depends on the assumptions one is willing to make about the distribution of the error term e. If the individual observations of the error term can be assumed to be independent of one another and independent of the forecast inputs x, y, and z, then the ordinary least squares regression techniques will be most appropriate. This assumption about the error term is most often legitimate when lagged values of the variables x, y, and z do not appear in the forecast equation, and there is no time pattern to the errors.

In cases where lagged values of the forecast inputs are present in the forecast equation, and/or the error term exhibits a complex time pattern, the model builder may need to employ a set of estimation techniques recently developed by Box and Jenkins.[2] These techniques are considerably more complex to use than regression techniques because the estimation occurs in several stages, with considerable judgement applied at each stage. However, the Box-Jenkins technique is an extremely powerful forecasting tool that has been successfully applied to many forecasting situations, including cash forecasting in a large oil firm.

APPLICATIONS

In the remainder of this chapter, we describe two statistical forecasting models that have been implemented in U.S. firms: The Payments Pattern Model and the Distribution Model. These models differ primarily in the choices that are made regarding the forecast input, the functional form, and the assumptions about the error-term distribution.

The Payments Pattern Model[3]

Many components of the firm's cash flow are related to sources that originated on a prior date. For instance, monthly cash collections from credit sales are related to total credit sales in previous months. Similarly, the dollar amount of checks presented to the firm's bank on a given day is related to the dollar amount of checks mailed out on previous days. The Payments Pattern Model is designed to forecast cash components that fall in this category.

When a cash component is related to a source originating at a prior time, it is natural to forecast the value of the cash component from knowledge of the average time delay, or "payment pattern," between the occurrence of the source and its corresponding cash flow. To illustrate how knowledge of the typical payment pattern can be used to forecast the values of the future cash flow, consider the example displayed in Table 7.1. For this firm, the credit sales for the eight month period November to June are $6000, $7000, $3000, $4000, $5000, $6000, $4000, and $7000, respectively. It is assumed that the firm collects 10% of a given month's credit sales in the current month, 50% one month later, and 40% in two months. Thus, $300 of January's sales are collected in January, $1500 are collected in February and $1200 are collected in March.

Examination of Table 7.1 reveals that total collections in any month can be expressed as a linear function of credit sales in previous months. Under our assumptions, this function is

$$TCC_t = .1CS_t + .5CS_{t-1} + .4CS_{t-2} \qquad (7.3)$$

[2]G. E. P. Box and G. M. Jenkins, *Time Series Analysis: Forecasting and Control*, Holden-Day, San Francisco, 1970.
[3]The Payments Pattern Model was developed by B. K. Stone to forecast monthly cash collections from credit sales. (See B. K. Stone, "The Payments Pattern Model to Forecasting and Control of Accounts Receivable," *Financial Management*, Autumn 1976, pp. 65–82.)

Table 7.1 Example of Cash Collections from Credit Sales

Credit		Cash Collections					
Month	Sales	Jan.	Feb.	March	April	May	June
Nov.	6,000	2,400					
Dec.	7,000	3,500	2,800				
Jan.	3,000	300	1,500	1,200			
Feb.	4,000		400	2,000	1,600		
March	5,000			500	2,500	2,000	
April	6,000				600	3,000	2,400
May	4,000					400	2,000
June	7,000						700
	Total	6,200	4,700	3,700	4,700	5,400	5,100

where TCC_t is total cash collections in month t, CS_t is credit sales in month t, CS_{t-1} is credit sales in month $t-1$, and CS_{t-2} is credit sales in month $t-2$. Coefficients in this linear function measure the proportions of a given month's credit sales that are collected in the current and later months; that is, they measure the "payment pattern."

In practice, the firm will not know the values of the payment pattern coefficients, as assumed in this example. Instead, it must estimate these coefficients from historical data on total cash collections and credit sales. Given the above illustration, it is natural to estimate the coefficients from a regression of the form

$$\text{TCC}_t = p_0\,\text{CS}_t + p_1\,\text{CS}_{t-1} + \cdots + p_H\,\text{CS}_{t-H} + e_t \qquad (7.4)$$

where $p_0,\cdots,p_H$ are unknown payment pattern coefficients, H is the latest month in which collections are made. and e_t is an error term that represents uncertainty in the forecast. Several issues that arise in estimating these coefficients merit examination.

Constraints on Coefficients

If the firm has no bad debts, the payment pattern coefficients (in Equation 7.4) should theoretically sum to 1. However, there are a variety of reasons why the coefficients that are actually estimated rarely sum to 1 in practice. This anomaly can be handled in one of two ways. First, the coefficients can be rescaled so that

$$\hat{p}_i = p_i \bigg/ \left(\sum_{j=0}^{H} p_j\right), \qquad i = 0,\ldots,H \qquad (7.5)$$

where $\hat{p}_i$ is the scaled coefficient for month i, and p_i is the original estimated coefficient.

Second, the analyst can use an approach called constrained regression[4] that will

[4]See J. Johnston, *Econometric Methods,* McGraw-Hill, 1972, pp. 356–364 for a description of constrained regression.

assure that the payment pattern coefficients sum to 1. The latter approach is somewhat more complex, but is theoretically the correct way to impose the constraint.

Illustration

Assume a regression of historical data on the payment patterns of a firm yields the following relationship:

$$\text{TCC}_t = .12\text{CS}_t + .24\text{CS}_{t-1} + .47\text{CS}_{t-2} + .14C_{t-3} + e_t,$$

where $P_0 = 0.12$

$\quad\quad P_1 = 0.24$

$\quad\quad P_2 = 0.47$

$\quad\quad P_3 = 0.14.$

Summing the coefficients yields a value of 0.97. Therefore, each of the coefficients must be rescaled according to Equation 7.5:

$$P_0 = \frac{.12}{.97} = .124$$

$$P_1 = \frac{.24}{.97} = .248$$

$$P_2 = \frac{.47}{.97} = .484$$

$$P_3 = \frac{.14}{.97} = .144$$

The rescaled coefficients now sum to 1, yielding the following modified payment pattern forecast with the error term removed:

$$\text{TCC}_t = .124\text{CS}_t + .248\text{CS}_{t-1} + .484\text{CS}_{t-2} + .144C_{t-3}.$$

Treatment of Bad Debts

If the firm generally does not collect all of its credit sales, then the analyst must simultaneously estimate the proportion of bad debts and the payment pattern. If we let GCS_t denote gross credit sales in month t and BD_t denote the bad debts realized in month t, then the following two regressions can be used for the simultaneous estimation problem:

$$\text{BD}_t = B'_0\,\text{GCS}_t + B'_1\,\text{GCS}_{t-1} + \cdots + B'_H\text{GCS}_{t-H} + u_t, \tag{7.6}$$

$$\text{TCC}_t = p'_0\,\text{GCS}_t + p'_1\,\text{GCS}_{t-1} + \cdots + p'_H\text{GCS}_{t-H} + e_t, \tag{7.7}$$

where $B'_0, \cdots, B'_H$ are the jointly estimated bad debt coefficients, $p'_0, \cdots, p'_H$ are the jointly estimated payment pattern coefficients, u_t is the error term in the bad debt equation, and e_t is the error term in the cash collection equation. The two equations are subject to the joint constraint that

$$P'_0 + \cdots + p'_H + B'_0 + \cdots + B'_H = 1 \tag{7.8}$$

Illustration

Assume that the total credit sales regression for a firm is the same as in illustration 7.5. Also assume that the reason the coefficients do not sum to 1 is due to bad debts of the firm's customers. A regression on historical bad debt patterns yields the following relationship:

$$BD_t = 0.0GCS_t + 0.0GCS_{t-1} + .005GCS_{t-2} + .01GCS_{t-3} + .015GCS_{t-4},$$

where $B'_0 = 0,$ $B'_3 = .01$
      $B'_1 = 0$ $B'_4 = .015$
      $B'_2 = .005$

It should be noted that the bad debt regression is solved simultaneously with the total cash collection regression with a joint unity coefficient constraint. As given by Equation 7.8, our same regression provides the following coefficients:

$$P'_0 + P'_1 + P'_2 + P'_3 + B'_0 + B'_1 + B'_2 + B'_3 + B'_4 = 1.0 \tag{7.8}$$

$$.12 + .24 + .47 + .14 + 0.0 + 0.0 + .005 + .01 + .015 = 1.0 \text{ (sample coefficients)}$$

Shifting Payment Patterns

The firm's payment pattern may shift over time due to changes in the economy or customer habits. Shifting payment patterns may be detected by keeping track of the forecast errors that arise from using the Payments Pattern Model to forecast future collections. In particular, if forecast errors are negative for 4 or 5 months in a row, this may indicate that the firm's customers are now paying more slowly, and that the forecast equation may have to be re-estimated. An alternative to re-estimating the equation is to include in the original version of Equation 7.4 additional economic variables that may be determinants of changes in payment patterns—for example, the level of interest rates or national income. The coefficients of these economic factors would then be estimated at the same time as the payments pattern coefficients.

Serial Correlation in Error Terms

When a regression equation such as 7.4 contains lagged values of the right-hand-side variables as inputs, the assumption that the components of the error term are independent is untenable. This is a technical problem that can be handled through a regression procedure developed by Cochran and Orcutt.[5] The complexity of this topic precludes further discussion here.

---

[5]See J. Johnston, *Econometric Methods,* McGraw-Hill, 1972, Chapter 8 for a discussion of serial correlation and the Cochran-Orcutt method of treating this problem.

THE DISTRIBUTION APPROACH

Distribution is a statistically based approach to cash forecasting that is especially designed to forecast the firm's daily cash position.[6] This approach uses a dummy-variable regression equation to estimate the typical pattern of cash flows over the days of the week and the days of the month. The resulting pattern is then used to "distribute" the firm's monthly cash budget over the days within the month. Distribution can be used for both cash collections and cash disbursements.

Forecasting Book Balances or Bank Balances

The distribution approach can be used to forecast either the cash balances on the firm's books or the net collected balances at the firm's bank. The difference between these two values is equal to the firm's float, which in turn, is composed of disbursement float and deposit float. Thus,

$$\text{bank balance} = \text{book balance} + \text{disbursement float} - \text{deposit float}.$$

Typically, a firm would use a two-step approach to forecasting daily cash balances. First, the distribution approach would be used to forecast the firm's daily book balances. Second, either the payment pattern approach, or some other method, would be used to forecast float. The remainder of this discussion describes the distribution approach as it is used in a one-step procedure (i.e., the distinction between book balances and bank balances is ignored).

Weekly and Monthly Patterns

The firm's total monthly cash flow often displays both a weekly and a monthly pattern. The weekly pattern is caused by customer payment habits and the peculiarities of the U.S. mail system. The monthly pattern is due to the terms of trade as well as to customer payment habits. An example of a weekly cash flow pattern is shown in Figure 7.2. The vertical axis measures the total fraction of the weekly cash flow, while the horizontal axis shows the day of the week. In this example, the largest fraction of the weekly cash flow occurs on Monday and the smallest fraction occurs on Thursday.

An example of a monthly pattern is shown in Figure 7.3. Here the vertical axis measures the fraction of the total monthly cash flow, while the horizontal axis shows the working days of the month.

Measuring Weekly and Monthly Patterns

An obvious approach to measuring weekly and monthly patterns is to calculate the average fraction of the weekly and monthly totals that occur on each day from past data. For instance, the weekly pattern could be estimated by

---

[6]The Distribution Approach is described more fully in B. K. Stone and R. A. Wood, "Daily Cash Forecasting: A Simple Method for Implementing the Distribution Approach," *Financial Management*, Fall 1977, pp. 40–50.

$$b_d = \frac{1}{N}\sum_{n=1}^{N} f_{dn}, \qquad d = 1, \ldots, 5 \qquad\qquad (7.9)$$

where f_{dn} measures the fraction of the weekly total that occurs on workday d in week n, N is the number of past weeks for which data are available, and b_d is the average value of past fractions for day d. Likewise the monthly pattern could be estimated by

$$a_t = \frac{1}{N}\sum_{n=1}^{N} f_{tn}, \qquad t = 1, \ldots, 23 \qquad\qquad (7.10)$$

where f_{tn} now measures the fraction of the monthly total that occurs on workday t in month n, N is the number of past months for which data are available, and a_t is the average value of past fractions for workday t.

Illustration

Assume a firm has examined historical data and determined the following weekly cash flow for day 1 in weeks 1 through 6 (Day 1 is Monday).

Week (n)	Percent of Total Week Bank Balance (f_{dn})
1	.30
2	.33
3	.29
4	.34
5	.39
6	.25

Using Equation 7.9, the average percent of the total weekly bank balance for the prior six weeks is:

$$b_1 = \tfrac{1}{6}(.30 + .33 + .29 + .34 + .39 + .25)$$
$$= .317$$

This indicates that on average 31.7% of the weekly cash balance occurred on Mondays.

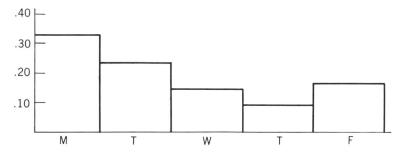

Figure 7.2 The day-of-week effect.

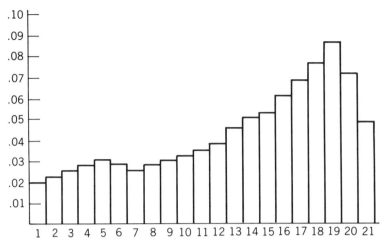

Figure 7.3 The day-of-month effect.

The above procedure breaks down, however, when the cash flow exhibits both weekly and monthly patterns at the same time. In this case, a dummy-variable regression equation can be used to measure simultaneously the weekly and monthly patterns. Let f_t again measure the fraction of the total monthly cash flow that occurs on workday t. Furthermore, let m_i be a dummy variable that equals 1 for day t and 0 otherwise, and let d_w be a dummy variable that is 1 when day t occurs on the wth day of the week and 0 otherwise. Then the regression

$$f_t = \sum_{i=1}^{M} a_i m_i + \sum_{w=1}^{5} b_w d_w + e_t. \tag{7.11}$$

where M is the number of working days in a month, can be used to estimate simultaneously weekly and monthly patterns.

Implementation

The distribution approach is implemented in the following manner:

1. The analyst employs the data structuring principles described in the first part of this chapter to segregate each cash flow component that lends itself to statistical cash flow forecasting[7] and whose monthly pattern is stable. Data on each cash flow component that satisfies these criteria are gathered from past monthly bank statements.
2. The dummy-variable regression procedure is used to estimate the coefficients a_i and b_w that characterize each cash flow component.

---

[7]See the discussion on pp. 126–127.

3. The projected monthly total of each cash flow component is obtained from the monthly cash budget. These monthly totals are computed in the manner described in Chapter 6.
4. The monthly total is then distributed over the days of the month through an equation such as

$$f_{12} = (a_{12} + b_3) \qquad (7.12)$$

where f_{12} is the forecasted fraction for workday 12, and a_{12} and b_3 are the estimated regression coefficients. In this case, it is assumed that workday 12 falls on weekday 3 (Wednesday). The total cash flow for workday 12, of course, is obtained by multiplying f_{12} by the monthly cash budget value of this component.
5. The statistical forecasts for each cash flow component are added together and the total is added to the forecasted value of the firm's major cash flows. As previously mentioned, the latter are generally known with some degree of certainty.

STATISTICAL ISSUES

Some other statistical issues related to the use of the distribution model concern the effects of holidays and changing monthly patterns.

Holidays   The normal monthly cash flow pattern is obviously affected by the presence of holidays. This is best handled by a two-step procedure: (1) the cash flow is first forecast in the absence of holidays, and (2) this figure is then adjusted for a typical holiday effect. For instance, if we know from past experience that 50% of the amount forecast for a holiday is delayed one working day and the remainder is delayed two working days, we would first forecast the total cash flow expected on the holiday and then shift 50% of this total to each of the next two days.

Changing Patterns   A change in the typical monthly pattern can usually be detected by observing forecast errors much in the manner described earlier in the section on the Payments Pattern Model. If the analyst can detect how previous forecast errors relate to future cash flows, a revised model can be estimated that allows for the possibility of such "error learning."

Calendar Day Effects   The monthly pattern in some cash flow components may be affected more by calendar days than by working days. In this case, the analyst should be careful to use dummy variables reflecting calendar days rather than working days.

SUMMARY

In this chapter, we have described a series of statistical techniques that can be used to provide improved cash forecasts in many situations. Three conclusions result from this discussion:

1. The user must take care at an early stage in the forecast process to structure the data in such a way that the stability assumption required for statistical analysis is satisfied.
2. There is no one statistical technique that yields good results for all cash forecasting problems. The user will have to think about the economic factors that most likely affect each cash flow component and choose a model that best allows her to capture these factors.
3. Statistical techniques are powerful but subtle tools that cannot be used in a mechanical fashion. The user must be aware of the underlying assumptions of each approach and must recognize that the models may need to be adjusted or fine-tuned after an initial trial period.

Statistical methods are highly successful in many industrial applications; financial management is no exception.

DISCUSSION QUESTIONS

1. Discuss the advantages and disadvantages of accounting-based approaches to cash forecasting.
2. How do statistical approaches to cash forecasting differ from accounting-based approaches?
3. Discuss the advantages and disadvantages of statistical approaches to cash forecasting.
4. Why is it important to properly structure the data before one uses a statistical forecasting model?
5. What is the difference between major and non-major cash flows?
6. Why is it important to divide the non-major cash flows into components?
7. What choices does one have to make in building a statistical cash forecasting model?
8. On what basis would you choose the forecast input?
9. On what basis would you choose the functional form of the relationship between forecast output and input?
10. Why are the assumptions about the error term important?
11. What are the typical assumptions one would make about the error term?
12. How would you test the accuracy of these assumptions?
13. What can you do if the "typical" assumptions are invalid?
14. Define the term "payment pattern."
15. How are payment pattern coefficients estimated?
16. Why do the payment pattern coefficients have to sum to one?
17. What can you do if the payment pattern coefficients don't sum to one?
18. How are bad debts handled in the Payment Pattern Model?
19. Describe some of the statistical problems that arise in the use of the Payment Pattern Model?
20. Describe the Distribution Approach to cash forecasting.

21. What is the difference between a firm's book balances and its bank balances?
22. Why is this distinction important to the Distribution Approach?
23. Why must weekly and monthly patterns be estimated simultaneously?
24. Describe how the Distribution Approach is implemented.
25. Discuss the statistical problems that may arise in implementing the Distribution Approach.

PROBLEMS

1. The Tyco Toy Company has gathered the following data on cash collections from credit sales:

Month	Credit Sales	Jan.	Feb.	March	April	May	June
				Cash Collections			

Month	Credit Sales	Jan.	Feb.	March	April	May	June
Nov.	$5,000	$1,530	$1,250				
Dec.	9,000	2,680	2,730	$2,260			
Jan.	6,000	980	1,790	1,810	$1,490		
Feb.	8,000		1,250	2,390	2,380	$1,985	
Mar.	4,000			610	1,220	1,210	$1,010
Apr.	5,000				745	1,530	1,480
May	3,000					460	920
June	6,000						890

What is your estimate of the payment pattern on Tyco's credit sales?

2. The marketing department at Tyco Toys has made the following forecast of credit sales for the next six months:

Month	Forecasted Credit Sales
July	$2,000
Aug.	3,000
Sept.	7,000
Oct.	6,000
Nov.	8,000
Dec.	7,000

Using this data and your answer to Problem 1, prepare a forecast of cash collections for the July to December period.

3. If the actual cash collection in July, August, and September turn out to be $4,950, $3,950, and $4,100, what would you conclude about the payment pattern on Tyco's credit sales?

4. Mitchell's Pharmacy has gathered the following data on cash receipts for the last three weeks:

Day/Date	Receipts		Day/Date	Receipts
Monday, 8/1	$4,200		Monday, 8/15	$4,600
Tuesday, 8/2	2,300		Tuesday, 8/16	2,500
Wednesday, 8/3	1,600		Wednesday, 8/17	1,650
Thursday, 8/4	3,100		Thursday, 8/18	3,150
Friday, 8/5	3,900		Friday, 8/19	4,100
Monday, 8/8	3,650			
Tuesday, 8/9	1,900			
Wednesday, 8/10	1,200			
Thursday, 8/11	2,300			
Friday, 8/12	2,950			

What is your estimate of the weekly pattern of cash receipts?

5. If the manager of Mitchell Pharmacy predicts that total cash receipts for the week beginning Monday, 8/22 will be $18,000, what would be your forecast of daily cash receipts for this week? *Hint*   Use your answer to Problem 4 and assume that there is no monthly pattern to cash receipts.

6. Suppose that Mitchell Pharmacy has hired you to develop a cash receipts forecasting model. You begin by running a dummy-variable regression on the daily cash receipt data that they provide you. Describe how you would organize the data matrix for the dummy variable regression. *Hint.*   Assume that there is both a monthly and a weekly pattern to the cash receipts data.

ADDITIONAL READINGS

1. Boyd, Kevin and Vincent A. Mabert, "A Two-Stage Forecasting Approach at Chemical Bank of New York for Check Processing," *Journal of Bank Research,* Summer 1977, pp. 101–107.

2. Lewellyn, Wilbur G. and Robert O. Edmister, "A General Method for Accounts Receivable Analysis and Control," *Journal of Financial and Quantitative Analysis,* March 1973. pp. 195–206.

3. Shim, Jae K., "Estimating Cash Collection Rates from Credit Sales: A Lagged Regression Approach," *Financial Management,* Winter 1981. pp. 28–30.

4. Stone, Bernell K., "The Payments Pattern Approach to the Forecasting and Control of Accounts Receivable," *Financial Management,* Autumn 1976, pp. 65–82.

5. Stone, Bernell K. and Tom W. Miller, "Daily Cash Forecasting with Dummy Variable Regression using Multiplicative and Mixed-Effect Models for Measuring

Cash Flow Cycles,'' Working Paper No. MS-79-18, College of Industrial Management, Georgia Institute of Technology, December 1979.

6. Stone, Bernell K. and Robert A. Wood, ''Daily Cash Forecasting: A Simple Method for Implementing the Distribution Approach,'' *Financial Management,* Fall 1977, pp. 40–50.

CHAPTER 8

Forecasting Daily
Disbursement Float

Forecasting daily disbursement float is one of the most important cash forecasting problems faced by financial managers. It is especially important to financial managers who wish to delay the funding of disbursement accounts until checks are presented for collection at the firm's bank. This practice of "playing the float" allows the financial manager to increase interest earnings on the firm's investments, but it also subjects her to the risk of having insufficient funds in the firm's account at the time checks arrive for payment. The financial manager can minimize the risk of insufficient funds by using better forecasting methods.

A forecast of daily disbursement float is also important to the financial manager who needs to plan the maturity structure of the firm's investment/borrowing portfolio. In this case, the forecast of disbursement float is used in conjunction with a schedule of book disbursements to help the financial manager earn the higher interest associated with longer term investments, without incurring the costs of liquidating investments before their maturity date.

This chapter discusses two statistical models of the firm's daily disbursements that follow the logic of the Payments Pattern Approach to cash forecasting. The first model generates daily cash forecasts from data on the *aggregate* dollar amount of the checks that were mailed to vendors on previous days. The distinctive feature of this model is that it corrects for the distorting effects of weekends in a novel manner.

The second model generates daily cash forecasts from the mailing date and dollar amount of *individual* vendor disbursements made, or scheduled to be made, during a time horizon not expected to exceed 90 days. Based on the historical distribution of the time between mailing date and clearing date, the model predicts when each disbursement item will be presented to the demand deposit account on which it is written.

The individual vendor disbursement forecasting model has three distinct features. First, it dynamically revises its cash forecast for future periods, as previously written checks are paid. Second, it tracks and updates the distribution of check processing times for the firm's largest vendors as new information becomes available. Third, it produces reports that alert the manager to significant changes in a particular vendor's check processing time, caused perhaps by a change in her lockbox site.

THE DAILY FORECASTING PROBLEM: AGGREGATE APPROACH

The Payments Pattern Approach was described in the last chapter as a method for forecasting the firm's monthly cash collections. When this method is applied to daily cash forecasting problems, an adjustment is required to correct for the distorting effects of weekends and holidays. To illustrate how this distorting effects comes about, we present the following example.[1]

Consider a firm that mails a total of $500,000 in checks over a five-day period in February: $100,000 on day 1, $100,000 on day 2, $100,000 on day 3, $100,000 on day 4, and $100,000 on day 5. Assume that 30% of the total amount mailed on a given day is presented to the firm's bank in three days, 50% in four days, and 20% in five days. (These assumptions are summarized in Table 8.1.)

If there are no weekends or holidays, Table 8.2 illustrates that the amount presented to the firm's bank on day t can be related to the amounts mailed on previous days by the simple equation:

$$d_t = .3m_{t-3} + .5m_{t-4} + .2m_{t-5},\tag{8.1}$$

where d_t is the amount disbursed from the bank on day t, m_{t-3} is the amount mailed three days ago, and so on.

Suppose now that both the firm and its bank are closed on days six and seven (the "weekend"). Since the firm's bank does not receive checks on the weekend, the dollar amounts of checks that would have been presented on days six and seven is shifted to the beginning of the next week. The precise pattern of this shift depends on how the check clearing system operates over the weekend.

To illustrate what can happen, assume that there is no check clearing over the weekend (i.e., checks continue to move through the system, but cannot be presented for payment). Under this assumption, the resulting pattern of presentations is summarized in Table 8.3.

Analysis of this table indicates that Monday presentments are considerably larger than they were when there were assumed to be no weekends. This is because the amount presented on Monday is equal to the sum of the Saturday, Sunday, and Monday presentments in the no-weekend model. Also, we note that the presentations

---

[1]This example assumes that there is only one weekend effect. In practice, there may be two weekend effects: one associated with the time a mailed check arrives at the vendor's office and another associated with the time the check is presented for payment at the firm's bank. Our studies indicate that the first weekend effect may be negligible. (See the discussion on p. 152.)

Table 8.1   Payment Pattern Assumptions

Amount Mailed by Date (in 000's)		Payment Pattern	
		Days Delay	Fraction
2/1	$100	3 days	.3
2/2	100	4 days	.5
2/3	100	5 days	.2
2/4	100		
2/5	100		

for the remaining days of the week are unaffected by weekends under this assumption. In particular, they are still described by the equation

$$d_t = .3m_{t-3} + .5m_{t-4} + .2m_{t-5}, \qquad (8.2)$$

with the exception that some m_{t-j}'s may be 0, because they refer to mailings on the weekend.

The above discussion suggests that the payment pattern may be estimated in the presence of weekends in the following manner:

1. Collect data on the daily amounts disbursed from the firm's bank and mailed from the firm for each *calendar* day in the sample period.
2. Use a regression equation of the form

$$d_t = a_1 m_{t-1} + a_2 m_{t-2} + \cdots + a_H m_{t-H} + e_t \qquad (8.3)$$

to estimate the underlying payment pattern in the absence of weekends. Only values of t corresponding to Tuesday, Wednesday, Thursday, and Friday will be included on the left-hand side of this regression, but mailings on all previous days up to H days ago are included on the right-hand side. (Recognize that the values of m_{t-j} will be 0 if the jth prior day is a Saturday or a Sunday.)
3. Use the forecast equation

$$\hat{d}_t = \hat{a}_1 m_{t-1} + \hat{a}_2 m_{t-2} + \cdots + \hat{a}_H m_{t-H} \qquad (8.4)$$

Table 8.2   Payment Pattern When There Are No Weekends

Date Mailed	Date Presented							Total Mailed (in 000's)
	1/4	1/5	1/6	1/7	1/8	1/9	1/10	
2/1	30	50	20	0	0	0	0	100
2/2		30	50	20	0	0	0	100
2/3			30	50	20	0	0	100
2/4				30	50	20	0	100
2/5					30	50	20	100
Total presented	30	80	100	100	100	70	20	

Table 8.3 Payments Pattern in the Presence of Weekends

Date Mailed	Date Presented												Total Mailed
	1/4	1/5	1/6	1/7	1/8	1/9	1/10	1/11	1/12	1/13	1/14	1/15	
1/1	30	50	0	0	20	0	0	0	0	0	0	0	100
1/2		30	0	0	70	0	0	0	0	0	0	0	100
1/3			0	0	100	0	0	0	0	0	0	0	100
1/4				0	80	20	0	0	0	0	0	0	100
1/5					30	50	20	0	0	0	0	0	100
1/6						0	0	0	0	0	0	0	0
1/7							0	0	0	0	0	0	0
1/8								30	50	0	0	20	100
1/9									30	0	0	70	100
1/10										0	0	100	100
1/11											0	80	100
1/12												30	100
Total presented	30	80	0	0	300	70	20	30	80	0	0	300	

to forecast disbursements for each future day. (The "$\hat{\ }$" in this forecast equation denotes an estimated value.)

4. Use the forecast values of $\hat{d}_t$ obtained from Equation 8.4 to forecast presentation values for days falling on Tuesdays, Wednesdays, Thursdays, or Fridays. However, to forecast Mondays' disbursements, we employ a trick: sum the forecast values obtained from Equation 8.4 for Saturday, Sunday, and Monday (just as if checks could have been presented on Saturday and Sunday). This sum is then our forecast for Monday.

Application

Assume we are given the data shown in Appendix A and are asked to prepare a forecast of the firm's cash disbursements for the next ten days. Our initial examination of the data encourages us to try the disbursement float forecasting model described above. However, there are several fundamental problems that are noted in advance.

1. Approximately 90% of the dollar amount of the firm's checks are mailed on just two days of each month. (Economies of scale in check disbursing encourages many firms to restrict the number of disbursing days to several each month.) This means that we only have at most 26 significant observations on which to base our forecast. It also means that we may have to be satisfied with something less than a "perfect forecast."

2. There are several points in the data set where the "typical" payment pattern is obviously affected by the occurrence of holidays. For instance, the $7,980,000 mailed on November 16 is disbursed later than usual because of Thanksgiving. We

Table 8.4 Regression Results

Variable[a]	Parameter Estimate	T-Ratio	Prob $\|T\|$
M_3	0.080	2.11	0.0361
M_4	0.125	3.04	0.0028
M_5	0.153	3.11	0.0022
M_6	0.321	6.60	0.0001
M_7	0.395	9.12	0.0001
M_8	0.170	4.94	0.0001
M_9	0.070	1.96	0.0513
M_{10}	0.075	1.81	0.0724
M_{11}	0.123	3.36	0.0010
M_{12}	0.027	0.61	0.5457

F-Ratio	Prob $\|F\|$	R-Square
23.04	0.001	0.6056

[a]Here, M_3 denotes the dollar amount of checks mailed three days ago, M_4 the dollar amount of checks mailed four days ago, and so on. M_1 and M_2 have been omitted because it was evident from observing the data that no checks were ever presented in one or two days.

Table 8.5   Dollar Amount Mailed by Day
(in 000's)

Day	Dollar Amount
−10	86
−9	0
−8	0
−7	212
−6	73
−5	2,328
−4	18
−3	64
−2	0
−1	0
0	14
1	162
2	41
3	17
4	80
5	0
6	0
7	102
8	33
9	90
10	1,968

may have to delete data points surrounding holidays in order to obtain an accurate picture of the "typical" payment pattern.
3. The data for the first half of November is suspect on the grounds that the $3,438,000 mailed on November 5 is not followed by disbursements of similar magnitude. We should probably delete these data as well.

Since the data problems noted in 2 and 3 would appear to seriously affect our results, we decide to delete the troublesome data from the set used in our regression. We then run a regression similar in form to Equation 8.3 with $H=12$. The results are shown in Table 8.4.

Suppose now that we have the data shown in Table 8.5 on the dollar amounts mailed on the last ten days and the dollar amounts forecast to be mailed on the next ten days. (The forecast of amounts to be mailed on the next ten days is quite accurate because the bills are already "in-house.") With these data and the regression results shown in Table 8.4, we prepare the forecast of disbursements for tomorrow (Day 1, a Tuesday) as follows:

$$\hat{d}_1 = 0.080(0)) + 0.125(64) + 0.153(18) + 0.321(2,328) + 0.395(73)$$
$$+ 0.170(212) + 0.070(0) + 0.075(0) + 0.123(86)$$
$$= 833.495.$$

Table 8.6   Disbursement Forecast
for Days 1–10

Day	Adjusted Disbursement Forecast
1	833
2	962
3	446
4	238
5	0
6	0
7	1186
8	100
9	62
10	100

The initial forecasts for the next ten days are prepared in a similar manner. The initial forecasts for days 5, 6, and 7 are then adjusted as described above. In particular, the adjusted forecast for days 5 and 6 are 0, because these correspond to a Saturday and Sunday, respectively; while the adjusted forecast for day 7 (a Monday) is the sum of the initial forecasts for Saturday, Sunday, and Monday. The set of adjusted forecasts for the next ten days is shown in Table 8.6.

SUMMARY

It is apparent that an adapted version of the Payments Pattern Model can be used to forecast daily presentation. The appropriate adaptation depends on one's assumptions about how firms, banks, and the post office operate over the weekend. The simplest assumption is that both the firm and its bank are closed over the weekend, but the mail and clearing agents continue to move at the same pace. For this case, we have outlined a straightforward approach for estimating the payment pattern coefficients and forecasting future days' presentations.

AN INDIVIDUAL VENDOR DISBURSEMENT FORECASTING MODEL

The previous section describes a model for forecasting aggregate daily presentations, using information on the aggregate dollar amount of checks mailed out on previous days. This model has the advantage that it is relatively easy to understand and implement. Once the payment pattern coefficients have been estimated, the user can forecast future presentations on the back of an envelope.

The individual vendor disbursement forecasting model described in this section is considerably more complex than its purely aggregate counterpart. However, the individual vendor model also has several advantages. As noted earlier, these are:

1. It dynamically revises its cash forecast for future periods as previously written checks are paid.
2. It tracks and updates the distribution of check processing times for the firm's largest vendors as new information becomes available.
3. It can produce reports that alert the manager to significant changes in a particular vendor's check processing time, caused perhaps by a change in his lockbox site.

For the remainder of this chapter we refer to the individual vendor model as the Disbursement Float Forecasting Model.

THE DISBURSEMENT FLOAT FORECASTING MODEL

The Disbursement Float Forecasting Model generates disbursement cash flow forecasts for individual large vendors based on a history of clearing times for each vendor. This history includes the minimum pay time (from mail date to presentation date), the expected time, and the variance.

The forecast of disbursements for a given day is prepared on a check-by-check basis for individual vendor checks. The expected dollars to be disbursed on or before the forecast day is found by multiplying the check amount by the estimated probability that the check will clear. For example, if there is a 75% chance that a $1000 check will clear by June 5. the single check forecast amount for June 5 would be $750. The estimated probabilities will increase with the forecast date (i.e., as the check becomes older). Thus, the forecast for June 6 might be $830 (83% chance of clearing) and $900 for June 7.

There is often considerable variation in the length of time it takes for a particular check to clear. For this reason, the model generates both an expected value ("best guess") projection and a more conservative forecast.

The individual check values for each forecast day are added together to produce a single disbursement estimate. The variance figures allow the model to obtain the conservative estimates by increasing each day's expected cumulative disbursement amount by an appropriate safety factor.

The method works well when good estimates (i.e., estimates we feel confident about) of the probabilities can be obtained. Because check disbursement times change periodically (for example, when a vendor opens a new lockbox or an existing mail route is changed), the probability estimates must be adjusted from time to time. The update method used insures that the system will "learn" the payment patterns for the company's checks as clearing times are observed.

Probability Estimates

The probability that a particular check (or group of checks) will clear on or before a given date depends on a number of important factors:

1. The day of the week on which the check was mailed.
2. The distance of the vendor from the mailing point of the check.
3. The use of a lockbox by the vendor or slower internal processing methods.

4. The location of the vendor's deposit bank and the extent to which it uses accelerated check clearing methods.
5. The amount of the check. (Large checks are often given priority treatment by vendors and banks. This occurs because large checks are generally routed to lockboxes and many banks send such large items directly to the drawee bank to expedite the clearing process.)
6. Environmental factors. (For example, mail service is notoriously slow during the Christmas season and may be delayed at other times by such factors as strikes and bad weather.)

Rather than consider each of the above effects separately, the model summarized the clearing history in terms of three statistics for each vendor. The three statistics computed for each check group are:

1. The expected time for a check to clear (in days).
2. The minimum time for a check to clear (in days). This is the smallest observed time.
3. The standard deviation of the time for a check to clear. This is computed as usual; that is, if n checks have been observed and the ith check cleared in d_i days, the standard deviation would be

$$ \text{SD} = \left[\frac{1}{n} \sum_{i=1}^{n} d_i^2 - \frac{1}{n} \left(\sum_{i=1}^{n} d_i \right)^2 \right]^{1/2} . \tag{8.5} $$

The probability distribution of the number of days for an item to clear is the key variable in the model. In a study performed by the authors, a fairly large sample of these items was analyzed on a vendor-by-vendor basis, and the following conclusions were reached:

1. There is a characteristic minimum clearing time for each vendor; this varied from one to ten days in the sample.
2. Once the data are transformed by subtracting the observed minimum time, the remaining values show a variety of distributions. A good characterization of such positive random variables is the coefficient of variation:

$$ \text{CV} = \frac{\text{standard deviation}}{\text{mean}} . $$

Coefficients of variation between 0.5 and 5.5 were observed.
3. A generally good fit to the observed distribution was obtained by selecting a discrete probability distribution based on the coefficient of variation:
   (a) A binomial distribution when $\text{CV} \leq 0.95$.
   (b) A Poisson distribution when $0.95 \leq \text{CV} \leq 1.05$.
   (c) A negative binomial (or Polya) distribution when $\text{CV} \geq 1.05$.
   The parameters for each of the three distributions are selected so that they match the observed times in both mean and standard deviation.

Forecast Production

The Disbursement Float Forecasting Model uses the vendor probability distributions to produce forecasts of expected *cumulative* payments. This forecast amount is determined by the following formula:

$$F_t = \sum_{i=1}^{n} A_i P_{it}, \tag{8.6}$$

where

F_t = the cumulative amount predicted to clear by day t

A_i = the amount of the ith check

P_{it} = the probability that check i clears on *or before* day t (computed using the probability distribution and parameters as determined by observation of previous check clearing times as discussed in the last section)

n = the total number of outstanding checks.

The amount predicted to clear on a given day t is computed from

$$f_t = F_t - F_{t-1}. \tag{8.7}$$

That is, it is the difference between two successive expected cumulative amounts.

The conservative forecast amounts are computed using the estimated standard deviation of F_t. This value is derived from

$$SD = \left[\sum_{i=1}^{n} A_i^2 P_{it}(1 - P_{it}) \right]^{1/2}. \tag{8.8}$$

That is, the square root of the sum of the variances of the individual check clearing times. It should be noted that this formula assumes that the probability distributions for individual checks are independent. The authors have found this assumption to be reasonably accurate, especially when weekend effects are accounted for. (Users of the model must realize that certain phenomena such as unusual weather could cause this assumption to be violated.) If n (the number of outstanding checks) is large, F_t will have an approximately normal distribution, and a 95% confidence limit on the daily amount cleared is:

$$C_t = F_t + Z_{95} SD_t, \tag{8.9}$$

where $Z_{95} = 1.645$ is the 95% point of the standard normal distribution and C_t is the value of F_t that will be exceeded only 5% of the time.

The conservative forecast amounts are modified somewhat to insure consistency. Thus, C_t will never be larger than the total amount of the outstanding checks on day t and it will be adjusted if necessary so that $C_t - C_{t-1} \le 0$. The conservative daily clearings c_t are determined in the same way as f_t, that is,

$$c_t = C_t - C_{t-1}. \tag{8.10}$$

Note that c_t may well be less than f_t in some cases, but the conservative cumulative disbursement forecast will always be higher than the expected forecast.

Parameter Updating

Each time an individual vendor check is paid, the parameters for the vendor are updated. The minimum number of days is changed to a new lower value if the observed clearing time is below the previous minimum, and the sample standard deviation is revised using Equation 8.5. The expected clearing time is treated somewhat differently.

To understand the treatment of expected values, consider the situation where one of the company's vendors opens a new lockbox in the company's city. Mail, clearing, and processing times are likely to decrease substantially, which must be rapidly detected and allowed for in the forecast. This would not occur if the overall average clearing time were used in the forecast as the expected clearing time. For example, if 40 checks had been previously written to the vendor with an average clearing time of 7 days, and the new clearing time were 4 days, about 200 more checks would have to be observed at this level before the expected clearing time for the forecast would be equal to 4.5 days.

The expected clearing time is instead updated using exponential smoothing. In this technique, the most recent observed clearing time and the previous expected time are used to create a new expected time using the following formula:

New Expected Time $= (1 - \lambda) \cdot$ Previous Expected Time $+ \lambda \cdot$ Observed Time.
In the formula, the parameter λ is the smoothing weight; its value is between 0 and 1. When λ is small, little weight is given to the new observation, and the model tends to retain the existing expectation. When λ becomes larger, the model's values change more rapidly. Our experience to date suggests that smaller values of λ (0.1 to 0.3) work better than larger ones.

The Impact of Weekends

The impact of weekends on the model's ability to predict cumulative cash disbursements on day t can be explained in terms of the difference between two types of forecasting error: systematic error that affects all or almost all checks in a similar way, and nonsystematic error that is unique to specific checks. Since the cash flow forecast is almost always the result of the sum of the predictions for a very large number of checks, the impact of nonsystematic error is reduced by the prediction process itself. Further reduction in forecast error is thus most likely to occur only through the identification of systematic effects. Weekends are such an effect.

For the purpose of disbursement float forecasting, two weekend effects must be examined. The first occurs when a mailed check arrives at the vendor's office. If the office is closed on the weekend, the check must wait until Monday to be processed. The second effect occurs when a check completes the Federal Reserve clearing process. A check that normally would take three business days to be cleared may become available for presentation to the drawee bank on the weekend, when the bank is closed, causing the actual clearing time to be four or five calendar days.

We examined the impact of the first weekend effect by comparing a weekend-adjusted and an unadjusted forecast. The first was computed using the sum of surveyed business day mail times, an adjustment for checks arriving on weekends, and surveyed calendar day clearing times. This was compared to a forecast based on the sum of calendar day mail and clearing times. The results of the analysis showed no appreciable difference in the two approaches. (The mail time and clearing time data were supplied by Phoenix-Hecht, Inc., a subsidiary of University Analytics, Inc., that provides such data to the banking industry.)

This result could be explained at least for the large vendors by the efficiency of their bank lockbox processing. The reason is that many but not all banks remain open throughout the weekend for receipt of items; some even initiate clearing the checks by depositing them with the Federal Reserve on Saturday.

The lack of an impact because of the first weekend effect has a very important side benefit. It turns out that, if we do not try to isolate the mail delay weekend effect, there is no need to distinguish between the mail time and clearing time components of the total disbursement time. This means that the corporation that uses the model will not need to have access to externally surveyed mail and clearing time data.

The impact of the second weekend effect was examined by comparing (1) a prediction based on the number of working days, adjusting if the check would have been presented for payment on a weekend, with (2) a simple calendar-day estimate of disbursement time. The studies indicate that predictions based on working days perform significantly better than simple calendar-day predictions. Thus, a correction for the second weekend effect appears to be worthwhile.

Summary

The Disbursement Float Forecasting Model may be summarized in terms of the flow chart shown in Figure 8.1. The analyst starts by gathering data on the dates checks were written to individual vendors and the dates they were presented for payment to the firm's bank. These data can be obtained from check reconciliation statements provided by the firm's bank. The analyst then calculates the following statistics for each vendor: mean clearing time, minimum clearing time, and standard deviation of clearing time. Depending on the values of these statistics, the analyst determines an appropriate probability distribution of each vendor's clearing times. After the appropriate probability distribution has been chosen, the analyst applies probability values to subsequent checks written by the firm to each vendor and calculates the percent of each check expected to be paid on the days after mailing. He then sums the individual daily check values to obtain a forecasted total of checks to be paid on that day. This is the forecasted bank balance requirement.

Example   The logic of the Disbursement Float Forecasting Model may be further clarified with an example. Suppose that historical clearing time data for the five most recent checks written to vendors A, B, C, D, and E has been collected as shown in

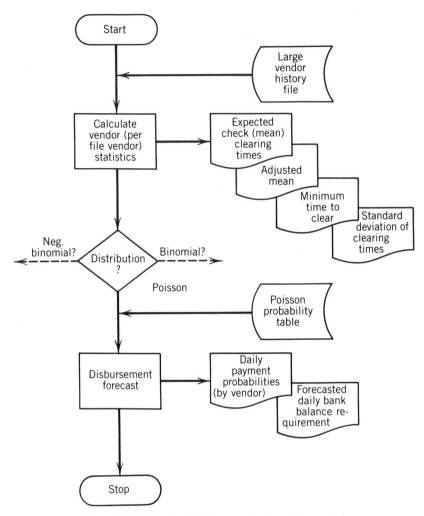

Figure 8.1 Flowchart-disbursements forcasting model.

Table 8.7

	Clearing Times for Five Sample Checks					Mean Clearing Time	Minimum Clearing Time	Adjusted Mean
A	2	2	3	3	3	2.6 days	2 days	0.6
B	5	6	5	7	6	5.8 days	5 days	0.8
C	4	4	4	2	5	3.8 days	2 days	1.8
D	6	6	5	6	4	5.4 days	4 days	1.4
E	8	5	6	5	5	5.8 days	5 days	0.8

Table 8.7. Using the table, and assuming a Poisson distribution, the following probability calculations can be derived for each day beginning with the minimum clearing time:

	Date of Mailing	Day 1	Day 2	Day 3	Day 4	Day 5	Day 6	Day 7	Day 8	Cumulative Probability
A	-0-	-0-	.55	.33	.10	.02	-0-	-0-	-0-	1.0
B	-0-	-0-	-0-	-0-	-0-	.45	.36	.14	.05	1.0
C	-0-	-0-	.17	.30	.27	.16	.10	-0-	-0-	1.0
D	-0-	-0-	-0-	-0-	.25	.35	.24	.11	.05	1.0
E	-0-	-0-	-0-	-0-	-0-	.45	.36	.14	.05	1.0

Now assume the following checks are mailed to each vendor today:

A—$240,000;   B—$490,000;   C—$1,150,000;   D—$620,000   E—$115,000.

The forecasted daily bank balance requirement can be computed for today's checks by applying the above probability to each check as specified, and totaling them by day as seen in the following chart.

KEY:	Probability	Amount of
		Check Expected to Be Paid This Date

Number of Days After Mailing Checks

	1	2	3	4	5	6	7	8	9
A $240,000	0	.55 132,000	.33 79,200	.10 24,000	.02 4,800	0	0	0	0 0
B $490,000	0	0	0	0	.45 220,500	.36 176,400	.14 68,600	.05 24,500	0
C $1,150,000	0	.17 195,500	.30 345,000	.27 310,500	.16 184,000	.10 115,000	0	0	0
D $620,000	0	0	0	.25 155,000	.35 217,000	.24 148,800	.11 68,200	.05 31,000	0 0
E $115,000	0	0	0	0	.45 51,750	.36 41,400	.14 16,100	.05 5,750	0 0
Total $2,615,000	0	327,500	424,200	489,500	678,050	481,600	152,900	61,250	0

As is evident from this sample problem, the firm would not expect to pay any of these checks on day 1, $327,500 on day 2, $424,200 on day 2, and so on. Using this model, the firm must arrange to deposit the forecasted amount into its checking account each day to cover the checks previously written. A more dynamic model would adjust the daily forecast as checks are actually paid and reported by the bank.

SUMMARY

Statistical methods are useful for forecasting the firm's daily disbursement float. Taken alone, these methods allow the financial manager to earn more interest by delaying the funding of the firm's disbursement account. When used in conjunction with more conventional forecasting techniques (i.e., scheduling), these methods help the financial manager to better manage his short-term investment/borrowing portfolio. Forecasting daily disbursement float is certainly one of the most important forecasting tasks facing the financial manager.

DISCUSSION QUESTIONS

1. How do weekends affect the application of the Payments Pattern Approach to daily disbursement float forecasting?
2. Describe how the underlying "payment pattern" can be estimated in the presence of weekends.
3. In the application discussed on pages 146–148, why were some of the data deleted from the data set?
4. Why do the coefficients displayed in Table 8.4 not sum to 1? What can be done about this problem?
5. Discuss whether or not the regression results shown in Table 8.4 are significant.
6. In what circumstances would the method described on pages 145–148 not work?
7. What are the principal advantages of the individual vendor disbursement float forecasting model? What are its principal weaknesses?
8. On what basis does the user decide to use the binomial, Poisson, or negative binomial distributions to summarize the clearing patterns for an individual vendor?
9. Why are these distributions used instead of other distributions such as the normal distribution?
10. Discuss how the parameters for the individual vendor clearing time distribution are updated.
11. What is the difference between the best forecast of presentations and the conservative forecast?
12. How does the individual vendor model handle the problem of weekends?
13. Under what circumstances would the individual vendor model not work?

PROBLEMS

1. Forman Electronics wishes to use the Payment Pattern Model to forecast the dollar amount of checks that will be presented to its bank for payment in the near future. It has gathered data on the daily amounts disbursed from its bank and the daily amount of checks mailed over a recent time period. Using this data, it has used a regression equation of the form

$$d_t = a_1 m_{t-1} + a_2 m_{t-2} + \cdots + a_H m_{t-H} + e_t,$$

where d_t is the amount disbursed from its bank on day t and m_{t-j} is the amount of checks mailed on day $t-j$, to estimate the underlying payment pattern. The regression produced the following results:

Variable	Parameter Estimate	T-Ratio	
M_1	0.001	0.18	
M_2	0.002	0.20	$R^2 = .67$
M_3	0.125	3.10	σ = standard error
M_4	0.382	7.28	of regression
M_5	0.397	9.42	= 469
M_6	0.093	2.47	

The Treasurer of Forman Electronics has also collected data on the dollar amount of checks that were mailed over the last six days and the dollar amount of checks that are forecast to be mailed over the next six days. These are given below:

Day	Dollar Amount
−6	1,616
−5	3,210
−4	2,098
−3	6,434
−2	0
−1	0
0	748
1	903
2	3,787
3	1,291
4	7,053
5	0
6	0

What amounts do you forecast will be presented to the firm's bank for payment today (day 0) and the rest of this week? *Hint.* Today is a Monday.

2. If the Treasurer of Forman Electronics wants to take no more than one chance in a thousand of having insufficient funds in his account, how much should he have in the account today.

3. The Treasurer of McBride Textiles has gathered historical data on the five most recent checks written to vendors, A, B, C, D, and E. A summary of these data is shown below:

	Clearing Times for Five Sample Checks					Mean Clearing Time	Minimum Clearing Time	Adjusted Mean
A	4	2	3	4	5	3.6 days	2 days	1.6
B	3	5	5	4	5	4.4 days	3 days	1.4
C	5	5	6	4	5	5.0 days	4 days	1.0
D	4	3	3	4	3	3.4 days	3 days	0.4
E	7	4	6	6	5	5.6 days	4 days	1.6

Using the above data, and assuming a Poisson probability distribution, specify the probabilities that each check will clear on each future day.

4. Now assume that the following checks are mailed to each vendor today:

A—$310,000,   B—$175,000,   C—$741,000,   D—$686,000,
E—$420,000.

What should be the Treasurer's forecast of the amounts to be presented to the firm's bank over the next eight days?

APPENDIX A

Dollar Amounts Mailed and Disbursed by Day
October 11, 1979–October 24,1980

Date	Mailed ($1,000)	Actual Disbursement ($1,000)
October 11	15	9
October 12	153	744
October 15	165	201
October 16	7,953	18
October 17	0	42
October 18	327	123
October 19	15	1,812

(*continued*)

Date	Mailed ($1,000)	Actual Disbursement ($1,000)
October 22	0	4,428
October 23	51	1,839
October 24	174	246
October 25	120	426
October 26	51	165
October 29	21	24
October 30	8,247	375
October 31	36	24
November 1	60	24
November 2	42	1,557
November 5	3,438	15
November 6	1,764	282
November 7	378	3
November 8	600	153
November 9	171	87
November 12	9	0
November 13	12	159
November 14	48	462
November 15	15	129
November 16	7,980	39
November 19	27	276
November 20	24	36
November 21	195	63
November 22	0	
November 23	0	1,863
November 26	33	1,890
November 27	0	3,915
November 28	48	231
November 29	39	297
November 30	132	78
December 3	6,000	66
December 4	0	21
December 5	570	30
December 6	84	480
December 7	150	1,398
December 10	390	3,336
December 11	15	717
December 12	24	153
December 13	0	603
December 14	147	198

(*continued*)

Date	Mailed ($1,000)	Actual Disbursement ($1,000)
December 17	21	51
December 18	11,766	270
December 19	57	141
December 20	96	102
December 21	0	159
December 24	0	1,866
December 25	0	0
December 26	0	5,307
December 27	0	1,932
December 28	0	1,665
December 31	0	420
January 1	0	0
January 2	0	195
January 3	57	12
January 4	0	144
January 7	1,689	24
January 8	183	249
January 9	372	30
January 10	6,033	15
January 11	243	276
January 14	81	6
January 15	66	2,511
January 16	39	2,682
January 17	147	939
January 18	177	1,626
January 21	0	324
January 22	120	216
January 23	249	108
January 24	51	39
January 25	12	141
January 28	0	270
January 29	8,229	33
January 30	21	195
January 31	1,104	99
February 1	60	609
February 4	726	4,194
February 5	72	1,794
February 6	243	210
February 7	30	1,440
February 8	372	1,023

(*continued*)

Date	Mailed ($1,000)	Actual Disbursement ($1,000)
February 11	36	450
February 12	21	624
February 13	36	60
February 14	192	486
February 15	8,646	27
February 18	204	0
February 19	102	30
February 20	33	570
February 21	30	4,731
February 22	48	1,056
February 25		1,536
February 26	18	804
February 27	27	120
February 28	84	447
February 29	8,970	66
March 3	54	21
March 4	318	18
March 5	552	63
March 6	0	1,011
March 7	855	4,896
March 10	33	1,155
March 11	24	1,209
March 12	18	366
March 13	48	936
March 14	6,651	795
March 17	45	30
March 18	234	771
March 19	12	2,331
March 20	18	1,632
March 21	30	1,125
March 24	81	528
March 25	42	792
March 26	21	42
March 27	18	261
March 28	753	39
March 31	8,370	2,610
April 1	24	57
April 2	63	24
April 3	36	1,638
April 4	0	0

(*continued*)

Date	Mailed ($1,000)	Actual Disbursement ($1,000)
April 7	2,046	408
April 8	69	6,267
April 9	0	192
April 10	93	117
April 11	60	1,089
April 14	2,280	657
April 15	45	171
April 16	9	618
April 17	3	1,443
April 18	198	576
April 21	54	225
April 22	27	195
April 23	246	33
April 24	57	156
April 25	9	180
April 28	12	18
April 29	6,417	105
April 30	33	2,580
May 1	78	252
May 2	132	771
May 5	1,248	1,752
May 6	18	2,934
May 7	3	402
May 8	36	411
May 9	24	1,551
May 12	7,584	27
May 13	84	237
May 14	348	24
May 15	21	1,875
May 16	354	4,353
May 19	6	372
May 20	0	813
May 21	78	132
May 22	36	243
May 23	6	24
May 26	0	0
May 27	45	495
May 28	99	27
May 29	9	30
May 30	6,339	69

(*continued*)

Date	Mailed ($1,000)	Actual Disbursement ($1,000)
June 2	63	21
June 3	0	303
June 4	0	1,335
June 5	15	2,511
June 6	4,677	1,011
June 9	0	1,092
June 10	69	1,203
June 11	63	1,458
June 12	6	1,515
June 13	6	315
June 16	150	165
June 17	21	375
June 18	222	24
June 19	12	36
June 20	15	30
June 23	51	33
June 24	477	213
June 25	327	9
June 26	27	36
June 27	3	132
June 30	7,605	9
July 1	21	705
July 2	0	177
July 3	1,635	90
July 4	0	0
July 7	402	4,752
July 8	45	1,758
July 9	42	558
July 10	0	279
July 11	165	297
July 14	2,115	1,440
July 15	54	108
July 16	48	54
July 17	12	99
July 18	597	1,266
July 21	42	681
July 22	9	243
July 23	24	603
July 24	1,563	255
July 25	0	66

(continued)

Date	Mailed ($1,000)	Actual Disbursement ($1,000)
July 28	0	27
July 29	4,626	633
July 30	0	615
July 31	3	276
August 1	0	105
August 4	0	15
August 5	0	2,889
August 6	0	96
August 7	1,110	1,305
August 8	36	204
August 11	0	147
August 12	69	252
August 13	132	984
August 14	0	33
August 15	4,602	6
August 18	0	21
August 19	0	146
August 20	33	18
August 21	213	18
August 22	0	39
August 25	48	2,685
August 26	135	885
August 27	27	783
August 28	12	252
August 29	1,683	72
September 1	0	0
September 2	21	33
September 3	576	564
September 4	36	390
September 5	27	168
September 8	18	716
September 9	12	618
September 10	3	21
September 11	102	72
September 12	21	111
September 15	3,222	24
September 16	216	18
September 17	27	3
September 18	333	441
September 19	9	1,887

(*continued*)

Date	Mailed ($1,000)	Actual Disbursement ($1,000)
September 22	210	453
September 23	0	501
September 24	33	72
September 25	21	492
September 26	0	54
September 29	39	33
September 30	3,936	219
October 1		15
October 2	747	15
October 3	15	966
October 6	27	1,668
October 7	1,041	756
October 8	24	312
October 9	27	213
October 10	2,526	1,059
October 13	0	0
October 14	27	45
October 15	66	792
October 16	0	897
October 17	0	1,398
October 20	144	150
October 21	0	54
October 22	255	102
October 23	180	6
October 24	0	57

SECTION IV

MANAGING THE MARKETABLE SECURITIES PORTFOLIO

CHAPTER 9

The Money Market

As caretaker of the firm's short-term investment/borrowing portfolio, the financial manager deals extensively in money market securities. To do so effectively requires a great deal of knowledge about the primary money market participants, the terms on which trades are made, and the risk and return characteristics of the various securities traded. This chapter provides a basic set of knowledge required for dealing in money market securities.

DEFINITION

The money market is that segment of the financial marketplace where short-term credit instruments such as treasury bills, commercial paper, and certificates of deposit are bought and sold daily. Trading in the money market does not take place at a single location. Instead, thousands of participants throughout the world communcate by telephone with the securities dealers and brokers who trade the securities. It is a compliment to modern technology that the money market operates efficiently despite its decentralized nature.

The competitive character of the money market is one of its most salient features. Although trading in money market instruments often occurs in multi-million dollar units, the market is so large and the participants are so numerous and well-informed that no one trader has a significant impact on market price. Because of its competitive nature and the sparsity of regulation, the money market is characterized by a high degree of innovation; new securities are constantly introduced to meet the needs of market participants.

Money market securities have several characteristics that make them a safe and convenient haven for the firm's cash surpluses and a low-cost means of financing the firm's cash deficits. First, since they are generally issued by borrowers with excellent credit ratings, money market securities have a very low default risk. Safety of principal is, of course, the financial manager's primary concern. Second, money market securities are available in maturities ranging from as short as one day to as long as one year. This gives the financial manager the ability to select a combination of risk and return that best meets his liquidity goals. Third, money market securities generally are traded in large and active secondary markets. Should the financial manager wish to liquidate his money market position, he can do so on short notice with minimal transaction costs and little risk of capital loss.

MONEY MARKET PARTICIPANTS

There are three types of participants in the money market: the Federal Reserve, the dealers and brokers who make the markets, and the primary borrowers and lenders.

The Federal Reserve

The Federal Reserve is the largest participant in the money market. As noted in Chapter 2, the Open Market Trading Desk of the Federal Reserve Bank of New York buys and sells money market securities to control the supply of bank reserves. Although the Fed's open market operations are concentrated primarily in the T-bill market, it occasionally conducts open market operations in other segments of the market as well.

In addition to its open market activities, the Federal Reserve buys and sells money market securities as an agent for foreign banks and governments. In recent years Federal Reserve transactions for this purpose have increased significantly. Because of the stability of the dollar and the strength of the U.S. political system, the U.S. money market is considered to be the safest place for foreign currency reserves held by foreign institutions. Given the sharp rise in oil prices of the last decade, it is not surprising that oil exporting countries have become particularly large investors in the U.S. money market, especially since the dollar is the primary currency in which oil trades are made.

The Federal Reserve transacts its money market business through a selected group of dealers in money market securities. To get on the Fed's list of approved dealers, the firm must have an adequate capital base, do a significant amount of transactions in various segments of the money market, especially the T-bill market, and possess a highly qualified management group.

Dealers and Brokers

Money market trading takes place primarily in the offices of dealers and brokers in various money market securities. The distinguishing characteristic of a dealer is that she buys and sells for her own portfolio. This requires her at times to take substantial positions (i.e., to hold substantial amounts) in money market securities and subjects her to much risk. In addition to the dealers, there is a small group of brokers who bring buyers and sellers together for a fee, but do not take a position in the market themselves. They operate primarily in the inter-dealer part of the market.

Activities of Dealers   Money market dealers perform several activities that help the market operate smoothly. Their primary activity is to trade securities with retail customers and other dealers for their own account. Dealers' trades with customers are said to occur in the "retail market," while dealers' trades with other dealers are said to occur in the "inside market."

In the inside market, dealers quote bids and offers for every security and maturity they are willing to trade with other dealers. The quotes are made through brokers who often provide a video television screen displaying the quotes of all dealers. If the dealer sees a particular bid or offer she thinks is especially favorable, she will "hit" that offer and the deal is made.

Dealers also do a significant amount of business with their retail customers. Since competition for customer business is fierce, bids and offers in the retail market tend to follow closely those found in the inside market.

The competitive nature of dealer trading in both the retail and inside markets assures that a single price will normally prevail for any instrument at any moment in time. This means that retail customers do not have to waste a lot of time shopping around for the best deals. In addition, the high degree of competition between dealers and the dealers' willingness to trade with all comers assure that money market instruments are highly liquid.

A second dealer activity is to underwrite new securities issued by federal, municipal, and local governments. Many new issues of municipal securities are purchased entirely by dealers and then resold to the public, hopefully for a higher price. Dealers also purchase approximately 40% of the T-bills auctioned by the U.S. Treasury.

Third, in some parts of the money market, dealers act very much like brokers. Commercial paper dealers are especially noteworthy in this respect. They help large corporate customers sell their paper to the public by (1) advising them on rates and maturities, (2) finding customers who will purchase large blocks of the firm's paper, and (3) positioning the paper (i.e., holding it for their own portfolio) and selling it later to retail customers. Dealers prefer to position only that part of their customers' paper for which there are no ready buyers. Since this tends to be a small part of the total, commercial paper dealers' role as matchmakers is more important than their role as market makers.

Dealer Profits   Dealer profits arise from four sources. First, they earn small commissions for selling CD's and commercial paper to their retail customers. This helps to cover some of the dealers' fixed expenses, but it is hardly enough to justify their staying in business.

Dealers also profit from what is commonly called "carry." This is the spread, frequently positive, between the dealers' financing costs and their return on investments. Since dealers frequently finance security positions with extremely short-term borrowings, they tend to profit from carry whenever the yield curve is upward sloping.

However, carry is a risky source of profits. When the yield curve inverts or changes levels, the dealer can find herself in a situation where she is offering funds at a lower rate than that which she receives, such as investing in 90-day T-bills at 10%, but having financed this with 11% money. Surely this is no easy road to riches.

Third, dealers sometimes earn large profits from positioning money market securities in accordance with their views of interest rate trends. At times when they believe interest rates will decline, dealers will increase both the amount and maturity of the securities they hold in their portfolio; at times when they believe interest rates will increase, dealers reduce the amounts and maturities of securities held in their portfolio or take short security positions. As noted below, increased activity in the market for repurchase agreements (RP's)[1] has encouraged dealers to take short positions more frequently than they have in the past.

Finally, dealers earn some profits on a day-to-day basis by buying securities at a slightly lower price than they sell them. These arbitrage activities of dealers, called market makers, are also important to the efficient working of the money markets.

Dealer Financing   Dealers finance their positions in money market securities in one of two ways. In recent years, the most popular financing method has been to sell securities to their customers with an agreement to buy them back sometime later at a fixed price. This agreement, commonly known as a repurchase agreement or repo, is actually a form of borrowing from customers, with the money market instruments serving as security for the loan. The maturity on repos is typically one day, but some are issued with indefinite maturities (open repos) and some are issued with fixed but longer maturities (term repos).

Bank dealers often obtain repo financing as part of a cash management service offered by the corporate services division of the bank. In this service the bank offers the corporate financial manager the opportunity to invest automatically cash balances in excess of a specified minimum in repurchase agreements with the bank. This service is actually a clever way to offer interest on checking account balances, something that the bank would ordinarily be forbidden to do under Regulation Q.

Overnight repurchase agreements are a convenient, but risky form of financing for securities dealers. As noted above, the dealer will experience positive carry on this form of borrowing as long as interest rates do not rise significantly. However, if interest rates do rise, the dealer may experience a situation where her borrowing costs exceed her return on investment.

Some dealers use short-term dealer loans from commercial banks as an alternative to financing under repurchase agreements. Dealer loans are more expensive than repo financing, but are more convenient for small levels of borrowings.

Brokers

Trading in the interdealer market for money market securities and in the interbank market for Fed funds is facilitated by brokerage firms that charge commissions for bringing buyers and sellers together. To see how brokers can provide a valuable market

[1]Repurchase agreements were defined in Chapter 2. They will be discussed in more depth later in this chapter.

service, consider how difficult it would be for each dealer to call all the others to find out their bids and offers. Considerable time and expense can be saved when each dealer calls in bids and offers to a single broker and the broker calls back when the quoted prices suggest the possibility of interdealer trades. The information services provided by the broker can be quite valuable and dealers are willing to pay for this service.

In recent years, several organizations have introduced a new system for reporting dealer quotes. The system works by having all dealers agree to input quotes via a computer terminal to a central electronic information location. Individual dealers have access to the quotes in the system through display terminals located in their offices. Since bids and offers can be changed and fed in continuously, the dealer is kept abreast of current conditions in the market. If she finds any of the bids favorable, she can arrange a transaction by calling her broker.

The second important function that brokers serve is to provide anonymity. Dealers prefer to arrange trades through brokers because they do not want to reveal their strategy to the other dealers. The importance of this factor is evidenced by the fact that about 70% of all dealer trades in some money market instruments are done through brokers.

Primary Borrowers and Lenders

Primary participants enter the money market to borrow and lend cash resources for short periods of time. Borrowers tend to be large, credit-worthy institutions who find they can obtain short-term financing more cheaply by selling short-term IOU's directly to the public rather than borrowing from an intermediary such as a bank. Lenders tend to be portfolio managers who want to earn interest on liquid balances without incurring much risk.

The list of money market borrowers includes the U.S. Treasury, commercial banks, non-bank financial institutions, federal government agencies, and large, well-known non-financial corporations. The U.S. Treasury is by far the largest money market borrower because it finances a large percentage of the federal government deficit through the issuance of T-bills with maturities of three months, six months, or 1 year. Sales finance companies float large volumes of commercial paper in the money market to finance loans to consumers; non-financial corporations float commercial paper to finance short-term cash deficits; state and local governments float short-term notes to finance expenditures in advance of tax, bond, or other specific receipts, and commercial banks sell certificates of deposit and purchase federal funds to finance their loan and securities portfolios.

Money market lenders often belong to the same economic sectors as money market borrowers. Within these sectors, however, they tend to be those units with cash surpluses rather than cash deficits. One exception to the above rule is that the Treasury is almost never an investor in the money market. Another exception is that some individuals invest in the money market by purchasing T-bills and agency securities or by investing in money market mutual funds, while individuals never borrow in the money market.

Apart from the U.S. Treasury, commercial banks in the aggregate are the largest money market participants. As noted in Chapter 2, commercial banks often act as both borrowers and lenders in this market. They purchase large amounts of Treasury bills and securities of state and local agencies, lend to government securities dealers, and sell excess reserves to other banks who are short. However, they also sell large volumes of CD's, commercial paper, and repos, and purchase large volumes of federal funds from other banks with surplus reserves. In addition to their borrowing and lending activities, commercial banks frequently act as dealers in money market securities.

MONEY MARKET INSTRUMENTS

This section surveys the money market instruments that are found most frequently in the firm's short-term investment portfolio. It includes a description of treasury bills, commercial paper, certificates of deposit (CD's), bankers acceptances (BA's), repurchase agreements (RP's or repos), and Eurodollars.

Treasury Bills

Treasury bills are the short-term debt obligations of the United States Government. They are sold to the public at a discount through regular weekly and monthly auctions, with 91- and 182-day maturities sold weekly and 365-day maturities sold monthly. In addition to the regularly scheduled bill offerings, some unique bills are offered periodically. These bills are called cash management bills, and their maturities range from 2 to 170 days. An unusual characteristic of Treasury bills is that they are issued primarily in book entry form. This means ownership is only recorded on the books of the Treasury; investors do not receive the bill itself.

Investment Characteristics   T-bills possess several characteristics that distinguish them from other money-market instruments. First, because they are backed by the full taxing authority of the U.S. Government, T-bills are generally considered to be free of default risk. This makes them an eligible investment for many portfolio managers who are precluded from investing in other money market instruments. State and local government authorities and commercial banks invest heavily in T-bills for this reason.

T-bills also possess a high degree of liquidity. Most investors define liquidity as the ability to sell an asset at short notice with little or no loss in price. The active secondary market for T-bills and their minimum price fluctuations give them this characteristic.

Unlike other money market instruments, T-bills may be purchased in denominations as low as $10,000. This makes them available to many individual investors with insufficient wealth to purchase other money market instruments. For this reason, investments in T-bills tend to increase dramatically when interest rates rise above those permitted on individual savings accounts under Regulation Q.

A final characteristic of T-bills is that they are exempt from state and local taxes. This advantage can be significant in periods of high interest rates. An individual or firm in a marginal state and local tax bracket of 6% would have to earn an extra 90 basis points[2] on commercial paper to earn the equivalent of 15% on T-bills (15% × .06 = .90%).

T-bill Yields   T-bills are non-interest bearing securities that are sold at a discount and redeemed at full face value at maturity. The investor who holds T-bills until maturity receives a gain equal to the difference between the face value and the discounted price. To compare the yield on T-bills with that on other money market securities, it is necessary to express this gain on a percentage basis. In practice, there are two ways to do this: the bank discount method and the bond equivalent method. The bond equivalent method is generally considered to be the best to use for the purpose of comparison with rates on alternative investment opportunities.

The bank discount method expresses the investor's gain as a percent of the face value of the security. Let

P = the discounted price
F = face value
D = the amount of the discount
d = the yield on a bank discount basis
t = time remaining to maturity (in days).

Then the annual yield on a bank discount basis may be expressed by the formula

$$d = \left(\frac{D}{F}\right) \div \left(\frac{t}{360}\right) = \frac{F - P}{F} \div \frac{t}{360} . \tag{9.1}$$

where the term $t/360$ is needed to adjust for the fact that the gain is normally experienced over a period less than a year.

In contrast, the bond equivalent method expresses the investor's gain as a percent of the price he actually pays. Let r denote the annual yield expressed on a bond equivalent basis. Then we have

$$r = \left(\frac{D}{P}\right) \div \frac{t}{365} = \left(\frac{F - P}{P}\right) \div \frac{t}{365} . \tag{9.2}$$

Since T-bills are frequently quoted on a bank-discount basis, while some other money market investments are quoted on a bond-equivalent basis, it is helpful to have an expression relating the bond-equivalent yield r to the bank-discount yield d. This is given by

$$r = \frac{365 \times d}{360 - (d \times t)} . \tag{9.3}$$

Example   To illustrate the above formulas for determining the yield on a T-bill, consider the example of an individual who purchases a 180-day T-bill with a face amount of $10,000 at a price of $9500. Substituting into Equation 9.1, the bank discount yield on this bill is found to be

---

[2]A basis point is 1/100 of a percentage point.

$$d = \frac{10,000 - 9,500}{10,000} \div \frac{182}{360} = 0.0989.$$

Substituting into Equation 9.2, the bond equivalent yield is found to be

$$r = \frac{10,000 - 9,500}{9,500} \div \frac{182}{365} = 0.1055.$$

Alternatively, substituting into Equation 9.3, the bond equivalent yield is given by

$$r = \frac{365 \times .0989}{360 - (.0989 \times 182)} = \frac{36.0985}{342.0002} = 0.1055.$$

Purchasing T-bills   The simplest way to purchase T-bills is to buy them from a bank or non-bank dealer. The transactions costs of purchasing T-bills from a dealer are low, especially if the amount purchased is large (over $200,000) and the bills are held to maturity. However, the investor should shop around to get the highest rate. Even though the T-bill market is highly competitive and rates will normally be close, at a particular point in time some dealers may not be eager to sell. They typically indicate this lack of eagerness by quoting yields 20 or 30 basis points below the market. (A basis point is 1/100 of a percent. Thus, bills yielding 9.50% and 9.30% differ by 20 basis points.) The investor who is unaware of this may accept the first quote he hears and end up earning less than market rates.

T-bills may also be purchased at one of the Treasury's regular or irregular auctions. When the investor chooses to purchase T-bills at the Treasury auctions, he must decide whether to bid competitively or noncompetitively. In a competitive bid, the investor indicates the quantity of bills he desires and the price he is willing to pay. In a noncompetitive bid, the investor states the quantity of bills he wishes to purchase and agrees to pay the average price on all accepted competitive bids. The alternative of entering a noncompetitive bid is only available to those who wish to purchase T-bills in amounts less than $200,000.

The investor who enters a competitive bid should recognize that his bid may not be accepted. The Treasury allocates the amount of securities it wishes to sell first to foreign central banks, foreign governments, and the Federal Reserve. It then allots whatever is needed to satisfy the noncompetitive bids. Once the noncompetitive bidders have been satisfied, the remainder is allocated to competitive bidders, starting with the highest bid. In most cases, it is not possible to award securities to all competitive bidders. Instead, there is a closeout price at which all lower prices are rejected.

T-bill Dealers   At the center of the T-bill market are 36 dealers who report daily to the Federal Reserve Bank in New York. Twelve of these dealers are associated with commercial banks and 24 are non-bank dealers. These dealers make money in much the same way as dealers in other money market securities. They earn profits from a positive carry on the T-bills in their portfolio, from taking a position in T-bills when they have a definite opinion about the future course of interest rates, and from their ability to buy at a few basis points less than they sell. The large number of T-bill dealers and the large size of the federal debt make the T-bill market extremely competitive, even by money market standards.

Commercial Paper

Commercial paper is an unsecured promissory note that is sold by a corporation at a discount to the public. Since the investor must rely entirely on the issuer's good faith and credit, commercial paper can only be sold by the most credit-worthy corporations. Commercial paper is usually issued in denominations of $100,000 and multiples thereof, with the average purchase equaling about $2 million. Maturities of commercial paper tend to fall in the range of 15 to 45 days. It is never issued with maturities greater than 270 days because the Securities & Exchange Commission requires time-consuming and expensive registration procedures on maturities exceeding this limit.

Issuers and Investors   Finance companies, nonfinancial corporations, and bank holding companies are the largest commercial paper issuers. Finance companies such as General Motors Acceptance Corporation, Sears Roebuck Acceptance Corporation, and Household Finance issue commercial paper primarily for the purpose of financing loans to individuals who wish to purchase consumer durables; nonfinancial corporations issue commercial paper both to finance seasonal increases in inventories and receivables and to finance construction expenditures during the interim before long-term bonds can be sold; and bank holding companies issue commercial paper to finance the leasing, real estate, and consumer finance activities of their subsidiaries.

The major investors in commercial paper are state and local governments, pension funds, nonfinancial corporations, commercial banks, and individuals who buy shares in money market investment pools. Like investors in Treasury bills, these investors are concerned about safety of principal and liquidity. However, they also appreciate the fact that commercial paper yields frequently exceed T-bill yields by a substantial margin.

Growth of Commercial Paper Market   The commercial paper market has grown rapidly in recent years. In 1965 there were only about 300 firms issuing commercial paper, and the total commercial paper outstanding was approximately $15 billion. By the end of 1981 there were over 1000 firms issuing commercial paper annually, and the total outstanding volume was $165 billion.

The large increase in commercial paper financing in the period 1965–1980 is explained by two factors. First, there was a tremendous growth during this period in purchases of consumer duables and an increased consumer willingness to borrow. Second, there were times in the late 1960s when firms had a difficult time obtaining financing from their commercial banks. This is because rates on CD's were limited at that time under Regulation Q and banks could not fund new loans. Firms that had traditionally borrowed at banks used the commercial paper market for the first time and discovered that commercial paper financing was actually less expensive than bank financing. These firms continued to use the commercial paper market even after the Regulation Q limits on CD's were lifted.

Quality Ratings   Although commercial paper is considered to be a relatively safe investment, there have been times when firms have defaulted on their commercial paper obligations. The most noteworthy example occurred in 1970 when the Penn Central Railroad Company defaulted on the $82 million of commercial paper it had outstanding. After the Penn Central crisis investors became more conscious of the issuing firm's creditworthiness and the rating of commercial paper by independent agencies became widespread.

Today firms who issue commercial paper are rated by one or more of three rating services: Moody's Investors Service, Standard & Poor's Corporation, and Fitch Investor Service. Although the rating classifications of these three firms differ, they all use basically the same criteria. In particular, they look at the quality of the firm's management, the trend in earnings, ability to borrow from other sources, liquidity, and strength of industry position. Quality ratings range from A-1 to A-3 for Standard & Poor's, P-1 to P-3 for Moody's, and F-1 to F-3 for Fitch. Since most investors only buy paper that receives a prime rating by every rating service, firms that do not receive a prime rating must pay a significantly higher yield to sell their paper.

Back-up Credit Lines   The majority of commercial paper issuers float commercial paper with an average maturity less than 30 days in order to finance investments with a maturity considerably greater than 30 days. This means that when their commercial paper matures, they can only pay it off by floating additional paper—that is, by rolling it over.

The practice of rolling over commercial paper creates many risks for both the issuer and the investor, as was entirely too evident in the Penn Central affair. To alleviate this risk, most investors will not purchase commercial paper today unless it is backed by a bank line of credit. The cost of this line of credit, whether it is paid for with fees or compensating balances, must be considered when calculating the total financing cost of the borrower.

Dealer Paper   A large percentage of the commercial paper issued each year is sold through dealers. In return for a commission of 1/8th of 1% the dealer provides many services normally provided by an underwriter. He advises the firm on market conditions, distributes the paper through his sales force to the public, and positions any paper that is not sold. Since there is great competition among dealers for the firm's business, yields on dealer paper tend to be as low as is consistent with market conditions.

Large, well-known, nonfinancial corporations are the major issuers of dealer paper. Since they enter the market on an infrequent basis, it is well worth the commission fee to obtain the dealer's services. Commercial banks, pension funds, and money market mutual funds are the major purchasers of dealer paper.

Direct Issue Paper   As noted above, the fee for issuing commercial paper through a dealer is 1/8th of 1%. This amounts to $175,000–$250,000 a year for a firm with $150–$200 million of commercial paper outstanding. Many large finance companies and a few bank holding companies regularly have commercial paper outstanding that exceeds this range. They find that they can substantially reduce the cost of issuing commercial paper by establishing a sales force to sell their paper to the market directly.

Directly issued paper differs from dealer paper in several respects. First, since directly issued paper is sold to investors on a personal basis, the maturities are often designed to fit the investor's needs. Thus, a corporate financial manager who wishes to invest surplus funds for, say five days, can frequently find a sales finance company that is willing to sell him commercial paper with this maturity. Second, although there is no secondary market for directly issued paper, the major issuers usually are willing to prepay the paper, should the investor need the money. Finally, issuers of direct paper are frequently willing to offer higher rates to large investors.

Recent Developments   A number of new participant groups have entered the commercial paper market in recent years. The list of new participants includes foreign nonfinancial corporations and banks, thrift institutions, and lesser-known corporations who obtain letters of credit[3] from banks. Although these participants frequently have to offer higher yields than those discussed above, they still find commercial paper yields to be attractive compared to their alternatives.

Certificates of Deposit

A negotiable certificate of deposit (CD) is a large denomination, fixed term, time deposit that is generally issued in bearer form so that the investor may sell it prior to maturity if he so desires. Both the interest and maturities on CD's is subject to negotiation between the issuing bank and the investor; however, Regulation Q of the Federal Reserve System requires that maturities exceed 14 days. Although CD's may be issued (under Regulation Q) in any denomination over $100,000, they are typically issued in units of $1 million or more. Unlike Treasury bills and commercial paper, the CD's are sold at face value with interest paid at maturity on CD's having a maturity less than 1 year, and semiannually on CD's having maturity greater than a year. Yields on CD's are quoted on a bond-equivalent basis, using a 360-day year. Interest rates on CD's may be either fixed or variable.

History   Negotiable CD's were first introduced in 1961 by a group of New York banks seeking additional sources of funding for their security and loan portfolios. Until that time nonfinancial corporations rarely invested in bank time deposits because of their lack of liquidity. If the firms experienced an unexpected outflow of cash, they could not withdraw funds from their time accounts, except at steep penalties, to help meet the cash drain. By creating an instrument that could be traded in secondary markets and reaching an agreement with several New York dealers to make markets in this instrument, the banks were able to overcome the traditional corporate disenchantment with time deposits. The market for CD's grew dramatically throughout the 1960s, reaching a total of about $10 billion at the beginning of 1969.

---

[3]A letter of credit is a written statement from a bank that the bank will "guarantee" the payment of the face amount of the commercial paper when it matures.

The market for CD's collapsed in 1969 when rising interest rates caused the Regulation Q interest ceiling to become a binding constraint. Major banks were able to lessen the effects of the dramatic loss of deposits in CD's by issuing CD's in the Eurodollar market through their offshore branches. This gave a major boost to the market for Eurodollar CD's and they have been an important factor ever since.

In 1970, after the collapse of the Penn Central Railroad, the Federal Reserve became worried about the financial health of the money markets. They were concerned that many firms would be unable to roll over commercial paper as it became due, and that these firms might go bankrupt if they could not borrow from an alternative source. Commercial banks were unable to be a major source of financing for firms at this time because they had no excess reserves to lend and they could not purchase additional reserves in the CD market due to the interest rate ceiling noted above. To solve these problems, the Federal Reserve removed the interest ceiling on domestic CD's over $100,000. By 1975 the market for CD's had grown again to about $90 billion. Although the volume of outstanding CD's fell off in 1976 and early 1977, it began growing again in the latter part of 1977. Today there are over $325 billion of domestic CD's outstanding.

Risk and Return The investor in large denomination negotiable CD's faces the risk that the issuing bank will go bankrupt before the CD matures. Since deposits in U.S. banks are only insured by the FDIC up to the first $100,000, this is not a significant source of protection. In addition to default risk, the investor faces the possibility that he may not find a ready secondary market for his CD in the event he needs to sell it before maturity. This is especially important for CD's issued by regional banks because the market for them is not as large.

The above factors have several important implications for the CD market. As shown in Figure 9.1, CD's tend to trade at yields that are at times significantly above those available on T-bills. The spread between the CD and T-bill yields becomes especially large in periods of market uncertainty when investor fears of bank collapse increase. A second implication is that regional banks with less well-known names may have to pay considerably higher yields to attract CD investors than the large money center banks. The large spreads that sometimes exist between regional and money center bank CD's do not seem to be justified in some cases. There are regional banks with conservative balance sheets and high credit ratings who pay more than some money center banks with less conservative balance sheets and lower credit ratings. Apparently, most CD investors equate risk with size.

The yields on bank CD's are also affected by the reserve requirements that banks must hold on CD's under Regulation D. In mid-1983, banks were required to hold reserves of 3% on CD's with original maturities of less than 2½ years, and 0% on CD's with original maturities greater than 2½ years.

Dealers At the present time, there are about 25 dealers active in the market for domestic CD's. Most of these dealers are located in New York City, but some have offices in other U.S. cities and in London. CD dealers make a secondary market in CD's by standing ready to buy and sell CD's from their own portfolio. Sometimes CD

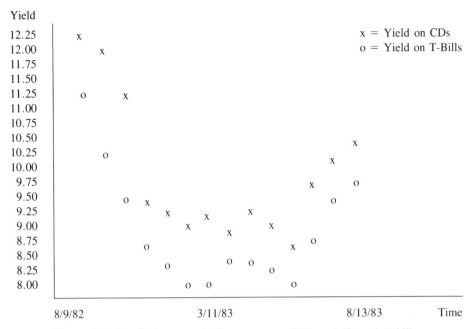

Figure 9.1 Spread between yields on one-year CD's and 52-week T-bills.

dealers also serve as brokers by helping banks line up major customers for particularly large issues they are unable to market themselves. Banks are somewhat reluctant to issue CD's through dealers because it costs more and because the CD's they issue through dealers may end up in the secondary market and compete with later issues. However, banks are forced to rely on dealers when the amounts they wish to issue are particularly large.

Dealers finance CD positions primarily with repurchase agreements (RP's). RP financing for CD's is more expensive than RP financing of T-bills, however, for two reasons. First, since the market perceives CD's to be more risky than T-bills, the underlying security of RP financing of CD's is not as great as that of RP financing of T-bills. Second, dealers are able to finance only the face value of CD's in the RP market, implying that accrued interest on CD's in their portfolio must be financed out of their own capital.

Variable Rate CD's (VRCD)   The CD market is no exception to the rule that competition encourages innovation. There have been many innovations in recent years that have made this market more appealing to investors. The most interesting of these innovations is the variable rate CD.

Variable rate CD's are longer-term negotiable CD's whose coupon is adjusted periodically to conform more closely to the then existing market conditions. On each VRCD there is a rollover period during which the interest rate doesn't change. At present, three- and one-month rollovers are the most common. If, for example, the rollover period is three months, then, at the end of the first three months, the investor may present the VRCD to the issuing bank[4] for collection of interest on the first period and have the VRCD stamped with the interest rate for the second period. Rates for the second period are set equal to the average dealer offer rates on three month CD's in the preceding day's secondary market. A similar adjustment is made each three months until the VRCD matures.

From the investors' point of view the VRCD has two principal advantages. The most obvious advantage is that he is not locked-in to a low rate when interest rates rise, as has happened so frequently in recent years. Second, VRCD's generally earn an interest premium compared with ordinary negotiable CD's.

Bankers' Acceptances

A bankers' acceptance is a low-risk, highly liquid money market instrument that arises primarily in the course of international trade. The instrument itself is actually a time draft, drawn on a bank, that specifies an amount and a date at which the bank will pay that amount to the bearer. Once the draft is accepted by the bank, it becomes a financial instrument that may be readily sold at a discount on the open market. Since only large U.S. banks with international reputations create bankers' acceptances, and the investor has secondary recourse to the bank customer involved in the financing, bankers' acceptances are considered to be an extremely safe money market instrument. In the 70 or so years that bankers' acceptances have been traded in this country, there is not a single example of a default.

Example   The typical economic circumstances under which a bankers' acceptance is created may be illustrated with an example. Suppose a furniture dealer located in New York City wishes to purchase Danish furniture from a manufacturer in Copenhagen. The dealer agrees with the Copenhagen firm that it will arrange for a letter of credit from Citibank in New York. The letter of credit will specify that the Copenhagen firm may draw a draft on Citibank for payment in 90 days. In its letter of credit application to Citibank, the New York dealer agrees to pay a fee of 1½% for the bank's letter of credit and also to pay the face value of the draft at the end of 90 days. The dealer then sends the purchase order to the furniture manufacturer in Copenhagen. After the application has been approved, Citibank sends the letter of credit to the Danish firm and instructs its correspondent in Copenhagen to honor the firm's draft. The Danish firm ships the furniture to New York and presents a time draft, along with the appropriate documents evidencing the shipment, to Citibank's correspondent in Copenhagen. The Copenhagen correspondent pays the furniture manufacturer the discounted value of the draft and sends the draft, along with the shipping documents, on to Citibank. When Citibank receives the draft, it marks it as ''accepted,'' and sells it to an acceptance dealer in New York (alternatively Citibank could hold the draft until maturity and earn the implicit interest on the draft in addition to the fee for the letter of credit). The acceptance dealer sells the draft, which is now known as a bankers' acceptance to an investor who presents it to Citibank for full face value at maturity. At each stage in the

---

[4]Alternatively, the rollover may be automatic.

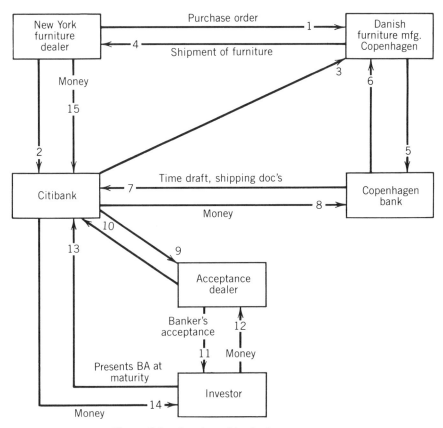

Figure 9.2   Creation of banker's acceptance.

process the price of the acceptance is determined by money market conditions at the time. A summary of the typical steps in the creation of a bankers' acceptance is displayed in Figure 9.2.[5]

Advantages of Acceptance Financing   The use of acceptance financing is advantageous to all parties concerned in the example previously described. Bankers' acceptance financing is advangeous to the furniture manufacturer in Copenhagen because he can sell his furniture without the risk of extending a loan to a New York dealer he knows little about. In addition he can obtain his funds immediately, if he so desires, rather than waiting the 90 days. BA financing is also advantageous to the furniture dealer in New York because it is often less expensive than bank credit, even though the implicit rate on the BA may exceed the bank's prime rate. This is because the bank requires the firm to keep compensating balances on a line of credit, and thus the true cost on bank financing exceeds the prime rate. Furthermore, BA financing is available

---

[5]This diagram is a modified version of a diagram that appeared in Jack L. Hervey, "Banker's Acceptances," *Business Conditions*, May 1976, pp. 3–11.

to firms whose credit is inadequate to float commercial paper. Third, BA financing is advantageous to Citibank because it can earn a fee for the use of its credit standing without necessarily tying up its funds. The secondary market in BA's allows it to sell the loan in the open market, something it could not do with a direct loan extended under a line of credit. Finally, BA's are advantageous to the investor because they allow him to earn money market interest without incurring much risk. Not only does the investor have recourse to both Citibank and the New York furniture dealer, he also has title to the furniture that was shipped.

Eligibility Requirements   Since its creation in 1913, the Federal Reserve has been involved in the acceptance market in at least four ways: (1) it sometimes purchases and sells BA's as part of its open market operations, (2) it permits member banks to rediscount BA's at the discount window, (3) it permits member banks to use BA's as security for a discount window loan, and (4) it sometimes enters the market as an agent for foreign central banks.

To be eligible for purchase or discount at the Federal Reserve, BA's must satisfy certain complex standards relating to the maturity of the BA, its security, and its marketability. Banks who create BA's try to meet these standards because BA's that are "eligible for purchase" and "eligible for discount" are more marketable, and hence more liquid than those that are not. In addition, the creating bank may sell BA's that are eligible for discount without incurring reserve requirements. For these reasons, BA's that are not eligible for Federal Reserve purchase or discount frequently sell at higher yields than those that are.

Growth   The volume of BA's outstanding has increased significantly since the late 1960s. A substantial part of this growth is due to the natural increase in foreign trade over this period. However, a large part of the growth is explained by the increased use of BA's to finance trade between two foreign countries. In the years after 1974 many countries began to use the BA market to finance oil imports that are paid for in U.S. dollars. Today, roughly half of the BA's outstanding arise from this kind of trade.

The growth in the BA market has caused a significant increase in the number of dealers who buy and sell BA's on a regular basis. BA dealers operate in much the same way as dealers in other money market securities and, like them, rely heavily on RP financing. At the present time, the BA market is considered to be almost as liquid as that for CD's.

Repurchase Agreements

A repurchase agreement (RP) is an agreement to sell a security, along with a simultaneous agreement to repurchase the same security at a later date. As such, the RP is essentially a collateralized loan from the buyer to the seller. The maturity of the loan is frequently one day, although longer term RP's are not unheard of. RP's are considered to have little risk because the securities that are sold serve as collateral for the investment. In addition, to protect against a decrease in price on the underlying securities there is frequently a positive margin between the market value of the underlying securities and the amount of the repo.

RP's are priced in one of two ways. In a method called flat pricing, the securities are bought and repurchased at the same price with an additional amount for interest paid at the maturity of the contract. Alternatively, the seller can simply agree to repurchase the securities for a higher price than he sold them for on the earlier date. In this case, the difference in price represents an implied interest on the investor's money. In both cases, the interest on the loan is generally less than the accrued interest on the underlying securities, because the term of the loan is less than the term of the securities.

The terms used to refer to RP's depend on whether one takes the buyer's or seller's point of view. From the seller's point of view, an agreement to sell a security and repurchase it at a later date is simply called an RP, as noted above. From the buyer's point of view, however, the same transaction is said to be a ''reverse RP,'' because it is an agreement to purchase a security, along with an agreement to sell it back at a future date.

Major Participants   The major participants in the RP market include securities dealers, commercial banks, nonfinancial corporations, state and local governments, and the Federal Reserve. As noted earlier in the chapter, securities dealers use RP's as a major source of financing for their large holdings of money market securities. A T-bill dealer, for instance, may purchase a large block of T-bills at the Treasury's weekly auction and immediately repo these securities overnight to a corporate treasurer. While the practice of financing longer term securities with overnight RP's is common, it also involves substantial risk, especially at times when interest rates rise. However, the cost of RP financing is usually significantly less than a dealer loan from a bank and so dealers continue to use them in large volume.

The growth of the market for reverse RP's has had significant implications for securities dealers. Previously dealers were reluctant to short securities at times when they thought interest rates were trending upwards because it frequently was too expensive to borrow the security and cover it at a later date. With the rise of the reverse RP market, however, dealers can obtain securities to cover shorts simply by reversing them in. This has given dealers a great deal of added flexibility in managing their portfolios.

In recent years, many security dealers have begun to act as financial intermediaries in the RP market. They borrow by selling RP's to investors and lend by selling reverses with the same maturity to institutions short of funds. They frequently can make money in this way because the cost of funds is less than the return on their investment.

Commercial bank use of the RP market as a source of funds has already been noted in Chapter 2. Banks typically limit themselves to doing RP's in government and federal agency securities because only RP's created with these securities are exempt from reserve requirements. Commercial banks began to use the RP market in significant volume in the late 1960s and early 1970s when high interest rates severely limited the growth of demand and time deposits, their traditional source of funds. Their participation was given further impetus in late 1974 by the Treasury's decision to hold deposits at Federal Reserve banks rather than at commercial banks. Since banks were required to keep government and agency securities as collateral for Treasury deposits, they were not free to use these securities to acquire funds in the RP market.

Nonfinancial corporations and state and local governments are the largest investors in RP's. Corporations invest in RP's because they are a convenient means to earn interest on overnight money. In fact, many banks offer firms a cash management service whereby any funds in the firm's demand deposit over a specified minimum at the end of the day are automatically invested in a RP with the bank. The opportunity to earn interest on overnight money is not as readily available in other money market instruments. For instance, the Federal Reserve requires that CD's be issued in maturities of greater than 14 days. Commercial paper and BA's can frequently be purchased with shorter maturities, but they are less convenient to arrange, their yields are often lower, and the transactions costs for such short maturities may be high.

State and local governments are the second major investor in the RP market. These governments frequently may invest only in government and agency securities and may not take a capital loss on their investments. The RP market permits them to earn interest on short-term loans collateralized by government and agency securities without the risk of taking a capital loss.

The Federal Reserve is the only participant that does not enter the market for the purpose of borrowing and lending short-term funds. Instead, it uses the RP and reverse RP markets to make temporary adjustments in the level of bank reserves. These adjustments may be necessary to offset the effects of rapid seasonal changes in Federal Reserve float or Treasury balances held in district Federal Reserve banks.

Federal Agency Securities

The federally sponsored credit agencies are financial intermediaries created by Congress for the purpose of encouraging investment in favored sectors of the economy such as housing and farming. Unlike many other financial intermediaries, the federally sponsored credit agencies are not involved in direct lending to ultimate borrowers. Instead, they achieve their goals by extending loans to other financial intermediaries (e.g., savings and loan associations, mutual savings banks, etc.) who are involved in making direct loans to ultimate borrowers and by purchasing packages of loans initiated by other financial institutions.

Federal agency securities are the debt obligations of the federally sponsored credit agencies. Since the credit agencies are sponsored by the federal government and serve important sectors of the economy, it is inconceivable that the federal government would let them default on their obligations. For this reason, federal agency securities generally trade at yields that are only slightly higher than those available on government securities with comparable maturities. Like government securities, federal agency securities trade in active secondary markets and are considered to possess a high degree of liquidity. The maturities of federal agency securities range anywhere from five days to 20 years. Since a significant volume of them are issued with maturities less than 1 year, they are a suitable topic for a chapter on money market securities.

The five major federally sponsored credit agencies are concerned primarily with encouraging investment in the housing and farming sectors of the economy. The Federal Home Loan Bank system and the Federal National Mortgage Association are federal agencies charged with the responsibility of encouraging investment in housing, and the Federal Intermediate Credit Banks, the Banks for Cooperatives, and the Federal Land Banks are agencies whose purpose is to encourage investment in farming-related activities. In addition to the five major federally sponsored credit agencies, there are a host of smaller credit agencies that are owned by the federal government.

Federal Home Loan Banks The Federal Home Loan Bank system (FHLB), established in 1932, regulates the savings and loan industry in much the same manner as the Federal Reserve System regulates the commercial banking industry. It consists of 12 regional Federal Home Loan Banks and a governing board in Washington. In addition to their regulatory functions, the Federal Home Loan Banks act as a lender of last resort to the member institutions in their region. In periods of tight money, depositors in S&L's shift their funds into alternative investments earning higher rates of interest. At these times, the FHLB helps the S&L's to stay afloat by purchasing mortgages from them with funds raised in the open market.

The FHLB issues two types of securities: bonds with maturities of a year or more and discount notes with maturities in the range of 30–270 days. Both types of securities are backed by the consolidated system of 12 Federal Home Loan Banks and by collateral typically consisting of government securities, insured mortgages, and so on. Although FHLB securities are not guaranteed by the U.S. government, it is inconceivable that the government would ever let the FHLB default on its obligations.

Federal National Mortgage Association The Federal National Mortgage Association (FNMA or ''Fannie Mae'') was created by Congress in 1938 for the purpose of providing liquidity to the market for government-insured mortgages. Originally, Fannie Mae was government owned with funding coming primarily from the U.S. Treasury. However, institutions who bought and sold mortgages with Fannie Mae had to purchase some of Fannie Mae's stock, and so it slowly was converted to private ownership. Today, Fannie Mae purchases government-insured mortgages with funds raised from the sale of short-term discount notes and debentures. The short-term discount notes are available in maturities ranging from 30 to 270 days, with the minimum purchase being $50,000. Fannie Mae short-term discount notes and debentures are considered to have a very low default risk, even though they are not expressly guaranteed by the federal government.

Farm Credit System The Farm Credit System is designed to serve the credit needs of the U.S. agricultural community. It consists of 12 Federal Land Banks, 12 Federal Intermediate Credit Banks, 12 Banks for Cooperatives, and a Central Bank for Cooperatives. Like the Federal Reserve Banks and the Federal Home Loan Banks, the Farm Credit Banks are owned by the financial intermediaries they serve. They are supervised by the Farm Credit Administration, an independent agency of the U.S. government.

The 12 Federal Land Banks make long-term loans to farmers who want to invest in land, machinery, and livestock. The loans are made through local Federal Land Bank associations and have maturities ranging from 5 to 40 years. The Federal Intermediate Credit Banks make short- and intermediate-term loans to financial institutions that provide seasonal financing for the production and marketing of crops, livestock, and other farm-related activities. The Banks for Cooperatives make short-term loans to farmers cooperatives engaged in marketing, distribution, and production of agricultural commodities.

In recent years, the 37 farm credit banks have obtained financing through the issuance of consolidated bonds and discount notes. The consolidated bonds are sold in minimum denominations of $5000 with maturities of six and nine months. The consolidated discount notes are sold in minimum denominations of $50,000 with maturities in the range of 5–270 days. Although neither the consolidated bonds nor the discount notes are expressly guaranteed by the U.S. government, they are considered to have very low default risk.

Eurodollars

A dollar-denominated deposit in a bank or bank branch located outside the U.S. is called a Eurodollar deposit. The term "Eurodollar deposit" is confusing to some because it seems to imply that the deposits must be held in European banks. Actually, the term "Eurodollar deposit" refers to dollar-denominated deposits in banks throughout the world, including such geographically diverse places as Hong Kong, Singapore, Bahrain, and the Cayman Islands. The prefix "Euro" merely indicates the importance of European banks in the early history of the market.

Because Eurodollar deposits are held in banks located outside the U.S., they fall beyond the reach of U.S. laws and banking regulations. In particular, there are no interest ceilings on Eurodollar deposits, banks do not have to hold reserves against Eurodollar deposits, and banks are not assessed a premium for FDIC insurance on Eurodollar deposits. The unregulated nature of the market for Eurodollar deposits has played an important role in its development.

The individuals, corporations, and governmental institutions who own Eurodollar deposits face at least two major types of risk. The first relates to the risk that banks offering Eurodollar deposits may become bankrupt before the deposit matures. In this regard, it is often noted that Eurodollar deposits are uninsured and there is no lender of last resort for Eurodollar banks. While these statements are both true. it is also true that a large portion of Eurodollar deposits are held in foreign branches of major U.S. banks or in large foreign banks with sound international reputations. The risk of these banks defaulting on their Eurodollar obligations is considered to be small.

A second source of risk is the possibility that a foreign government may block the movement of Eurodollar deposits out of the country. This risk, too, is considered to be slight because host countries receive considerable benefits from the Eurodollar banking business and the act of blocking funds movement would certainly preclude their enjoying these benefits in the future. Furthermore, for some foreign residents the risk of governmental restrictions on Eurodollar deposits is less than the perceived risk of U.S. government restrictions on deposits held in U.S. banks. This fact became painfully obvious after the Iranian oil crisis in 1979.

A large volume of trading in the Eurodollar market occurs in what might technically be called the interbank market. At any one time, there are some banks who accept more in Eurodollar deposits than they can profitably lend and others who can profitably lend more than they accept in deposits. These banks typically trade Eurodollar deposits much as banks in the U.S. trade Fed funds. Furthermore, the rate on interbank Eurodollar trades, commonly referred to as the London Interbank Offer Rate, or LIBOR, plays an important role in the pricing of Eurodollar loans just as the prime rate plays an important role in the pricing of domestic loans. (In fact, LIBOR is frequently used as a basis for domestic loans because it is a market established rate.)

History of the Market   The history of the Eurodollar market has been strongly influenced by U.S. laws and banking regulations that affect deposits held in U.S. banks, but not those held abroad. Ironically, the Eurodollar market was stimulated in the years following World War II by the need of Soviet-bloc countries to carry on international trade in dollars. These countries were reluctant to hold dollar deposits in U.S. banks because they thought the U.S. government might at some time block their ability to make withdrawals. To avoid this problem, Soviet-bloc countries began to hold dollar-denominated deposits in European banks. At times when their balance of payments were in deficit, the Soviet-bloc countries also had a need for dollar financings. The major European banks attracted dollar-denominated deposits from other sources in order to make loans to these countries.

The Eurodollar market was further stimulated in the mid-1960s by a set of government programs designed to eliminate U.S. balance of payments problems. The Interest Equalization Tax of 1964 penalized the use of money and capital markets by foreign borrowers; the Foreign Credit Restraint Program of 1965 constrained loans to foreign borrowers by U.S. banks; and the Foreign Investment Program of 1968 placed restrictions on the ability of U.S. corporations to use dollars raised in the U.S. to finance foreign investments. These programs greatly increased the demand for financing in the Eurodollar market and encouraged banks to accept additional deposits in this market to finance increased loan demand.

The period of high interest rates that began in 1968 gave additional impetus to the growth of the Eurodollar market. U.S. banks were suffering from financial disintermediation at this time because Regulation Q prevented them from offering market rates of interest on domestic time and savings deposits. They soon discovered that they could avoid Regulation Q limitations by attracting dollar-denominated deposits in the name of their foreign branches. As noted earlier, this stimulus to the development of the Eurodollar market was eliminated in 1974 when the Federal Reserve changed Regulation Q to allow banks to pay market interest rates on large denomination, negotiable certificates of deposit. However, the market had grown significantly in the mean time.

The sudden rise in oil prices following the Arab oil embargo of 1974 was yet another stimulus to the development of the Eurodollar market. Since international trade in oil is largely transacted in dollars, the oil exporting countries experienced a large increase in dollar holdings and the oil importing countries experienced a large increase in their need for dollar financing. Due to its freedom from regulation, the Eurodollar market was the natural place for this financial activity to occur.

Types of Eurodollar Deposits   Eurodollars are held primarily in the form of time deposits having a fixed rate and a fixed term to maturity. Most Eurodollar time deposits have maturities of less than six months, although there are some whose maturity extends out to a year. Corporations, governmental institutions, and wealthy individuals are all significant investors in Eurodollar time deposits; however, the major share of Eurodollar time deposits are held by banks who trade them in the interbank market.

Because Eurodollar time deposits lack liquidity, some investors prefer to hold Eurodollar CD's. This market is not as well developed as the domestic CD market, however, because Eurodollar banks, unlike U.S. banks, are extremely flexible in the maturities they offer on Eurodollar time deposits and the investor can thus choose a maturity that best matches his liquidity needs. Today, Eurodollar CD's are concentrated primarily in the longer-term maturity end of the Eurodollar market where the need for liquidity is greatest.

Investments in Eurodollar Floating Rate CD's and Eurodollar Floating Rate Notes have become common in recent years. These instruments are designed to protect the investor from the risk of rapid interest rate changes. Although these instruments typically have a maturity of anywhere from 1 to 7 years, their interest rate or coupon is reset every three or six months to reflect the current level of LIBOR. The secondary market for Eurodollar Floating Rate CD's and Eurodollar Floating Rate Notes is relatively thin (i.e., not heavily traded) at the present time.

Types of Eurodollar Loans   Banks who accept Eurodollar deposits also extend Eurodollar loans. Most of these loans are priced at LIBOR plus a spread that depends on both the borrower's credit rating and market conditions. The list of borrowers includes almost any type of organization that needs dollar-denominated financing, even some U.S. firms who need the dollars purely for domestic purposes.

Eurodollar loans take a variety of forms, including most of those found in the domestic market for U.S. dollars. A significant volume of Eurodollar loans are rollover loans, where the borrower has the option of taking either a three- or six-month loan at the then existing market rates whenever a rollover date occurs. He may continue to do this for the life of the loan contract, which may extend for several years.

In addition to rollover loans, many banks grant Eurodollar lines of credit that, unlike U.S. credit lines, are typically paid for on a strict fee basis. The interest on these credit lines is frequently cheaper than that on U.S. credit lines because of the absence of reserve requirements on Eurodollar deposits. Most Eurodollar credit lines are legal commitments for the life of the credit agreement.

Fixed rate term loans are significantly less common in the Euromarket than they are in the U.S. market for dollar loans. Since most banks consider Eurodollar deposits to be a fairly unstable source of funds, they are unwilling to make loans at fixed rates extending out for several years. However, there does exist a small volume of such loans with maturities averaging between 5 and 10 years.

In recent years the practice of loan syndication has become increasingly common on Eurodollar loans above a certain dollar amount. The lead bank in the loan syndicate reaches terms with the borrower and agrees to put the loan together on a fully underwritten basis. The lead bank or banks then attempt to sell whatever portion of the loan they do not want to other banks. The final loan agreement is signed once the entire set of syndicate members is set up. In addition to the usual spread over LIBOR, the borrower must pay the lead bank a fee for managing the syndicate agreement.

SUMMARY

The money market is a highly competitive, but informal segment of the financial marketplace where thousands of participants from around the world buy and sell short-term securities daily. The securities traded in this market are safe and highly liquid because they are issued by only the best credit risks and trade in active secondary markets. Since the maturities of these securities may be as short as one day, they are frequently traded in book entry form; that is, the transaction is recorded on the books of a dealer or large bank, but no paper is physically transferred.

The participants in the money market include the Federal Reserve, the dealers and brokers who make the market, and the primary borrowers and lenders. The Federal Reserve uses the money market primarily as a vehicle for conducting monetary policy, but it also sometimes enters the market as an agent of foreign governments or banks. Money market dealers trade in the market for their own portfolio, while brokers bring large borrowers and lenders together for a fee. The primary borrowers and lenders are large firms, financial institutions, and governmental units who experience short-term surpluses or deficits of funds. The market is generally open only to large participants with outstanding credit reputations because trading takes place in large units and there is almost no mechanism for extensive credit investigation.

The money market is useful to the corporate financial manager because it is a safe haven for temporary funds surpluses, and a convenient and inexpensive means of financing temporary funds deficits. To participate in this market, however, the financial manager requires a wide array of information on money market participants, interest rate trends and relationships, and the characteristics of the securities that are traded in the money market. This chapter has sought to provide some of the information needed to participate in the money market.

DISCUSSION QUESTIONS

1. Who are the major money market participants?
2. What role does the Federal Reserve play in the money market?
3. Describe the activities of money market dealers?
4. What are the major sources of dealer profits?
5. How do dealers finance their positions in money market securities?
6. Describe the services provided by money market brokers.
7. Who are the primary money market borrowers?
8. Who are the primary money market lenders?
9. Why are T-bills considered to be the most liquid of money market instruments?
10. How are T-bill yields quoted?
11. How are T-bills purchased?
12. Describe the primary characteristics of commercial paper.
13. What is the difference between directly issued and dealer paper?
14. Describe the characteristics of certificates of deposit.
15. How has regulation affected the growth of the CD market?

16. How are rates determined on variable rate CD's?
17. What is a banker's acceptance?
18. What are the principal advantages of acceptance financing?
19. What is a repurchase agreement?
20. Who are the major participants in the market for repurchase agreements?
21. Describe the major federally sponsored credit agencies.
22. What are the major purposes of these agencies?
23. In what ways do the federally sponsored credit agencies participate in the money market?
24. What is a Eurodollar deposit?
25. What are the major differences between Eurodollar deposits and domestic deposits?
26. What are the major types of Eurodollar loans?

PROBLEMS

1. Calculate the annual yield on a bank discount basis earned on a 91-day T-bill that is purchased at $97.80 for each $100 of face value and held to maturity.
2. Calculate the bond equivalent yield on the T-bill described in Problem 1.
3. Suppose a financial manager purchases a 91-day T-bill at a time when interest rates on such instruments are 9.20%. What price will he have to pay for this investment?
4. Suppose a financial manager purchases a 182-day T-bill at a time when interest rates on such instruments are 9.00%. He sells this T-bill 91 days later when newly issued 91-day T-bills are yielding 10.00%. What return does the financial manager earn on this investment?
5. What is the dollar value of one basis point on a $1 million investment in a 6-month CD?
6. Suppose you hold a $50 million portfolio of CD's with an average maturity of 6 months. If interest rates on 6-month CD's suddenly drop from 8.76% to 8.49%, how much has the value of your portfolio changed?
7. Consider a portfolio manager who invests in a 91-day T-bill yielding 8.40% and finances the first 30 days of this investment with a 30-day term repurchase agreement yielding 8.30%. What is the total *net* yield on this investment?

ADDITIONAL READINGS

1. Brick, John R., ed., *Financial Markets: Instruments and Concepts,* Robert F. Dame, Inc., Richmond, Va., 1981.
2. Cook, Timothy Q., ed., *Instruments of the Money Market,* Federal Reserve Bank of Richmond, Richmond, Va., 1977.
3. First Boston Corporation, *Handbook of the Securities of the United States Government and Federal Agencies and Related Money Market Instruments,* New York, 1978.

4. Hawk, William A., *The U.S. Government Securities Market,* Harris Trust and Savings Bank, Chicago, Ill., 1976.

5. Lindlow, Wesley, *Inside the Money Market,* Random House, New York, 1972.

6. Stigum, Marcia, *The Money Market: Myth, Reality and Practice,* Dow Jones-Irwin, Homewood, Ill., 1978.

CHAPTER 10

Portfolio Management Strategies

Management of the firm's marketable security portfolio is one of the most difficult tasks in financial management. It requires a great amount of institutional knowledge of money market securities and how they are traded, an understanding of complex economic relationships, and an ability to compare alternatives in a very short period of time. In the previous chapter, we provided much of the institutional background required to make portfolio management decisions. This chapter discusses the major economic concepts governing short-term portfolio management. A computer model that helps the financial manager to rapidly compare alternative strategies is described in the appendix.

CASH VS. MARKETABLE SECURITIES

The portfolio manager is responsible for deciding how much of the firm's liquidity balances should be held as cash and how much should be invested in money market securities. This decision has been studied extensively in the economics and management literature. We begin this chapter with a review of several conceptual models of the cash/marketable securities decision that highlight the important economic factors affecting this decision.

The Baumol Model

Baumol was the first to recognize that the decision to hold cash can be treated as a problem in inventory management. He assumed (1) the firm had a known and steady demand for cash over some period of time, say a year, (2) the firm replenishes cash when it runs out by selling marketable securities, (3) the firm incurs an opportunity cost for holding cash of $i\%$ per year per dollar held, representing the lost interest on the dollar holdings, and (4) the firm incurs a fixed transaction cost of b dollars each time it makes a security transaction.

Under the above assumptions, the firm's cash balances will follow the pattern shown in Figure 10.1 over time. In this figure, the firm starts with C dollars in cash and returns the cash balance to the level C each time it sells securities. Between securities sales, the cash balance moves steadily downward until it reaches zero, so that the average cash balance is $C/2$. The financial manager's problem is to choose that level of C that minimizes the total cost of the cash management policy.

To solve the financial manager's cash management problem, we have to express total cost in terms of the fundamental decision variable C. We know that total cost is the sum of the transactions cost for selling securities and the holding cost of the cash balances. Furthermore, the transactions cost is equal to the fixed rate per transaction times the number of transactions, and the holding cost is equal to the interest rate i times the average cash balance. Since the number of transactions is equal to T/C, where T is the total demand for cash over the planning period and the average inventory is $C/2$, the expression for total cost is simply

$$\text{Total Cost} = b \times \frac{T}{C} + i \times \frac{C}{2}.$$

The process of adding the transactions cost to the holding cost associated with the cash management policy is shown graphically in Figure 10.2. For a given value of T, the number of transactions decreases with increases in C. Thus, the transactions cost component of total cost decreases as C increases. However, larger values of C produce higher average cash balances, and hence higher holding costs. Thus, the financial manager's problem is to find the optimal tradeoff between the two cost components. The optimal value of C may be found in two ways. First, the financial manager can simply calculate the total cost associated with a representative sample of C values, and choose that value of C which produces the lowest total cost. Alternatively, the value of C that minimizes total cost may be found by using the familiar rule from calculus that the derivative of total cost with respect to C must be zero when total cost is a minimum.

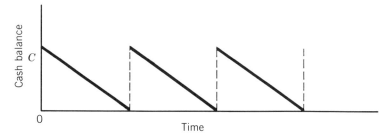

Figure 10.1   Time pattern of cash balances.

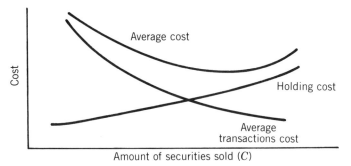

Figure 10.2 Average total cost, holding cost, and average transaction costs of cash management policy.

This rule produces a formula for the optimal level of C that has come to be called the Economic Order Quantity (EOQ) formula. It is

$$C* = \sqrt{\frac{2bT}{i}},$$

where $C*$ is the optimal level of C.

Example   Suppose the financial manager has estimated that he will have to make cash payments of $100 million over the next year. Suppose also that the fixed transactions costs for selling marketable securities is $150 and that the interest rate is 9% per year. Using the EOQ formula, we find that the optimal transaction size is given by

$$C* = \sqrt{\frac{2bT}{i}} = \sqrt{\frac{2 \times 150 \times \$100,000,000}{0.09}} = \$577,320.$$

Thus, the average cash balance is $288,660, and the firm ends up selling securities every two days.

Weaknesses of the Baumol Model   Although the Baumol model provides considerable insight into the economic factors affecting the firm's cash balance (and hence marketable securities) decision, it suffers from several weaknesses that have diminished its importance in practice. First, the assumption of a known and steady demand for cash is rarely met. Not only is the demand for cash highly uncertain in practice, but it is also subject to large seasonal fluctuations. Under these circumstances, the EOQ formula doesn't provide much help.

Second, the assumption that there are no cash receipts other than from sales of marketable securities is clearly at variance with reality. Once we allow for cash receipts, the sawtooth pattern of cash holdings shown in Figure 10.1 no longer applies, and the total cost is no longer given by the simple equation used in deriving the EOQ formula.

Finally, the Baumol model fails to recognize the existence of compensating balance agreements that many firms have with their banks. When the transactions cost is relatively low and the interest rate is relatively high, as has recently been the case, the optimal C from the EOQ formula produces average balances that are well below those required to compensate the firm's bank for a credit line and other services. Thus, the firm's cash balances are determined by bank compensating balance agreements, rather than by the EOQ formula.

The Miller-Orr Model

Recognizing some of the weaknesses of the EOQ model, Miller and Orr formulate a model of the cash balance problem that assumes that cash balances fluctuate randomly in either direction. The financial manager is assumed to control her cash position by setting two control points, H and U, and a return point, Z.

When the randomly fluctuating cash balance reaches the upper control point H, the financial manager transfers enough cash into the marketable securities portfolio to return the cash position to the level Z. When the randomly fluctuating cash balance reaches the lower control point U, the financial manager sells enough marketable securities to return the cash position to the point Z. Thus, the time path of the firm's cash balances will follow the pattern shown in Figure 10.3.

If we assume, for the sake of discussion, that the lower control point U is zero, then the financial manager's problem is to choose a return point Z and an upper control point H such that the sum of the expected transactions cost and the expected holding cost of the cash management policy are minimized. Miller and Orr show that the optimal value of Z is given by the formula:

$$Z = \sqrt[3]{\frac{3b\,\sigma^2}{4i}},$$

where

$$b = \text{fixed cost of security transactions}$$
$$\sigma^2 = \text{variance of daily net cash flows}$$
$$i = \text{interest rate per day.}$$

The optimal value of H is equal to $3Z$.

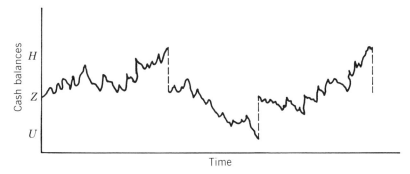

Figure 10.3   Typical time path of daily cash balances in Miller-Orr model.

Weaknesses of the Miller-Orr Model

Although the Miller-Orr Model also provides important insights into the firm's cash balance problem, it too suffers from several weaknesses that have diminished its importance. While the Baumol model assumes that the firm's cash flows are certain, the Miller-Orr Model assumes that they are completely uncertain. In practice, there are some components of the firm's cash flows that are known with certainty and others that are uncertain. However, even for those components that are uncertain, the financial manager is likely to have some information about their trend. Thus, the Miller-Orr assumption about independence in the daily cash flows is not likely to hold in practice.

In addition, the control parameters H and Z are determined by the cost minimization process, and there is nothing to guarantee that the average cash balance will satisfy any compensating balance requirements imposed by the firm's bank. The ability to handle compensating balance requirements is one of the advantages of the model to be considered next.

Stone's K-day Look-Ahead Model

Stone's K-day Look-Ahead Model recognizes that most banks allow firms to satisfy compensating balance requirements by averaging balances over a specified period such as a month or a quarter. Since there is no need to meet the compensating balance requirement each day, the policy calls for the financial manager to let the balance amount drift up or down until a control point is reached. In this respect, the K-day Look-Ahead policy is similar to the Miller-Orr Model, with the exception that the control points must be set heuristically in such a way that the average cash balance satisfies the compensating balance requirement.

The major difference between the K-day Look-Ahead strategy and the Miller-Orr Model relates to what happens when the control point is reached. Rather than taking an action that will immediately move the cash position to the return point, the financial manager looks at the cash forecasts for the next K days, where K is a parameter whose value depends on the firm's ability to accurately forecast future cash flows. If the cash balance is expected to exceed the control point in K days, securities are bought or sold in sufficient quantities that the target balance will be reached at the end of the K-day horizon.[1] If, however, the cash balance is expected to fall within the control point in K days, no action is taken at the present time; that is, the cash balance is allowed to drift for a while longer.

To illustrate the differences between Stone's K-Day Look-Ahead Model and the Miller-Orr Model, consider the set of data on the cash flow forecast and the actual cash flow shown in Figure 10.4. The pattern of transactions occurring using a three-day look-ahead policy with a target balance of 20, an upper control point of 27, and a lower control point of 13 compared to those occurring using no look-ahead are also shown in this figure. (The no look-ahead policy corresponds roughly to the policy recommended in the Miller-Orr Model.) Evidently, the three-day look-ahead policy involves fewer

[1]This is actually a slight simplification. Stone suggests that securities should be bought or sold whenever the cash balance is expected to be within a margin of $\$\delta$ of the control limits. For the purposes of our discussion, we shall assume that δ is zero.

	Cash Forecast and Cash Flow Data			Three-Day Look-Ahead		No Look-Ahead	
Day Number	Cash Flow Forecast	Actual Cash Flow	Forecast Error	Transaction Cash Flow	Final Cash Position	Transaction Cash Flows	Final Cash Position
1	1	1	0	—	21	—	21
2	2	1	1	—	22	—	22
3	3	6	−3	—	28	−8	20
4	−1	−1	0	—	27	—	19
5	−2	−3	1	—	24	—	16
6	−3	−3	0	—	21	+7	20
7	−8	−9	1	—	12	+9	20
8	5	6	−1	—	18	—	26
9	6	4	2	—	22	−10	20
10	4	6	−2	−17	11	—	26
11	5	3	2	—	14	−9	20
12	4	4	0	—	18	—	24
13	0	1	−1	—	18	—	25
14	2	−1	3	—	18	—	24
15	−3	−2	−1	—	16	—	22
16	1	2	−1	—	18	—	24

Figure 10.4   Cash flow, security transactions, and cash position data.

transactions and a larger dollar value for each transaction. The no look-ahead policy (i.e., Miller-Orr policy), however, reduces the average cash balances.

The reason for the differences between the two policies is especially apparent when the firm's daily cash position under the two policies is shown graphically, as in Figures 10.5 and 10.6. We see that, under the the three-day look-ahead policy, the firm does

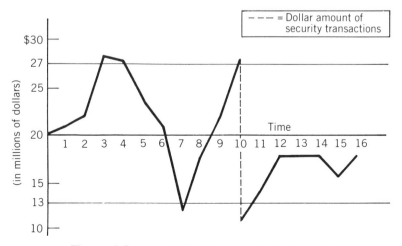

Figure 10.5   Cash position with three-day look-ahead.

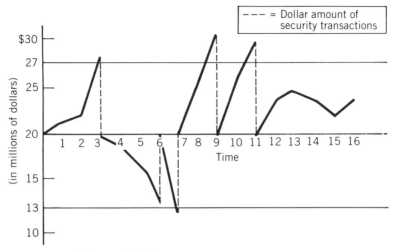

Figure 10.6   Cash position with no look-ahead.

not necessarily make a transaction when its cash position reaches the upper or lower control limits. It only makes a transaction when its cash position reaches either the upper or lower control limit *and* its cash position is expected to still be outside the control limits in three days.

The major advantage of Stone's *K*-day Look-Ahead Model is that it is easy to understand and implement. In addition, the policy takes advantage of any information the financial manager has about the trend in the firm's cash flows. This leads to a further reduction in the number of transactions, and hence the transactions cost. The major disadvantage of the policy is that it is not easy to find optimal values for the control limits and control points, once we allow for trends in the cash flows. Stone suggests that these be obtained by trial and error.

FACTORS AFFECTING PORTFOLIO PERFORMANCE

Once the financial manager has determined what proportion of liquid balances should be held in cash and what proportion should be held in marketable securities, he must choose a strategy for managing his marketable securities portfolio. The financial manager's ability to manage the marketable securities portfolio can be measured along three dimensions: (1) the return, or yield, he earns on the portfolio, (2) the risk he incurs, and (3) his ability to satisfy the firm's cash requirements. Thus, to perform his duties effectively, the portfolio manager should understand the factors that affect these three dimensions of portfolio performance.

Measuring Portfolio Return

Before we discuss the factors that affect portfolio return, it is important we agree on exactly how portfolio return is to be measured. For one-period investments, of course, there is little controversy about the measurement of portfolio return; it is simply the percentage change in the value of the investment from the beginning to the end of the period, stated on an annualized basis. If the portfolio manager purchases a security with a 1-year maturity at a discounted price of $890 and receives $1000 when the security matures, then most would agree that the return on the portfolio managers' investment is given by

$$R_1 = \frac{1000 - 890}{890} = 12.36\%.$$

However, the concept of portfolio return is more difficult to understand and measure for multiperiod investments, especially when the portfolio manager invests in a sequence of shorter term securities, each of which is earning at a different rate. In this case, we must distinguish between returns measured over different time periods; and we must be careful in comparing returns of different portfolio managers, or of different management strategies, to make comparisons over a common period of time. We shall call this period of time the planning horizon, under the assumption that it is only fair to calculate a manager's performance over one complete planning cycle. The value of the manager's portfolio at the end of the planning period will be called the horizon value of the portfolio.

In addition to distinguishing between returns over different time periods, we need to distinguish between returns that are actually achieved and those that are merely expected. We will denote one period returns by the lower case letter r and returns corresponding to more than one period by the capital letter R. If the return is expected rather than actual, we will use a lower case e as a superscript. Subscripts will be used to indicate the beginning and end of the period for which the rate applies. Thus, we will use the notation $R_{2,4}^e$ to indicate the expected return on a two-period investment purchased at the beginning of period 2 and matures at the beginning of period 4, and the notation $r_{3,4}$ to refer to the actual return earned on a one-period security that is purchased at the beginning of period 3 and matures at the beginning of period 4. For the purposes of discussing how to compute multiperiod portfolio returns, we will restrict our attention to actual, or earned, returns on investments. When we turn our attention to theories of the relationship between returns on securities with different maturities, we will need to talk about expected returns.

Consider now three portfolio managers who have made the investments shown in Table 10.1 over the last 4 years. Manager 1 made a single investment in a 4-year security yielding 12% per year; manager 2 made a sequence of investments in 2-year securities, the first yielding 10% per year and the second yielding 16% per year; and manager 3 made a sequence of investments in 1-year securities yielding 6%, 9%, 15%, and 15%, respectively. We want to know which of these portfolio managers earned the highest average return over the 4-year period.

To determine which portfolio manager earned the highest return over the 4-year period, we proceed much as we would for a single-period investment, namely, we calculate the horizon value of each portfolio and then find the average annual return that would make the initial investment grow to the horizon value by the end of the fourth year.

Consider portfolio manager 1. For each $1 of initial investment, the horizon value of

Table 10.1 Results of Three Alternative Investment Strategies

Year	Portfolio Manager 1	Portfolio Manager 2	Portfolio Manager 3
1	12%	10%	6%
2			9%
3		16%	15%
4			15%

Portfolio Manager 1
  Horizon Value $= (1.12)^4 = 1.5735$
  Average return $= \sqrt[4]{1.5735} - 1 = 12\%$
Portfolio Manager 2
  Horizon Value $= (1.10)^2(1.16)^2 = 1.6282$
  Average return $= \sqrt[4]{1.6282} - 1 = 12.96\%$
Portfolio Manager 3
  Horizon Value $= (1.06)(1.09)(1.15)(1.15) = 1.5280$
  Average return $= \sqrt[4]{1.5280} - 1 = 11.18\%$

his portfolio is $(1.12)^4 = 1.5735$. Thus, his average annual return is found by solving the following equation for r:

$$(1 + r)^4 = 1.5735.$$

Not surprisingly, the solution turns out to be 12%.

Likewise for manager 2, we see that the horizon value of his portfolio for each \$1 initially invested is $(1.10)^2 (1.16)^2 = 1.6282$. Thus, the average return on his portfolio is that value of r which satisfies the following equation:

$$(1 + r)^4 = 1.6282.$$

The solution to this equation is 12.96%.

This example teaches us several lessons about the problems of measuring portfolio performance.

1. The portfolio return is a complex weighted average of the returns on the individual securities comprising the portfolio over the horizon period. Although it is indicative of the "average growth" in portfolio value over the horizon period, it does not say anything about the range of returns earned on individual securities over various intervals within the horizon period.
2. The portfolio return can be very sensitive to the length and dates of the horizon period. In the above example, portfolio manager 1 earned the highest return in year 1 and portfolio manager 3 earned the highest return in year 4. However, portfolio manager 2 earned the highest return over the entire 4-year period.
3. It is difficult to compare returns on securities with different maturities. At time period 0, the 4-year security had a significantly higher yield than the 2-year security. The 2-year security turned out to be a better investment, however, because

interest rates rose to 16% at the beginning of period 3. The only way to compare returns on different securities is to look either at the wealth they provide, or the average return they earn, over a common time period.

4. The return on a portfolio is rarely known at the time the initial investment is made. As already noted, portfolio manager 2 earned a higher return over the horizon period than portfolio manager 1, because interest rates rose to 16% at the beginning of period 3. At the time he made his initial investment, however, portfolio manager 1 did not know for sure in which direction interest rates would move, and so his ultimate outcome was at least partly due to chance.

Factors Affecting Portfolio Returns

Having described the difficulties in measuring and comparing portfolio returns, we now discuss four major economic factors that determine portfolio returns: (1) maturity, (2) default risk, (3) taxability, and (4) special supply and demand factors.

Maturity   Table 10.2 shows the yields on Treasury issues with different maturities, as reported in the *Wall Street Journal* of February 17, 1984. It is evident from these data that maturity has a very strong influence on yield. In fact, for these data the yield quite consistently increases with increases in the term to maturity. The difference between the yield on the shortest maturity, the March 1984 issue, and the yield on the longest maturity, the November 2003 issue, being 380 basis points.

The relationship between yield and maturity is so important that financial managers have given it a name; it is called the yield curve. Several explanations for the shape of the yield curve are discussed below under the heading the Term Structure of Interest Rates.

Default Risk   The yield on a money market security is also strongly affected by the risk that the issuer will default on either the payment of interest or principle. Government T-bills are generally considered the safest of money market securities because

Table 10.2   Yields on Treasury Issues
with Different Maturities[a]
Thursday, February 16, 1984

Maturity Date	Yield
March 1984	8.17%
April 1984	8.48%
May 1984	8.91%
August 1984	9.44%
December 1984	9.70%
December 1985	10.51%
November 1990	11.68%
November 2003	11.97%

[a]Taken from *The Wall Street Journal.*

they are backed by the full faith and credit of the U.S. government. Thus, U.S. T-bills usually offer the lowest yields available in the money market. The short-term obligations of the federal government agencies and banker's acceptances are also considered very safe investments. There is no example in the history of the U.S. money market where the issuers of these instruments have defaulted. Bankers acceptances and federal agencies usually trade at yields only slightly above those available on U.S. T-bills. Certificates of deposit and commercial paper are generally considered to have slightly higher risk of default than the three previously mentioned securities. Their yields are thus above those available on the other instruments.

A feeling for the magnitude of the yield premium required to compensate the investor for the risk of default in the money market can be obtained from the data shown in Table 10.3. We see that the portfolio manager could earn an extra 75 to 100 basis points by investing in Eurodollar deposits rather than U.S. T-bills in early 1984, a period of relative optimism in the market. During periods of high market uncertainty, the yield premium for bearing risk would, of course, increase significantly.

Taxability   Money market instruments that have special tax features offer yields that cannot be explained by their maturity and risk of default alone. Since income from investments in the securities of state and municipal governments are exempt from federal income taxes, their yields are generally quite low on a before tax basis compared to the yields on other money market securities.

Special Supply and Demand Factors   There are times when special supply and demand factors distort the usual relationships between money market yields. This is especially true in the T-bill market, where yields are strongly affected by the supply of new issues and the need of corporate treasurers to have a safe haven for funds that will soon be used to pay taxes.

Table 10.3   Interest Rates on 90-Day Money Market Securities[a] Thursday, February 16, 1984

Security	Yield
U.S. T-bill	9.04%
FNMA note	9.32
Bankers acceptance	9.40
Commercial paper	9.45
Certificates of deposit	9.50
Eurodollar deposits	9.78–10.00

[a]Taken from *The Wall Street Journal.*

The Term Structure of Interest Rates

Given the importance of the yield curve to the thinking of portfolio managers, it is not surprising that economists have devoted considerable effort to explaining its shape. Their work has produced three theories of the term structure of interest rates: the Expectations Theory, the Liquidity Preference Theory, and the Market Segmentation Theory. Although these theories have different implications concerning the term structure, it appears that there is some truth in each. An understanding of these theories is an important part of the tool kit of portfolio managers.

Expectations Theory   To help in explaining the Expectations Theory of the term structure of interest rates, consider again the data shown in Table 10.1, but this time assume that the interest rates for periods other than period 1 are expectations rather than realizations. Under this assumption, the portfolio manager has three ways she can invest her money over the horizon period. If she chooses Alternative 1, she expects to earn a return of 12% per year; if she chooses Alternative 2, she expects to earn a return of 12.96% per year; and if she chooses Alternative 3, she expects to earn a return of 11.18% per year.

The proponents of the Expectations Theory argue that the above results could never occur in practice. If the portfolio manager expected to earn a higher return from Alternative 2 than from Alternatives 1 and 3, she would surely choose that alternative, as would all other portfolio managers with the same expectations. The rash of orders to purchase the 2-year investment included in Alternative 2 would tend to increase its price and reduce its yield. Likewise, the weak demand for the 1- and 4-year investments found in Alternatives 1 and 3 would tend to lower their price and increase their yield. Ultimately, a new equilibrium would be reached where each alternative had the same expected return over the horizon period.

The requirement that each investment have the same expected return over the horizon period imposes certain constraints on the term structure of interest rates. In particular, if $R_{1,3}$ is the known return on a 2-year security in today's market and $r_{1,2}$ is the known return on a 1-year security in today's market, then the relationship between $R_{1,3}$ and $R_{1,2}$ must be given by the following equation:

$$(1+R_{1,3})^2 = (1+r_{1,2})(1+r_{2,3}^e). \qquad (10.1)$$

This equation implies that the rate on a 2-year security, $R_{1,3}$, will exceed the rate on a 1-year security, $r_{1,2}$, whenever the rate expected on a 1-year security in the future $(r_{2,3}^e)$ exceeds the current rate on the 1-year security. Likewise, the equation implies that the rate on the 2-year security will be less than the rate on the 1-year security whenever the expected rate on the 1-year security is less than the current rate on the 1-year security.

Since the relationship between the current rates on the 1- and 2-year securities is exactly what is captured in the yield curve, the yield curve will be upward sloping when 1-year interest rates are expected to increase, and it will be downward sloping whenever 1-year interest rates are expected to decrease (see Figure 10.7). The expected

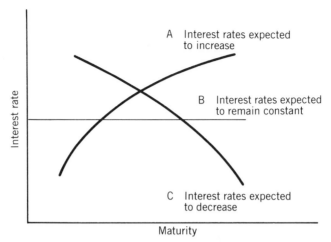

Figure 10.7 The shape of the yield curve implied by the expectations theory.

rate on a 1-year security at a future point in time that is embodied in the yield curve is sometimes called "the forward rate of interest."

Using the data from our example and Equation 10.1, we see that the forward rate of interest, $r^e_{2,3}$ is equal to:

$$[(1+R_{1,3})^2 \ / \ (1+r_{1,2})] -1 \text{ or } [(1.10)^2 \ / \ 1.06] -1 = 14.15\%.$$

Thus, the portfolio manager's expectation on the one-period return at the beginning of period 2 (9%) is far out of line with the forward one-period rate implied in the yield curve.

Liquidity Preference Theory   Under the Expectations Theory, the yield curve will be flat whenever the short-term interest rate is expected to remain unchanged. The Liquidity Preference Theory asserts that it is possible for the yield curve to be upward sloping (i.e., it is possible for the current rate on the 1-year security to be less than the current rate on the 2-year security), even though the 1-year rate is expected to be the same at the beginning of period 2 as it is today. The proponents of the Liquidity Preference Theory argue that this may occur because portfolio managers have a preference for liquidity; that is, they may accept Alternative 3 in spite of its lower expected return, because it is more liquid.

In terms of our previous notation, the Liquidity Preference Theory suggests that the relationship between the short and long rate is given by the equation:

$$(1+R_{1,3})^2 = (1+r_{1,2})(1+r^e_{2,3} + \text{Liq. Prem.}),$$

where Liq. Prem. is the yield investors are willing to forego in order to maintain liquidity. A summary of the yield curve relationship under the Liquidity Preference Theory is shown in Figure 10.8.

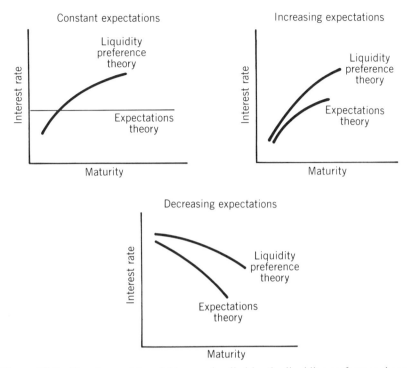

Figure 10.8 The shape of the yield curve implied by the liquidity preference theory.

Market Segmentation Theory   Whereas the Expectations and Liquidity Preference Theories rely heavily on the assumption that portfolio managers are willing to shift funds from one maturity to another depending on relative returns, the Market Segmentation Theory suggests that portfolio managers and security issuers have certain preferred habitats in the range of maturities available. Although corporate portfolio managers generally prefer to invest in short-term securities, portfolio managers working in insurance companies (or any other firm with long-term liabilities) prefer to invest in securities with longer term maturities. Likewise, there are some security issuers who naturally prefer to issue short-term securities (perhaps because their assets are mainly short-term) while there are other security issuers who naturally prefer to issue long-term securities. Thus, under the Market Segmentation Theory the yield curve depends more on the demand and supply factors in each segment of the market than it does on expectations concerning the future course of interest rates.

Portfolio Risk

The manager of the firm's short-term investment portfolio incurs three kinds of risk: default risk, interest rate risk, and liquidity risk. As the name implies, default risk refers to the possibility that the security issuer will be unable to pay either the interest or principle when they are due. Since money market securities are generally issued only by firms or institutions with outstanding credit ratings, this risk is small for most money market securities. However, holders of the commercial paper of the Penn Central Railroad Company in the early 1970s and holders of certificates of deposit in the Penn Square Bank in the early 1980s will testify that the risk is very real indeed. Since the primary purpose of the short-term security portfolio is to serve as a temporary storehouse of cash until it is needed in the firm's basic operations, it doesn't make any sense to incur a significant amount of default risk in return for a little higher yield.

Interest rate risk refers to the risk that the return on the short-term portfolio will be less than what was expected at the time the investments were made. The degree of interest rate risk that the portfolio manager faces is a function of the average maturity of his money market portfolio and the average maturity of the firm's cash requirements.

Consider again the three portfolio strategies shown in Table 10.1. It is easy to see that the interest rate risk associated with each strategy depends on the timing of the firm's cash requirements. If the firm has no need for cash until the horizon period, then strategy 1 involves no interest rate risk, because the return on the 4-year security over the horizon period is known with certainty. The other two strategies involve a significant amount of interest rate risk, however, because the proceeds of the maturing 1- and 2-year securities will have to reinvested at unknown interest rates.

On the other hand, the interest rate risk of strategy 1 may be substantial if the firm has cash requirements before the end of the horizon. For in this case, the 4-year security will have to be sold before it matures at an unknown price. If the firm has a need for cash at the beginning of period 2, then it is the 1-year security that has no interest rate risk; if the firm's need for cash is at the beginning of period 3, then it is the 2-year security that has no interest rate risk.

The above discussion suggests that interest rate risk is largely a function of the degree of "mismatch" in the maturity of the firm's securities and the maturity of the firm's cash requirements. Intuitively, the portfolio manager incurs no short-term interest rate risk whenever the weighted average maturity of the firm's money market assets is equal to the weighted average maturity of the firm's short-term cash requirements.[2] Although this principle is not easy to implement when the firm's cash requirements are uncertain, an understanding of the principle should help the portfolio manager to minimize interest rate risk.

The final risk that the portfolio manager incurs is called liquidity risk. It refers to the possibility that the portfolio manager will have a difficult time financing an unexpectedly large cash requirement because of an inability to sell the assets in his portfolio at short notice with little loss in value. To protect against this risk, some portfolio managers invest only in securities with very short maturities. To us this seems a bit extreme. The portfolio manager can feel comfortable investing in longer maturities as long as the secondary market for these securities is well developed. However, he

---

[2]This statement assumes that short- and long-term interest rates change by the same percentage amount over time. If they do not change by the same percentage amount, then the weighted average maturity is only an approximate measure of interest rate risk. See Jess B. Yawitz, George H. Hempel, and William J. Marshall, "The Use of Average Maturity as a Risk Proxy in Investment Portfolios." *Journal of Finance*, May 1975, pp. 325–333.

should be wary of investing in longer term securities that have substantial penalties for liquidation prior to maturity.

Before we proceed to a discussion of the alternative strategies that financial managers use to manage their marketable securities portfolio, we should point out that liquidity risk can be significantly reduced through better cash forecasting.

ALTERNATIVE STRATEGIES

In managing their marketable securities portfolio, financial managers employ a variety of strategies that help them increase portfolio yields, while keeping risks and management costs to a minimum. For the purpose of discussion, it is convenient to group these strategies into four categories: passive, matching, riding the yield curve, and active.

Passive Strategy

In firms where the size of the marketable securities portfolio is rarely sufficient to justify large management costs, financial managers employ one of several passive portfolio management strategies. These strategies require little action on the part of the financial manager. Their goal is to earn an acceptable yield on invested funds, while minimizing the costs and risks of portfolio management.

One passive strategy, used by many small firms, is to invest any funds in excess of the required daily bank balance in an interest earning account maintained by the bank. These accounts are frequently called ''sweep'' accounts, because any amount in excess of the required daily balance is automatically ''swept'' into the interest-earning account. Although these accounts are extremely convenient for the financial manager, they generally earn an interest yield somewhat below the market rate. This is because the bank must invest the funds in money market instruments, and it requires an incentive to perform this service.

Matching Strategy

The passive strategy described above allows the firm to earn some interest on its excess cash, while incurring almost no risk of loss due to market fluctuations; however, the interest earned is generally quite low because the investment is essentially one day in length. The financial manager can sometimes improve his interest earnings at very little additional risk by investing in securities whose maturity is matched to the dates of expected cash outflows. Thus, if the financial manager expects a large cash outflow in two months, he might invest in a 60-day CD.

The matching strategy allows the financial manager to earn a higher yield on his investment by matching the maturity of his investment portfolio to periods of expected cash drains. This strategy is slightly more risky than the passive strategy, however, because the financial manager's cash forecast may be inaccurate. In this case, he would simply sell some of his investments before maturity, thereby incurring the risk of a possible loss. For securities in the less than 90-day maturity range, this risk is not large.

Riding the Yield Curve

The yield curve—the relationship between the yield on a security and its term to maturity—is the basis of many portfolio strategies. One such strategy, called "riding the yield curve", calls for the financial manager to purchase securities with maturities greater than her expected investment horizon. To understand this strategy, consider what happens when the yield on a 30-day T-bill is 9%, the yield on a 60-day T-bill is 9.40%, interest rates are constant over time and the financial manager has a 30-day investment horizon.

If the financial manager purchases the 30-day T-bill, she will earn 9% for sure over this horizon. If she purchases the 60-day T-bill, her yield is composed of two elements: the underlying interest rate and the capital gain or loss on the instrument. However, if interest rates are constant, we know that the capital gain on the 60-day T-bill will be positive, because at the end of 30 days the 60-day T-bill will be trading like a 30-day T-bill, whose yield is assumed to be 9%. Thus, in these circumstances, the 60-day T-bill is a better buy. An example of the effect of riding the yield curve in these circumstances is described in Table 10.4.

Although the logic of the riding the yield curve strategy sounds convincing, its major drawback is that interest rates rarely remain constant. If interest rates rise, as they have frequently done over the last 20 years, the financial manager might take a capital loss on her investment in the 60-day T-bill. Studies of the strategy over this period indicate that this is exactly what has happened. On average, financial managers would have earned a slightly higher yield by riding the yield curve, but the additional risk would have been much larger as well. Thus, over this period at least, the strategy was of doubtful value. An example of the effect of riding the yield curve when interest rates rise is described in Table 10.5.

Active Strategy

The fourth strategy, followed only by firms whose marketable security portfolio is consistently large, is to buy and sell securities much like a money market dealer. This involves a willingness to (a) sell securities before maturity, (b) buy and sell securities for extremely short periods to take advantage of conditions in the market, and (c) invest

Table 10.4 Effect of Riding the Yield Curve When Interest Rates Do Not Change

Date	Alternative 1	Alternative 2
Aug. 3	Purchase 91-day T-bill at $97.75 (discount yield = 9%)	Purchase 182-day T-bill at $95.30 (discount yield = 9.40%)
Nov. 2	91-day T-bill matures at $100	Sell 182-day T-bill at $97.75 (discount yield = 9.00%)
	Bond equivalent yield $= \dfrac{100-97.75}{97.75} \times 4$ $= 9.21\%$	Bond equivalent yield $= \dfrac{97.75-95.30}{97.75} \times 4$ $= 10.03\%$

Table 10.5 Effect of Riding the Yield Curve When Interest Rates Rise

Date	Alternative 1	Alternative 2
Aug. 3	Purchase 91-day T-bill at $97.75 (discount yield = 9.00%)	Purchase 182-day T-bill at $95.30 (discount yield = 9.40%)
Nov. 2	91-day T-bill matures at $100	Sell 182-day T-bill at $97.50 (discount yield = 10.00%)
	Bond equivalent yield $= \dfrac{100 - 97.75}{97.75} \times 4$ $= 9.21\%$	Bond equivalent yield $= \dfrac{97.50 - 95.30}{97.50} \times 4$ $= 9.03\%$

in a wide variety of sophisticated instruments, including futures and instruments denominated in foreign currencies.

The active portfolio manager is generally willing to take a stand on the future course of interest rates; she shortens the average maturity on her portfolio when she believes interest rates will rise, and she lengthens the average maturity on her portfolio when she believes interest rates will fall. Unlike the financial manager who follows the matching strategy, the active manager is only secondarily concerned with the time pattern of the firm's operating cash flows; that is, she does not attempt to match the maturity of her securities to the time pattern of the firm's cash flows.

An active portfolio management strategy can be rewarding for the extraordinarily sophisticated financial manager. However, this strategy involves a significant management cost, because the skills required to play the game at this level are scarce and the backup support is expensive.

COMPUTER AIDS TO SHORT-TERM PORTFOLIO MANAGEMENT

Managing the short-term securities portfolio is a difficult task that involves an ability to process large volumes of data, forecast future financial requirements, and make complex interest rate calculations rapidly. Fortunately, computer models have been developed that significantly reduce the difficulty of this task. These models provide the following benefits to the portfolio manager:

1. *Balance reporting.* In a world where firms may have cash in accounts at banks throughout the country, it is sometimes difficult for the financial manager to obtain timely information on the amount of funds he actually has available for investment. Computerized balance reporting systems, offered as a cash management service by many banks, provide information on deposit amounts in all of the firm's bank accounts via a computer terminal in the financial manager's office. In addition to simple deposit information, most balance reporting systems provide information on average cash balances versus compensating balance requirements, lockbox collections, and cash disbursements.

2. *Portfolio information.*   When the firm's portfolio is large, it is sometimes difficult to obtain adequate information on types and maturities of various securities in the portfolio, accrued interest, initial yields, and cash flows from maturing securities. Computer-based portfolio management systems provide ready access to this kind of information. They also allow this information to be fed into other files, such as a cash forecasting system or the firm's accounting records.

3. *Interest rate information.*   Current market rate information on money market securities and foreign exchange is provided electronically by a number of firms for a fee. The information provided by these services is obviously essential to the financial manager who is following an active portfolio management strategy.

4. *Evaluating alternative strategies.*   Computer models are now available that allow the manager to evaluate the financial impact of alternative portfolio management strategies. Some of these models rely on sophisticated mathematical programming algorithms that help the manager find the portfolio strategy that maximizes return for a given level of risk.

LINEAR PROGRAMMING APPROACHES TO PORTFOLIO MANAGEMENT

In Chapter 6, we briefly described how linear programming could be used to help the financial manager evaluate alternative short-term financial plans. The portfolio management problem is very similar in structure to the short-term financial planning problem. Both problems require that the financial manager (1) develop a cash forecast for each period in the planning horizon, (2) identify alternatives for satisfying the cash requirements, and (3) evaluate each alternative in terms of some objective. Thus, it would seem that linear programming can also be used to improve portfolio management.

Unfortunately, the difficulties of applying linear programming to portfolio management are greater than they at first seem. While short-run financial planning frequently encompasses a 1-year horizon period with monthly intervals, portfolio management frequently involves a three- to six-month horizon period with daily intervals, at least during the first few weeks. In addition, while it may be suitable for short-run financial planning to treat loans as having a small number of maturities that coincide with the beginning of various months in the planning horizon, this approximation is not very suitable for portfolio management. Money market securities may be purchased with virtually any maturity in the range one day to one year, and the securities that mature at the beginning of the various periods in the planning horizon may not have the most attractive yields. Since the portfolio manager needs to be prepared to satisfy cash flows that occur daily and there are a great many investment alternatives, a linear programming formulation of his problem frequently becomes too unwieldy to be practical. This is especially important since portfolio management decisions must be made within a period of 30 minutes to an hour in the morning.

Although the above difficulties present major problems for the application of linear programming to portfolio management, the advantages of using linear programming are such that it is worthwhile to see if they can be overcome. The authors have been involved with several major banks in developing a linear programming approach to portfolio management that solves many of the practical difficulties noted above. It is programmed in an interactive mode that greatly reduces the amount of work involved in inputting data, checking for errors, and interpreting results. The model in described in the appendix to this chapter.

SUMMARY

Management of the firm's marketable security portfolio involves decisions about the optimal mix of cash and marketable securities, as well as decisions about the type and maturity of securities to hold. The decision to hold cash instead of marketable securities, depends on the level of interest rates, the cost for making security transactions, the firm's ability to forecast future cash flows, and the level of compensating balance requirements the firm may have to hold with its banks. This chapter reviews three conceptual models of the cash/marketable securities decision that highlights the important economic factors affecting this decision. Although these models are useful instructional tools, they have been sparsely used in practice.

To make decisions regarding the type and maturity of securities to hold in his portfolio, the financial manager must understand the factors that affect the portfolio's return, risk, and liquidity. The portfolio's return depends on several characteristics of the securities, including maturity, degree of default risk, and taxability. In addition, the portfolio return may depend on special supply and demand factors in the money market.

Since the relationship between the portfolio return and its average maturity is so important to the portfolio manager's thinking, we discuss three theories about the form of this relationship: the Expectations Theory, the Liquidity Preference Theory, and the Market Segmentation Theory. A sound understanding of these theories helps the financial manager to make better portfolio maturity decisions.

In addition to the portfolio's return, the financial manager must obviously be concerned with its risk. Three kinds of risk are important: default risk, interest rate risk, and liquidity risk. Default risk refers to the possibility that the security issuer will default on his obligation to pay either principal or interest when due. Since this risk depends on the issuer's credit standing, the financial manager must be careful to investigate this credit standing before he makes security purchases.

Interest rate risk refers to the risk that the portfolio's return will be less than what was expected at the time the investments were made. Interest rate risk depends on the average maturity of the marketable securities portfolio and the average maturity of the firm's cash requirements. The financial manager can minimize interest rate risk by matching the average maturity of his portfolio to the average maturity of the firm's cash requirements.

The final risk that the portfolio manager incurs, liquidity risk, refers to the possibility that the portfolio manager will be unable to satisfy unexpectedly large cash requirements. The portfolio manager can minimize this risk by restricting his investments to short-term securities that are traded in highly active secondary markets.

An understanding of the factors that affect portfolio performance helps the financial manager to choose an investment strategy. Four frequently used strategies are discussed in this chapter: passive, matching, riding the yield curve, and active. The appropriate strategy for a given portfolio manager depends on his knowledge of money market conditions, his ability to forecast the firm's cash requirements, and his tolerance for risk. The passive and matching strategies are most appropriate for financial managers who have little confidence in their ability to play the market and who have a low risk tolerance. Most corporate portfolio managers fall in this category. The exceptional few portfolio managers who actively manage their portfolios so as to increase return without accepting undue risk generally work for firm's with very large investments in marketable securities.

DISCUSSION QUESTIONS

1. Describe the duties of the manager of the firm's short-term securities portfolio.
2. What managerial decision is the Baumol model designed to address?
3. What are the major assumptions of the Baumol model?
4. How useful do you think the Baumol model is likely to be in practice?
5. What are the major weaknesses of the Baumol model?
6. How does the Miller-Orr model differ from the Baumol model?
7. In what circumstances are the conclusions of the Miller-Orr model likely to be more applicable than the Baumol model?
8. What are the major weaknesses of the Miller-Orr model?
9. How does the Stone *K*-Day Look Ahead model differ from the Baumol and Miller-Orr models?
10. Describe the criteria financial managers generally use in selecting marketable securities. Why are these reasonable?
11. What are the major factors that affect portfolio returns?
12. What are the major factors that affect portfolio risk?
13. In what circumstances is the matching strategy likely to be optimal?
14. In what circumstances are passive strategies preferable.
15. What does it mean to ''ride the yield curve''?
16. Why is riding the yield curve not always a successful strategy?
17. Describe the various computer aids that are available to help the manager of the firm's short-term portfolio?
18. What are the major data inputs required to make short-term portfolio management decisions?
19. How does the portfolio management problem relate to the short-run financial planning problem described in Chapter 6?
20. Discuss how arbitrage might arise in short-term portfolio planning.
21. How does the maturity of the firm's assets and liabilities affect its risk?

22. Describe the typical constraints that might be placed on the portfolio manager's decision making ability.
23. What are some of the major problems involved in using linear programming to help make portfolio management decisions?

PROBLEMS

1. The financial manager of Litton Electronics has decided to use the Baumol Model to help her make cash management decisions. The manager has determined that the total demand for cash over the next year is $172 million; the transactions cost for selling securities is $90 per transaction, including the cost of managerial time, telephone expenses, and so on; and the average interest rate on marketable securities is 10%. What is the optimal cash management policy?
2. Consider a firm that has annual sales of $300 million. If the firm has average cash balances of $1 million over the year, do you believe that there is sufficient evidence to recommend that the firm reprimand its cash manager for being inefficient?
3. Consider a firm whose cash forecast and actual cash flows are given in the following table.

Day Number	Cash Flow Forecast	Actual Cash Flow
1	2	2
2	3	2
3	2	8
4	-3	-2
5	-1	1
6	2	2
7	-1	-2
8	-4	-7
9	-2	-4
10	3	1
11	2	3
12	0	2
13	-1	1
14	-3	-2
15	4	3
16	2	2

If this firm starts day 1 with a cash balance of $50 and it employs a Four-Day Look-Ahead Policy with an upper control point of $60, a lower control point of $40, and a return point of $50, how many transactions will it make over the 16-day period shown? How many transactions will it make if it employs a No-Day Look-Ahead Policy?

4. Calculate the average cash balances under the two policies discussed in Problem 3. Which policy should the firm adopt?

5. You have been asked to evaluate the performance of three portfolio managers over a 4-year period. Manager 1 invested in a 4-year government security earning 10% per year. Manager 2 initially invested in a 2-year government security earning 8.5% per year and then invested the proceeds in another 2-year government security earning 11.5% per year. Manager 3 made four consecutive investments in 1-year government securities yielding 7%, 9%, 11%, and 15%, respectively. What returns did each of these portfolio managers earn on their investments over this 4-year period?

6. Consider a firm that has expected cash requirements over the next four months as follows:

Month	Cash Requirement
1	(100)
2	(300)
3	(400)
4	(200)

Suppose that the financial manager for this firm currently has $1000 to invest on the firm's behalf, and that over the next four months he expects interest rates on T-bills with 30-, 60-, 90-, and 120-day maturities to be:

	Instrument			
Month	30	60	90	120
1	8.0	8.2	8.4	8.5
2	8.3	8.5	8.7	7.8
3	8.8	8.9	9.0	9.1
4	8.9	9.1	9.3	9.4

Suppose also that this financial manager can borrow for any length of time at 20 basis points over the yield on the 120-day instrument and that all securities will be liquidated at the horizon at their market value.

(a) Describe three alternative investment/borrowing strategies that satisfy the firm's cash requirements in every period. Identify these strategies as being either passive, matching, riding the yield curve or active. *Hint.* Review how we identified feasible strategies to the short-run financial planning problem in Chapter 6.

(b) Determine which of your three feasible strategies has the highest horizon value.

(c) Suppose that interest rates actually follow the pattern shown below rather than that which was expected at the beginning of the investment horizon.

Interest Rates on 30-, 60-, 90-, and 120-Day
Instruments Over the Four Months

	Instrument			
Month	**30**	**60**	**90**	**120**
1	8.0	8.2	8.4	8.5
2	7.7	7.9	8.1	8.2
3	7.4	7.6	7.8	7.9
4	7.1	7.3	7.5	7.6

What happens to the horizon value of your three feasible strategies when interest rates follow this pattern instead of the expected pattern?

(d) Which of your three feasible strategies has the greatest risk? Why?

(e) How many feasible strategies do you think there are to this investment problem?

(f) If you were the President of this firm, would you want to place any constraints on the portfolio manager's decisions?

ADDITIONAL READINGS

1. Austin, J., S. F. Maier and J. H. Vander Weide, "General Telephone's Experience with a Short-Run Financial Planning Model," *Cash Management Forum,* June 1980, pp. 3–6.

2. Baumol, William J., "The Transactions Demand for Cash: An Inventory Theoretic Approach," *Quarterly Journal of Economics,* November 1952, pp. 545–556.

3. Daellenbach, Hans G., "Are Cash Management Optimization Models Worthwhile?" *Journal of Financial and Quantitative Analysis,* September 1974, pp. 607–626.

4. Eppen, Gary D. and Eugene F. Fama, "Cash Balance and Simple Dynamic Portfolio Problems with Proportional Costs," *International Economic Review,* June 1969, pp. 110–133.

5. Maier, S. F. and J. H. Vander Weide, "A Practical Approach to Short Run Financial Planning," *Financial Management,* Winter 1978, pp. 10–16.

6. Mao, J. C. T., "Application of Linear Programming to the Short-Term Financing Decision," *The Engineering Economist,* July 1968, pp. 221–241.

7. Miller, Merton H. and Daniel Orr, "A Model of the Demand for Money by Firms." *Quarterly Journal of Economics.* August 1966, pp. 413–435.

8. Orgler, Y. E., *Cash Management: Methods and Models,* The Wadsworth Publishing Company, Inc., Belmont, Calif., 1970.

9. Osteryoung, Jerome S., Gordon S. Roberts and Daniel E. McCarty, ''Riding the Yield Curve-A Useful Technique for Short-Term Investment of Idle Funds in Treasury Bills?'' Reading 15 in *Readings on the Management of Working Capital,* 2nd ed., Keith V. Smith, ed., West Publishing Company, St. Paul, Minn., 1980.
10. Pogue, G. A. and R. N. Bussard, ''A Linear Programming Model for Short-Term Financial Planning Under Uncertainty,'' *Sloan Management Review,* Spring 1972, pp. 69–98.
11. Robichek, A. A., D. Techroew and J. M. Jones, ''Optimal Short-Term Financing Decision,'' *Management Science,* September 1965, pp. 1–36.
12. Srinivasan, V., ''A Transshipment Model for Cash Management Decisions,'' *Management Science,* June 1974, pp. 1350–363.
13. Stone, Bernell K., ''The Use of Forecasts and Smoothing in Control-Limit Models for Cash Management,'' *Financial Management,* Spring 1972, pp. 72–84.

APPENDIX TO CHAPTER 10

THE PORTFOLIO MANAGER

In this appendix, we describe a computer aid to short-run portfolio management that has been found to be useful by managers at several large firms. For the purposes of our ensuing discussion, we will call this computer aid the Portfolio Manager. However, it should be recognized that the Portfolio Manager is not really a manager at all, it is only a useful device for helping the real portfolio manager explore the implications of various future economic scenarios.

The Portfolio Manager is a user-oriented version of the type of short-run planning model considered at the end of Chapter 6. Although it is based on a sophisticated linear programming formulation, it addresses many of the practical problems associated with earlier linear programming formulations of the portfolio manager's decision problem. In particular, the Portfolio Manager has three characteristics that differentiate it from earlier formulations: (1) efficient interactive data entry, (2) an ability to handle practical problems of implementation, and (3) an ability to describe and incorporate the firm's existing portfolio.

Efficient Interactive Data Entry

The Portfolio Manager is programmed in an interactive mode that greatly reduces the amount of work involved in inputting data and checking for errors. The user can input all necessary data and explore several economic scenarios in a session lasting no longer than 20–30 minutes. In fact, once the model has been run the first time, the user can evaluate a particular decision problem in as little as 10 minutes.

New Features

The Portfolio Manager has the capacity to handle a number of practical problems that are ignored in the previous contributions: variable maturities, instruments that mature beyond the planning horizon, borrowing and investment maturity mismatches, and the possibility of arbitrage.

Current Status

The model provides reports on the characteristics of the firm's current portfolio of investment/borrowing instruments and automatically incorporates these characteristics into its constraints. The ability to automatically incorporate the cash flows from maturing securities in the firm's current portfolio is especially useful when the amount of the dollars to be invested (borrowed) is small relative to the total existing portfolio.

INPUT REQUIREMENTS FOR THE MODEL

The Portfolio Manager is user-oriented. All information is entered via computer terminal in a time-sharing conversation. Since data from previous runs are stored, the model is particularly easy to use, once the first scenario has been run. Only data changes need be entered on subsequent runs.

The input is conveniently grouped into six types.

Period Duration and Cash Flow Projection

The financial manager must specify the starting date of each time period within the planning horizon. He is also asked to specify the cash flows that are expected at the beginning of each time period within the horizon. The current model specification allows for a maximum of 25 time periods, with no limitations on the length of these periods. Cash flows may be either positive or negative.

Experience has shown that it is best to keep the first few periods in the time horizon relatively short. For example, it is frequently convenient to use daily periods for the first few days, followed by a three-day period corresponding to a weekend. Later periods can be longer, often a week or two. It is also helpful to have one final period of relatively long duration to incorporate the firm's long-run cash flow and interest rate projections.

Instrument Description

The second input section presents a description of the available investment/financing instruments. Each instrument is described by name, maturity length, yield, and interest rate projection.

The maturity may be specified as a constant (e.g., a 91-day Treasury Bill would be specified as 91 days). Since some financial instruments may have the same yield over a range of possible maturities, the model also permits the user to specify a range. For example, commercial paper with a yield of 9.5% could be purchased with a maturity of between 15 and 37 days.

The yield on an instrument is always computed as if the interest will be paid upon maturity. If the instrument is sold or bought at a discount, the discount rate can be specified and the model will automatically convert the discount rate of interest to the interest yield, as if the interest had been paid at maturity.

Flexible maturities and user-selected lengths for the time periods within the planning horizon cause unique problems for any model. In particular, one must deal with instruments that mature in the middle of a planning period. (Note that in a linear programming formulation only investment and borrowing that take place at the start of an investment period are under model control.) In order to bridge from a mid-period maturity, the model takes two actions. First, if the instrument can be rolled-over, the model will automatically do so until the start of the next planning period is reached. The second action depends on whether it is a maturing investment or borrowing instrument. If the funds are in a maturing investment instrument, the system automatically puts the money into an over-night repurchase agreement and rolls this over to the next decision point. If a borrowing instrument is maturing in the middle of a period, then as of the date of the just previous decision point, money is set aside in a repurchase agreement, which with compounding will just equal the amount of the required repayment. These actions preserve the unique characteristics of both flexible maturities and variable time-period lengths without overly distorting the reality of how portfolio managers actually manage their financial portfolios.

Interest-Rate Projections

The financial manager can specify an interest rate projection as a single interest rate projection (and use it to modify the yields on a group of investment instruments), or he can specify an independent interest rate projection for each of his investment or borrowing instruments.

The interest-rate projections incorporate into the model the financial manager's forecast of the movement of interest rates during the planning horizon. Using this information, the model can then help the financial manager select whether to invest/borrow long or short. This involves looking at economic tradeoffs such as whether paying a premium for longer term borrowings is justified when it is expected that interest rates will increase.

Borrowing and Investing Limits

The model allows a financial manager to limit the amount of borrowing or investing associated with any instrument or group of instruments. This limit allows him to incorporate judgments about the risk of various instruments, or to include company policy restrictions (e.g., do not invest more than $3 million of the portfolio in commercial paper).

Average Maturity Constraints

Upper and lower limits may be placed on the average maturities of the borrowing and/or investing side of the portfolio. This type of constraint is useful in limiting the degree of interest rate risk to which the firm is exposed. Professional investment managers often refer to a portfolio with differing average maturities of the investment and borrowing instruments as a "mismatched book." These constraints allow limits to be placed on the level of mismatch the company is willing to tolerate. In the absence of such constraints, and with a normal shaped yield curve, the model would tend to always invest long and borrow short, which at times can produce a severely mismatched book.

Ratio Mix Constraints

Ratio mix constraints are similar to borrowing and investing limits, except that the bounds are specified as percentages rather than dollars. These constraints enable the financial manager to further define personal or company policy restrictions. For example, a constraint can be included to keep the ratio of bank borrowing to commercial paper at 50-50. A constraint of this form can be used to determine the cost of maintaining good bank relationships, when commercial paper appears to be significantly cheaper.

OUTPUT REPORTS

The Portfolio Manager provides several types of output reports.

Cost Summary

The cost summary gives four types of information for each period (Figure 10.9):

- Period length.
- Cash flow projection.
- Interest expense.
- Cumulative interest expense.

Period	Cash Flow	Interest Expense This Period	Cumulative Interest Expense
1/26–2/1	−$2,300,000.00	$8,191.79	$8,191.79
2/2–2/8	2,100,000.00	$1,006.23	$9,198.02
2/9–2/15	−1,300,000.00	$6,713.48	$15,911.50
2/16–3/1	−4,360,000.00	$41,554.61	$57,466.11
3/2–3/15	3,950,000.00	$14,227.11	$71,693.22
3/16–3/29	2,500,000.00	$−3,056.85	$68,636.37
3/30–4/26	3,100,000.00	$−50,046.91	$18,589.46
4/27–5/24	−5,200,000.00	$21,454.00	$40,043.46
5/25–6/21	4,600,000.00	$−42,858.93	−$2,815.47

Figure 10.9 The optimal short-term financial plan cost summary.

The number of days in the period and the projected cash flows are user-specified. The interest expense takes into account all instruments purchased or sold during the period, and all instruments that were activated before the start of the period and will mature at some later date. (A negative interest expense indicates interest earned.) The cumulative interest expense is the interest expense for the current and all previous periods.

Action Summary

The action summary (Figure 10.10) lists the following information for each instrument bought or sold:

- Date on which the action is initiated.
- Instrument name.
- Type of action (buy or sell).
- Amount of capital involved with the original purchase/sale of the instrument.
- Maturity date.
- Maturity value of the instrument.
- Yield of the instrument.

An instrument is only listed in this report on the day the initial action is taken. (To obtain a list of both initial and concluding actions within a period, a separate detailed report is available, although not shown in this Chapter.)

Date	Instrument	Act	Amount	Mature Date	Maturity Value	Yield
1/26	Credit line	B	$1,866,541.98	2/2	$1,873,136.94	18.171%
1/26	CM paper	B	529,986.99	3/2	539,270.01	18.016%
1/26	30-day CD	I	7,932.91	3/2	8,041.89	14.130%
1/26	60-day CD	I	52,916.69	3/30	54,245.56	13.000%
1/26	Daily repo	I	35,679.37	2/2	35,769.70	13.000%
2/2	60-day CD	I	50,211.20	3/30	51,352.26	14.609%
2/2	Daily repo	I	212,421.56	2/9	212,959.85	13.013%
2/9	CM paper	B	2,456,790.07	3/16	2,500,000.00	18.090%
2/16	Credit line	B	2,986,777.06	3/2	3,007,958.65	18.200%
3/2	30-day CD	I	410,813.23	3/30	415,765.82	15.500%
3/30	30-day CD	I	3,547,110.58	4/27	3,596,110.40	17.761%
3/30	90-day CD	I	74,253.05	6/23	77,431.75	18.131%
4/27	Credit line	B	854,540.72	5/25	866,762.43	18.278%
4/27	CM paper	B	854,540.72	6/6	871,362.51	17.717%
4/27	30-day CD	I	105,191.83	5/25	106,687.69	18.283%
5/25	30-day CD	I	2,972,363.16	6/22	3,015,421.14	18.625%
5/25	Repo	I	867,562.11	6/6	871,362.51	13.119%

Figure 10.10   The optimal short-term financial plan action summary.

Date	Credit Line	Comm. Paper	30-Day CD	60-Day CD	90-Day CD	Daily Repo
1/26	.18171	.18016	.14130	.14350	.14500	.13000
2/2	.18184	.18075	.14389	.14609	.14759	.13013
2/9	.18194	.18090	.14595	.14815	.14965	.13023
2/16	.18200	.18074	.14762	.14982	.15132	.13029
3/2	.18208	.18040	.15500	.15720	.15870	.13037
3/16	.18201	.18005	.17250	.17470	.17620	.13030
3/30	.18226	.18000	.17761	.17981	.18131	.13055
4/27	.18278	.17717	.18283	.18503	.19653	.13107
5/25	.18290	.17250	.18625	.18845	.18995	.13119

Figure 10.11   The optimal short-term financial plan interest rate summary.

The "action" column indicates, with a "I" or "B," whether the instrument represents an investment or borrowing. The action date is the first day of the period in which the instrument is activated and the maturity date is the day the instrument matures.

The instrument yield is set initially as part of the instrument's description; it can be revised by the user-defined interest rate projection.

Interest Rate Summary

Figure 10.11 gives an example of the Interest Rate Summary Report, showing in matrix form the yield of each instrument at the start of each period. The instruments are listed across the top of the matrix. The first column in the matrix lists the starting date of the period.

With this information, the financial manager can check how his interest rate projections have modified the yield on each instrument. If there was no projection for the instrument, the same yield will appear throughout the column.

For instruments purchased at the start of a planning period, the yield can be found directly in this report. For instruments purchased in the middle of a planning period, such as would occur due to an automatic rollover, the yield is a linear extrapolation of the yields given in this report.

Risk Summary

The risk summary (Figure 10.12) prints the average maturities of the portfolio for each period in the planning horizon. In addition to the starting date of the period, the following data are given:

- Total dollars invested as of the start of the period.
- Average investment maturity as of the start of the period.
- Total dollars borrowed as of the start of the period.
- Average borrowing maturity as of the start of the period.

This report is used to monitor the mismatch of the portfolio.

	Investments		Borrowing	
Date	**Total Dollars Outstanding**	**Weighted Average Maturities**	**Total Dollars Outstanding**	**Weighted Average Maturities**
1/26	$ 96,528.97	40.000	$2,396,528.97	13.192
2/2	323,651.81	23.152	531,843.60	28.000
2/9	1,481,292.24	10.012	2,990,490.27	32.501
2/16	111,854.41	39.998	5,987,765.92	19.764
3/2	515,249.91	28.000	2,482,716.03	14.000
3/16	518,306.77	14.000	0.00	0.000
3/20	3,621,363.63	29.169	0.00	0.000
4/27	180,491.98	40.099	1,709,081.43	34.000
5/25	3,916,272.52	24.475	866,315.97	12.000

Figure 10.12   The optimal short-term financial plan risk summary.

Input Summary

The input summary lists the data in a particular model file, giving users a consolidated look at all additions and deletions made during a computer session. It includes information on six major input categories: (1) period duration and cash flow projection; (2) borrowing and investing limits; (3) instrument description; (4) interest rate projections; (5) average maturity constraints; and (6) ratio mix constraints.

BENEFITS FROM USING THE MODEL

The Portfolio Manager provides several benefits.

First, the model makes the financial manager sensitive to variables that affect his day-to-day borrowing decisions. This in turn leads to increased awareness of economic trade-offs associated with short-run financial decision making.

Second, the model provides a means of comparing alternative instruments on the basis of "effective" vs. "posted" interest rates. This is especially important when the firm uses both commercial paper and CDs, because interest rates on these instruments are quoted differently.

Third, the model helps the financial manager to quickly and efficiently compare borrowing instruments that have variable maturities, providing a quantitative measure of risk and the expected value of different financing strategies. This important feature allows a financial manager to analyze risk/return relationships.

Finally, the model's flexibility facilitates identification of the strengths and weaknesses of the present cash management system and forecasting methods, and offers ways to improve them.

SUMMARY

This appendix describes a decision support system the financial manager can utilize to improve the short-run financial planning process. The system allows the financial manager to evaluate the economic trade-offs involved in short-run financial decision making without having to make a great many complex calculations. Although the system employs a linear programming formulation of the short-run financial decision problem, it does not alleviate the need for managerial skill and judgement in short-run financial decision making. It allows the financial manager to manage effectively the firm's short term investment/borrowing portfolio by improving his ability to develop intelligent short-run financial plans.

CHAPTER 11

Futures Contracts and Markets

The recent development of financial instrument futures contracts offers the financial manager an opportunity to reduce the risks associated with short-term portfolio management. To take advantage of this opportunity, however, the financial manager must become familiar with the institutions and economics of futures markets, so that she can understand how they can best be used to her benefit. Chapters 11 and 12 are designed to help the financial manager obtain the familiarity with futures markets institutions and understanding of futures markets economics necessary to achieve the benefits these markets offer.

CASH AND FORWARD CONTRACTS

To understand futures contracts, we need to understand the difference between a cash contract and a forward contract.

A cash contract is an agreement between two parties to exchange a commodity for cash, with the delivery of the commodity and the exchange of cash taking place immediately. The cash contract is one of the most common forms of conducting business today. A farmer who takes his grain to market, and sells it for cash, implicitly or explicitly signs a cash contract. The market for trading in cash contracts is called the cash market.

In contrast, a forward contract is an agreement between two parties to exchange a commodity for a fixed amount of cash, with the delivery of the commodity and the exchange of cash taking place at a specified future date. The purpose of a forward contract is to allow individuals or firms to reduce the price uncertainties associated with anticipated future transactions. Consider the farmer who seeks a loan in March to finance the cost of producing a corn crop that will not be harvested until September. His bank may be reluctant to extend the loan because it is uncertain whether the price of his crop at harvest time will be sufficient to pay back the cost of the loan plus interest. The farmer can assure the banker of his ability to pay back the loan by signing a contract in March with a grain dealer to sell his crop in September at a fixed price. The farmer's situation is typical of those that led to the widespread use of forward contracts in the agricultural states around Chicago in the middle of the last century.

Although forward contracts have existed for many centuries and are still in use today, there are several inherent problems with them that limit their usefulness. First, it is tempting for the seller in a forward contract to deliver commodities of less than average quality. The Book of Genesis records that the Jewish patriarch Jacob reached an agreement with his uncle Laban to work 7 years in return for the hand of Laban's beautiful daughter Rachael in marriage. At the end of the 7 years, however, the shrewd Laban delivered his daughter Leah instead. To marry Rachael, Jacob was forced to work another 7 years. Similarly, farmers are tempted to deliver a lower quality crop than they promised at the time the forward contract was arranged.

Second, if the current market price on the forward date named in the contract (the "delivery date") is more favorable for either the buyer or the seller than the previously agreed forward price, that individual is tempted to renege on the forward contract. This can be done by simply not showing up to make final delivery, as happened frequently in mid-19th century America.

Finally, it may be convenient for one of the parties to the forward transaction to sell the contract for cash to a third party. The original buyer of the farmer's corn, for instance, may decide in mid-summer that it is better to allocate his resources to some other venture. He would prefer to sell his contract to buy the farmer's corn to someone else. The lack of a good secondary market for forward contracts makes it difficult to liquidate contracts when it becomes desirable.

FUTURES CONTRACTS

A futures contract, like a forward contract, calls for the exchange of a commodity for cash at a later date. However, the futures contract differs from the forward contract in several important aspects. First, futures contracts are traded on a formal exchange, such as the Chicago Board of Trade or the Chicago Mercantile Exchange. The exchange provides space for trading to take place, approves the contracts that are to be traded, establishes a set of trading rules, and guarantees that the terms of the contract will be fulfilled. Because it is traded on an exchange, the futures contract typically possesses a lower degree of risk and a higher degree of lquidity than the forward contract.

Second, futures contracts in a particular commodity are standardized with respect to the quality and quantity of the commodity that is to be traded, the place of delivery, the time within the month delivery occurs, and the effect of delivering other than the standard quality. Contracts differ only with respect to the delivery month and the price.

Standardization of contracts greatly increases the number of traders in each contract and helps assure that the economic benefits of a competitive marketplace will be realized.

Third, trading in futures contracts tends to be for entirely different purposes than trading in forward contracts. The buyer of a forward contract fully intends to take delivery on the commodity, because she has a need for that commodity in her basic line of business. The buyer of a futures contract frequently has no business need for the exact commodity described in the contract. Instead, she is using the contract either as a vehicle for hedging business risk or as a vehicle for speculating on the future course of price. A large percentage of all futures contracts are canceled before the delivery date. The process by which futures contracts are canceled will be discussed later in this chapter.

THE FUTURES EXCHANGE

A futures exchange is a nonprofit organization whose purpose is to facilitate trading in futures contracts. The personnel operating the exchange are employees who are paid by revenues from the exchange's dues, fees, and investments. In order to trade futures contracts on the exchange one must be a member. The number of memberships is usually limited to a figure set by the board of directors of the exchange, subject to change by them as conditions warrant. Memberships are available only to individuals, though many are members because of their corporate affiliation. A prospective member must be certified to be of good character and financially trustworthy by two current members. If approved by the board of directors he may purchase a membership. Currently, memberships on most exchanges are selling at somewhat over $100,000. Membership has a value because: (1) it is a prerequisite to trade personally on the floor of the exchange and (2) lower commissions are charged members who trade through agents on the floor. Although all futures exchanges are operated independently, their objectives tend to be similar. They are:

1. To provide a marketplace with a specified layout and established trading hours.
2. To establish rules governing trading procedures, criteria of equitable business practices, and procedures for mediation of disputes among members.
3. To establish contract size, quality, procedure for delivery, and method of payment, along with a mechanism to guarantee that members perform their contracted obligations.
4. To collect and publish price and market information to interested members and to the public.

Marketplace

The exchange provides a physical location in which all futures trading occurs, with specified opening and closing times for the trading. The prospective traders in one commodity all gather in one ring (or "pit") where they call out their bids. When a trader accepts another trader's bid, both buyer and seller note on their card the price, quantity, and the delivery month, along with the name of the other party to the trade. These two cards are turned in to be recorded by the clearing house of the exchange at the close of trading. The traders are also required immediately to inform the observers present at the edge of the ring of the details of any trade made. These observers feed the information thus received into a ticker tape or computer information system that sends the price information to many locations throughout the world.

Trading Rules

The exchange establishes the rules governing trading in futures contracts. Usually they cover the following four areas:

1. The exchange establishes the units in which prices will be quoted for each commodity and the minimum price fluctuations allowed. Price quotations and minimum price fluctuations vary by commodity. Pork bellies are quoted in cents per pound with ¼¢ per pound the minimum price fluctuation. Treasury bills are quoted in basis points with 1/100 of a percent (i.e., 1 basis point) the minimum price fluctuation.
2. The exchange establishes a limit on the allowable daily price changes. The maximum daily price limit on commercial paper is 50/100 of a percent (50 basis points) above and below the previous day's settlement price. The purpose of the limit is to prevent speculators from driving the price too far in one direction. However, the limits have the disadvantage that trading may not occur when the limit is reached. Thus, the limit produces a loss of liquidity for those holding the contract.
3. The exchange limits the number of contracts that may be owned or traded by an individual speculator in any one day. This rule is designed to prevent individuals from cornering the market in a commodity.
4. The exchange establishes the times at which trading can occur in each commodity. This includes both the trading period within the day, and the specific times within the delivery month, at which trading in that month's commodity ceases.

Contract Terms

The exchange approves contracts that may be traded on the exchange floor. The contract defines in precise terms the commodity that is to be traded on the future date. The definition includes the quantity, the quality, the time and place of delivery, and the penalty for default. An example will illustrate the terms of a typical contract.

On June 1st one might buy a contract of December corn futures at $2.72. This would mean the buyer had contracted to pay $2.72 per bushel for 5000 bushels of #2 yellow corn (U.S. Department of Agriculture grain standards) delivered at one of the warehouses certified by the exchange. On any date in December (1st through 30th) *chosen by the seller,* with 24 hours notice, the buyer will be furnished an endorsed warehouse receipt for the corn, at which time he will be required to pay $13,600.00 in cash. Since warehouse receipts are, in fact, negotiable instruments, much of the cost of the commodity can be financed.

At the time the contract is made buyer and seller agree on a differential per bushel for delivery of a higher or lower grade than the standard #2. Let us say a figure of $.03

per bushel has been agreed on for the differential. The seller may elect to deliver corn of a quality one grade lower than that specified in the contract, and the buyer will pay only $13,450 ($.03 per bushel less). The seller may instead elect to deliver corn of a quality one grade higher than contracted, in which case the buyer must pay a premium of $.03 per bushel, a total of $13,750.00.

If the buyer should default on this obligation, the seller is empowered by the contract to sell the commodity on the open market for the account of the buyer, with the buyer required to supply any insufficiency. If the seller can only get $12,800 for his 5000 bushels of #2 corn, the seller has the right to receive the remaining $800 from the buyer. A default by the seller is more complicated as it probably would be caused by nonavailability of the commodity. In fact, the exchanges have taken such a firm position on the delivery of contracted commodities that defaults have been almost unknown.

Information Function

The exchange provides various kinds of information to the public concerning futures trading. As we have already noted, it provides facilities for sending price and volume information on each trade to customers throughout the world. It also provides educational materials on futures trading, conducts seminars and conferences, and supports research on futures contracts and markets at universities.

THE CLEARING HOUSE

The clearing house plays an important role in futures trading. It maintains trading records, guarantees fulfillment of contracts, facilitates delivery, and collects payment and margin from members. In general, the clearing house and the exchange are separate legal entities.

Membership

Although membership in the clearing house is limited to members of the exchange, not all members of the exchange need be members of the clearing house. The requirements of membership are simple. A member must purchase stock in the clearing house corporation in proportion to the volume of business he clears. He must deposit a sum in the clearing house guarantee fund and make margin deposits determined by the net open position the member represents. The margin serves as a good faith deposit to help assure that contract obligations will be fulfilled.

Reconciliation of Trades

As noted earlier, the buyer and seller of a contract on the floor of the exchange turn in a card with information on the price, quantity, delivery month, and name of the other party to the trade. It is the clearing house that records these details and, if necessary, reconciles any differences in the terms between the buyer's and seller's reports.

Once the trade has been confirmed, the clearing house becomes the second party to all trades, the buyer to each seller and the seller to each buyer. This intervention serves three purposes. First, it provides a simple means for either the buyer or seller to cancel his contract. If an individual has previously bought a futures contract in, say, May soybeans, he can cancel his obligation to take delivery on the soybeans by placing an order to sell a May soybeans contract. On the books of the clearing house he now has a position to buy and sell the same contract, a meaningless situation that will be canceled out by the clearing house bookkeeping system. Second, it allows a great simplification in recordkeeping as records of only open positions (i.e., noncancelled) need be maintained. Third, it puts the clearing house in a position to guarantee fulfillment of contracted obligations. This creates a climate of public confidence that broadens participation in the markets.

Margin

As an additional factor assuring fulfillment of contractual obligations, the clearing house collects a good faith deposit called margin from clearing members. The amount of the margin held varies from one commodity to another, depending on the maximum price fluctations in that commodity. Margin is always sufficient to cover the maximum daily loss on that commodity.

Margin accounts work as follows. At the time a trade is made, the clearing member deposits an amount in her account at the clearing house equal to the initial margin requirement. This requirement is the same for both buyers and sellers. At the end of each subsequent trading day, the member's account is debited or credited for price changes in that commodity. If the amount in the account falls below a level known as the "maintenance margin," the clearing member must make a deposit large enough to return the account to its initial margin position. If the amount in the member's account rises above the initial margin requirement, the surplus may be withdrawn.

The margin requirements pertain to the relationship between the member firm and the clearing house. Member firms frequently clear trades for exchange members who do not belong to the clearing house and for customers who are not members of the exchange. The clearing members normally will establish a separate system of margin requirements for parties who clear through them.

THE FUTURES COMMISSION MERCHANT

A large percentage of the trades on the floor of any exchange are executed by brokers for nonmembers. These brokers, called Futures Commission Merchants, provide the services needed by their nonmember customers who trade in futures contracts. These services include (1) the receiving and placing of customer orders, (2) rapid order execution, (3) being an agency for the customer in all transactions with the exchange, (4) bookkeeping services, and (5) research in the form of more or less extensive Market Letters according to customer involvement in trading.

COMMODITIES TRADED

The financial pages of *The Wall Street Journal* provide information on the futures contracts most actively traded on the U.S. futures exchanges. The most frequently traded commodities are grouped into six categories: (1) grains and oil seeds, (2) livestock and meat, (3) food and fiber, (4) metals and petroleum, (5) wood, and (6) financial instruments.

Of the various contracts reported in *The Wall Street Journal,* the financial manager is most interested in those pertaining to financial instruments. Table 11.1 shows information on the financial instrument futures contracts reported in *The Wall Street Journal* of Monday, April 30, 1984. It shows actively traded contracts in several foreign currencies, several debt instruments, and the S&P 500 stock index.

It is interesting to focus on at least one financial instrument to illustrate the typical terms in which these contracts are traded. Looking at Table 11.1, we see that there are eight Treasury bill contracts traded on the International Monetary Market at the Chicago Mercantile Exchange. The delivery month on these contracts extends from June 1984 to March 1986. Each contract calls for the delivery of 90-day Treasury bills with a maturity value of $1 million. The delivery is to occur on the Thursday after the third Monday of the month shown in the third column. Prices on Treasury bill contracts are quoted in terms of a price index constructed by deducting the T-bill yield from 100. Thus an opening price of 90.77 indicates that the discount yield is 9.23.

MARKET PARTICIPANTS

The futures market is frequented by individuals with various motives for entering the market. Although different groupings are possible, we find it helpful to distinguish between participants who are hedgers, speculators, arbitrageurs, and portfolio managers.

The Hedger

The hedger is an individual who uses the futures market to offset the price risks associated with his basic business activities. As already noted, farming provides many opportunities for hedging because of the seasonal nature of production, the long periods of storage required to meet continuing demand in the non-harvest season and the rapid price changes associated with most agricultural products. Recent changes in financial markets have encouraged the introduction of futures contracts in financial instruments and foreign exchange that allow for the possibility of hedging price risks in these markets as well.

The economics of hedging works on the documented fact that the cash and futures prices of a commodity tend to converge by the delivery date. By assuming a position in the futures market that is equal and opposite to his position in the cash market, the hedger establishes a situation where losses in the cash market are offset by gains in the futures market, and vice versa. Thus, the risk of price fluctuations are virtually eliminated. To illustrate how hedging works, we describe two situations that are of interest

Table 11.1   Actively Traded Financial Instrument Futures Contracts

Exchange	Financial Instrument	Trading Months	Contract Size	Price Quoted in
International Monetary Market (IMM)	British pound	June/Sept/Dec/March 85	25,000	$ per pound
IMM	Canadian dollar	June/Sept/Dec/March 85 June	$100,000	$ per Can. $
IMM	Japanese yen	June/Sept/Dec/March 85	12.5 million yen	$ per yen (.00)
IMM	Swiss franc	June/Sept/Dec/March 85 June	125,000 francs	$ per franc
IMM	W. German mark	June/Sept/Dec/March 85	125,000 marks	$ per mark
IMM	Eurodollar	June/Sept/Dec/March 85 June/Sept	$1 million	Pts. of 100%
London International Financial Futures Exchanges (LIFFE)	Eurodollar	June/Sept/Dec/March 85 June	$1 million	Pts. of 100%
LIFFE	Sterling deposit	June/Sept/Dec/March 85 June	250,000 pounds	Pts. of 100%
Chicago Board of Trade (CBT)	GNMA 8%	June/Sept/Dec/March 85 June/Sept/Dec/March 86 June	$100,000 principal	Pts. 32nd of 100%
CBT	Treasury bonds	June/Sept/Dec/March 85 June/Sept/Dec/March 86 June/Sept/Dec	$100,000	Pts. 32nd of 100%
CBT	Treasury notes	June/Sept/Dec/March 85	$100,000	Pts. 32nd of 100%
IMM	Treasury bills	June/Sept/Dec/March 85 June/Sept/Dec/March 86	$1 million	Pts. of 100%
IMM	Bank CD's	June/Sept/Dec/March 85 June/Sept	$1 million	Pts. of 100%
Chicago Mercantile Exchange (CME)	S&P 500 Index	June/Sept/Dec/March 85 June/Sept	500 times Index	
CME	S&P 100 Index	May/June/July/Sept	200 times Index	
New York Futures Exchange	NYSE Composite	June/Sept/Dec/March 85 June/Sept	500 times Index	
Kansas City Board of Trade	Value Line Index	June/Sept/Dec.	500 times Index	

to the financial manager. The first is called locking-in a lending rate and the second is called locking-in a borrowing rate.

Locking-in a Lending Rate Suppose that a financial manager has prepared a cash forecast and is quite confident that he will have approximately $3 million to invest in two months. Interest rates on T-bills are 12.5%, which seems high at the moment. The financial manager is afraid that if he waits until June, when the money becomes available, he may face a considerable reduction in the interest that can be earned on the money. To hedge against the possibility of an interest rate decline, he decides to purchase three June Treasury Bill contracts (each contract is for $1 million in T-bills) on the International Monetary Market at the Chicago Mercantile Exchange.

The results of the financial manager's hedging strategy are reported in Table 11.2. Two outcomes are considered, one where the yield on T-bills declines to 11% and one where the yield on T-bills increases to 13%. In Outcome 1 the financial manager gains 120 basis points on his futures contract because he bought it at a lower price ($100-12.20 = $87.80) than he sold it for on June 1. To calculate his net yield on the 91-day bill purchased in the cash market in June, we have to add the 120 basis point gain in the futures market to the nominal yield on the cash bill. The result is a net yield of 12.20, which is equal to the yield in the futures market on April 1.

In Outcome 2 the financial manager loses 80 basis points on his futures contract because he makes a reversing sale at a lower price ($100-13 = $87) than the price at which he purchased the futures on April 1 ($100-12.20 = $87.80). To calculate his net yield, we must subtract this loss of 80 basis points from the 13% nominal yield he receives on the new cash bill he purchases on June 1. Again the net yield is 12.20.

Table 11.2 Results of Hedging Strategy

Outcome 1

Date	Cash	Futures
April 1	T-bills in cash market currently selling at 12.50	Buys three June bill contracts at 12.20
June 1	Buys 91-day bill trading at 11.00	Sells three June bill contracts at 11.00
Results		Gain: 120 basis points
	Net yield on 91-day bill = 11.00 + 1.20 = 12.20	

Outcome 2

Date	Cash	Futures
April 1	T-bills in cash market currently selling at 12.50	Buys three June bill contracts at 12.20
June 1	Buys 91-day bill trading at 13.00	Sells three June bill contracts at 13.00
Results		Loss: 80 basis points
	Net yield on 91-day bill = 13.00 - 0.80 = 12.20	

Table 11.3   Results of Hedging Strategy

Outcome 1

Date	Cash	Futures
April 1	Commercial paper in cash market currently selling at 13.00	Sells three June commercial paper contracts at 13.30
June 1	Sells 90-day commercial paper at 14.50	Buys three June commercial paper contracts at 14.50

Results

Gain: 120 basis points

Net yield paid on 90-day commercial paper = 14.50 − 1.20 = 13.30

Outcome 2

Date	Cash	Futures
April 1	Commercial paper in cash market currently selling at 13.00	Sells three June commercial paper contracts at 13.30
June 1	Sells 90-day commercial paper at 12.00	Buys three June commercial papers at 12.00

Results

Loss: 130 basis points

Net yield paid on 90-day commercial paper = 12.00 + 1.30 = 13.30

Locking-in a Borrowing Rate   Suppose another financial manager prepares a cash forecast and discovers that she will very likely have to borrow $3 million for 90 days in the commercial paper market in June. However, she is afraid that interest rates will increase over the next two months and she would like to lock-in the rate that she pays on the future borrowing now. She does this by selling a June futures contract in 90-day commercial paper.

The results of the financial manager's hedging strategy are shown in Table 11.3. If interest rates rise as she feared, the financial manager gains 120 basis points on her futures transactions because she executes a reversing purchase of commercial paper at a lower price ($100–14.50 = $85.50) than she received on her previous sale ($100−13.30 = $87.70). Subtracting the 120 basis point gain on the futures transaction from the 14.50% yield paid in the cash market on June 1, results in a net yield paid of 13.30%.

On the other hand, if yields unexpectedly decline to 12%, the financial manager suffers a loss of 130 basis points on her futures contract. Adding this loss to the 12% paid in the cash market on June 1 again results in a net yield of 13.30%.

The Speculator

The speculator is an individual who takes a position in the futures market that is not offset by an opposite position in a basic line of business. Thus, the speculator seeks to profit from movements in futures prices; he buys the futures contract when he thinks the futures price will rise and he sells the futures contract when he thinks the price will fall.

Speculators serve at least three useful functions in the futures market. First, they assume the risk of price fluctuations that hedgers seek to avoid. This leads to a more efficient allocation of economic resources because it allows the hedger to concentrate on what he does best—his basic business operation—while letting those who are most capable of judging the future course of prices assume price fluctuation risk.

Second, speculators help to provide information to those operating in the cash market. As we have already noted, speculators will be net purchasers of futures contracts at times when they believe the futures price will rise. However, because the futures price and the cash price must be equal at the delivery date, a belief that the futures price will rise is tantamount to a belief that the cash price will rise. Thus, the actions of speculators in futures markets provide a consensus forecast of where cash prices are headed. Businessmen operating in the cash market can use this forecast to make better production decisions in that market.

Third, speculators may help to stabilize prices in the cash market. To see how this occurs, consider how a speculator could respond to a belief that prices will be higher at some future date. It has already been noted that the speculator might respond by purchasing a futures contract in the same commodity. But he also could purchase the commodity in the spot market and store it until the price rises. This action increases the demand for the commodity at the earlier date and increases the supply of the commodity at the later date. The result is an increase in the earlier price, a decrease in the later price and a more stable price pattern overall. It should be noted that this third point depends on the assumption that the speculator's forecast is correct. If speculators are on average poor forecasters of future prices, then their actions may be de-stabilizing.

The Arbitrageur

An arbitrageur is an individual who seeks to profit from a situation where the same commodity is trading at different prices in different markets. When this situation occurs, the arbitrageur buys in the market where price is low and sells in the market where price is high, thus forcing the two prices back into line with one another. In financial markets, the arbitrageur is especially interested in the relationship between interest rates in the futures markets and the forward rates of interest implied by the yield curve. We will elaborate on the relationship between futures and forward interest rates in the next chapter. For now, we merely note that the arbitrageur serves a useful economic function because he helps to assure that market prices provide accurate signals for resource allocation decisions.

The Portfolio Manager

There is evidence that a fourth type of participant has recently entered the futures market. This is the investor who recognizes that futures contracts offer an excellent opportunity for portfolio diversification. A recent study[1] has shown that returns on

[1]See Zvi Bodie and Victor Rosansky, "Risk and Return in Commodity Futures," *Financial Analysts Journal*, May/June 1980, pp. 27–40.

investments in futures contracts and returns on stock investments frequently are negatively correlated (i.e., they move in opposite directions). Negative correlation between two securities in a portfolio tends to reduce variation in the total portfolio return. Thus, investments in futures are a useful component of a widely diversified portfolio.

SUMMARY

This chapter introduces the basic features of futures contracts and the markets in which they are traded. Futures contracts differ from cash contracts in that they provide for a future exchange of goods for money. Futures contracts differ also from forward contracts in that they are traded on a formal exchange. The chapter describes the purposes and functions common to futures market, then discusses the different aims of various types of participants in futures markets. Finally, the chapter gives two examples of ways in which a financial manager might utilize the financial instrument futures market to lock-in current rates on anticipated future transactions.

DISCUSSION QUESTIONS

1. Why have interest rates and foreign exchange rates been so volatile in recent years?
2. How has the increased volatility in interest rates and foreign exchange rates affected the growth of futures market in financial instruments?
3. What is the difference between the cash contract and the forward contract?
4. How do futures contracts differ from forward contracts?
5. Why are so many futures contracts canceled before the delivery date?
6. What are the requirements for membership in a futures exchange?
7. Describe the major objectives of most futures exchanges.
8. Describe the marketplace in which futures trading occurs.
9. What rules govern trading in futures contracts?
10. What happens if the seller of a futures contract is unable to deliver a commodity of the same quality as that called for in the contract?
11. On what day in the delivery month does delivery occur?
12. Describe the role of the clearing house in futures trading.
13. How does "margin" on futures contracts differ from "margin" on stocks?
14. Describe the services provided by a Futures Commission Merchant.
15. Describe how financial instrument futures contracts differ from commodity futures contracts.
16. How do hedgers differ from speculators?
17. Why does the presence of speculators in futures markets not lead to instability of commodity prices?
18. Explain what is meant by the following statement: "Futures contracts offer an excellent opportunity for portfolio diversification." What do you suspect would happen to the overall portfolio return if futures were added?
19. Why is it a good assumption that on the delivery date of a futures contract, the cash price, and the futures price are equal?

20. What action can the financial manager take to lock-in a lending rate? A borrowing rate?

PROBLEMS

1. The financial manager at Alston Foods expects to have a temporary cash surplus of $5 million for three months beginning two months from now (January 15). Interest rates on T-bills are currently 9.70%, but the financial manager is expecting them to drop sharply over the next several months. To hedge against the possibility of an interest rate decline, the financial manager has decided to purchase five March 91-day T-bill contracts on the International Monetary Market at the Chicago Mercantile Exchange. The current yield on the March 91-day T-bill futures contract is 9.30%. Calculate the net yield on the financial manager's investment if the interest rate on the 91-day T-bills falls to 7.50% by March 15. What happens if it increases to 10.00%?

2. The financial manager at Webb Soft Drinks, Inc. expects to have a temporary cash deficit of $10 million for three months beginning six weeks from now (June 1). She would like to finance this deficit by floating 90-day commercial paper, but she is worried that interest rates may increase significantly by the time she needs the money.

(a) Can you suggest how the financial manager can hedge against the risk of an interest rate increase?

(b) Suppose that interest rates on the September 90-day commercial paper futures contract are 9.60% at the present time. What is the result of the financial manager's hedge if interest rates on 90-day commercial paper in the cash market are 10.20% on July 15, while interest rates on the September 90-day commercial paper contract in the futures market are 9.90% at that time? You may assume, if you want, that the current interest rate on 90-day commercial paper is 9.30%.

ADDITIONAL READINGS

1. Gold, Gerald, *Modern Commodity Futures Trading,* Commodity Research Bureau, Inc., New York, 1972.

2. Gould, Bruce E., *Dow Jones Guide to Commodities Trading,* Dow Jones-Irwin, Homewood, Ill. 1973.

3. Hieronymous, Thomas A., *Economics of Futures Trading for Commercial and Personal Profit,* Commodity Research Bureau, Inc., New York, 1971.

4. Kroll, Stanley and Irwin Shishko, *The Commodity Futures Market Guide,* Harper & Row, New York, 1973.

5. Loosigian, Allan M., *Interest Rate Futures,* Dow Jones-Irwin, Homewood, Ill. 1980.

6. Powers, Mark J. and David J. Vogel, *Inside the Financial Futures Markets,* John Wiley & Sons, New York, 1981.

CHAPTER 12

Economics of Hedging

The financial manager is interested in futures markets primarily because they allow her an opportunity to reduce the risks associated with rapid fluctuations in interest rates, commodity prices, and foreign exchange rates. This chapter discusses the economic principles underlying the use of futures markets as a tool for hedging business and financial risks. It contains several examples of hedging situations that confront the typical financial manager.

BASIC DEFINITIONS

Economists have developed a special vocabulary to help them distinguish between the many possible hedging strategies of interest to managers. An acquaintance with this vocabulary is essential to an understanding of the economic principles presented later.

Cash, Forward, and Futures Markets

As noted in Chapter 11, the cash or spot market for a commodity is the market for current delivery. It is the market all of us experience when we go to the supermarket for groceries. Without notifying the grocer in advance, we walk in, pick out some groceries, pay cash, and take the groceries home. In contrast, the forward market is the market where we agree now to exchange a commodity for a fixed amount of cash at a later date. This is the market we experience when we agree with a home builder to take delivery on a new house for a fixed price at a later date. Finally, the futures market is the market for standardized forward contracts that are approved by a futures Exchange.

Basis

The difference between the cash price and the futures price of a commodity at a point in time is termed the *basis*. The key to all hedging principles is that the cash price and futures price of a commodity tend to converge on the delivery date of the futures contract; that is, the basis tends to become zero on that date. Of course, prior to the delivery date, the cash price can be either above or below the futures price. A situation where the cash price is above the futures price is called a "normal backwardation"; one where the cash price is below the futures price is called a "contango".

To see why the basis tends to be zero on the delivery date, imagine what would happen if it were not. If the futures price is less than the cash price on that date, individuals who have previously bought the futures contract can simply take delivery and sell the commodity in the cash market for a nice profit. If the futures price exceeds the cash price, it is possible to make a profit by purchasing the commodity in the cash market and selling the futures at a higher price. The possibility of arbitrage operations of this kind forces the futures price to equality with the cash price at delivery.[1]

Perfect and Imperfect Hedges

A perfect hedge is one where the individual is able to eliminate all risk of price fluctuations. As will be shown later, the individual is able to eliminate price fluctuation risks because she knows that the cash and futures price of a commodity converge on the delivery date. By taking opposite positions in the cash and futures markets, and then reversing both positions on the delivery date (i.e., at the time the basis is zero), the individual achieves a gain in one market that offsets any losses in the other.

In practice, there are several reasons why a hedging strategy is frequently imperfect. First, the individual may have sound business reasons for reversing her cash and futures positions at a point in time before the delivery date on the futures contract. For example, a grain elevator operator may plan to sell corn from his inventory in June. Since there is no June corn contract on the Chicago Board of Trade, she may hedge the price on the anticipated future sale of corn by selling a July corn futures contract. However, when she sells her corn in the cash market in June and simultaneously reverses her futures position (by buying a contract in July corn), she cannot be assured that the basis will be close to zero. She is thus speculating on the value of the basis in June, and his hedge is imperfect.

Second, the individual may find that there are no futures contracts on the commodity she wishes to hedge in the cash market. Consider the financial manager whose firm plans to sell a large mortgage bond through an investment banker in three months. The financial manager is unable to find a perfect hedge against a rise in interest rates because there are no futures contracts on her firm's mortgage bonds. However, there is a futures contract on Treasury bonds, and the rates on Treasury bonds tend to be highly correlated with mortgage bond rates. Thus, she is not able to find a perfect hedge, but an imperfect hedge does exist.

---

[1]As noted later, the existence of transactions costs, transportation costs, and so on, may prevent the relationship from being an exact equality. However, arbitrage does cause the futures price to be very close to the cash price at delivery.

Third, the commodity the individual holds in the cash market may be stored at a location that is distant from the delivery point called for in the futures contract. The existence of transportation costs may invalidate the arbitrage opportunities necessary for the convergence of the cash and futures prices on the delivery date. Again, the futures market provides only an imperfect hedging opportunity.

Pure and Anticipatory Hedges

A *pure* hedge is one where the individual or firm assumes a position in the futures market equal and opposite to his current position in the cash market. Again, consider the grain elevator operator who has an inventory of grain. To protect himself from the risk of a price decline, the operator can sell one or more contracts in the futures market with delivery dates that are close to the time he expects to sell his grain in the cash market. If the price of grain declines in the cash market, it will decline in the futures market as well and the grain elevator operator will be able to make a reversing purchase in the futures market at a lower price than he had previously sold. Thus, his gain in the futures market offsets his opportunity loss in the cash market.

An *anticipatory* hedge is defined as taking a position in the futures market that is a temporary substitute for an anticipated position in the cash market at a later date. This type of hedge is appropriate for the financial manager who knows that she will have to purchase Deutsche Marks (DM) in 60 days to pay for machinery her firm has just imported from West Germany. To hedge against the risk of an increase in the price of Deutsche Marks, she buys a DM futures contract for delivery in about two months. Since the cash and futures DM price generally move in the same direction, any opportunity loss in the cash market caused by a price increase will be offset by a gain in the futures market.

Partial and Cross Hedges

A *partial* hedge and a *cross* hedge are two other types of hedging strategies that have important applications. A partial hedge is most useful where the manager has a definite opinion about the direction of price movements, but is not willing to bear the entire risk of being wrong. Thus, she takes a position in the futures market that is smaller than her position in the cash market. A cross hedge is useful when there is no futures contract in the commodity the manager is trading in the cash market. To hedge the risks of price fluctuations in the cash market, the manager must find a commodity in the futures market whose price movements are similar to (i.e., highly correlated with) those of the commodity she trades in the cash market. When the manager takes a futures position in a commodity that is not her cash market commodity, she is engaging in a cross hedge.

Long Hedges and Short Hedges

A situation where the hedging individual or firm buys a futures contract is called a long hedge; one where she sells a futures contract is called a short hedge. The long hedge is appropriate for an individual who has a future need to buy the commodity in the cash market; the short hedge is appropriate for an individual who has a future need to sell the commodity in the cash market.

HEDGING ECONOMICS

The economics of hedging is best explained in terms of polar cases. For purposes of our discussion, we assume that (1) there exists a futures contract calling for delivery of the same commodity that the individual holds, or plans to hold, in the cash market, (2) the delivery date on the futures contract is identical to the future date on which the individual needs to transact business in the cash market, and (3) there are no transportation or transactions costs that nullify the equality of cash and futures prices on the delivery date.

This section begins with an explanation of the economics of a pure hedge. This is the hedge strategy that applies to an individual who is already either long or short in the cash market. The financial manager who has just purchased Canadian dollars so that he can invest in a Canadian T-bill maturing in 90 days is a likely candidate for a pure hedge strategy.

Economics of Pure Hedges

The economics of a pure hedge may be illustrated in terms of the diagrams in Figures 12.1 and 12.2. The results of a pure hedge depend on the relationship of the cash to the futures price on the initiation date (the date on which the contract is purchased) and the direction in which the cash price moves. Assume first that the futures price is originally above the cash price and that the individual engages in a pure short hedge; that is, he sells a futures contract to cover his current long position in the cash market.

If the cash price falls (as shown in Figure 12.1a), the pure short hedger makes a profit on his transactions in the futures market, because the price on his reversing futures purchase is less than the price on his initial sale of the futures contract. At the same time, the pure short hedger suffers a loss in the cash market, because he must now sell the commodity at a price that is less than the cash price at which he purchased it on the initiation date. If the cash price rises (as shown in Figure 12.1c), the pure short hedger takes a loss on his futures transactions, because the price on his reversing futures purchase is now greater than the price at which he sold the futures contract on the initiation date. However, he achieves an offsetting gain in the cash market. In both cases, the pure short hedger has been able to eliminate all risk of price fluctuations. In fact, he has been able to lock in a profit of $F-C$, the value of the basis on the initiation

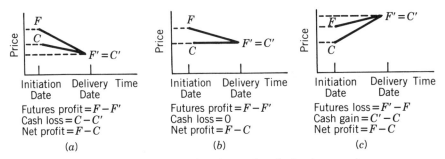

Figure 12.1 Economics of pure short hedge (contango).

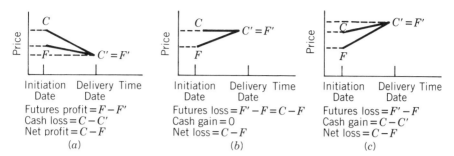

Figure 12.2   Economics of pure short hedge (normal backwardation).

date. This is because his gain in each case exceeds his offsetting loss by the value of the basis on that date.

Assume next that the futures price is less than the cash price on the initiation date, a normal backwardation. If the cash price falls (as shown in Figure 12.2a), the pure short hedger again suffers a loss in the cash market and achieves an offsetting gain in the futures market. However, since the futures gain is now less than the cash loss, the pure short hedger has a net loss of $C-F$, the value of the basis on the initiation date. On the other hand, if the cash price rises (as shown in Figure 12.2c), the pure short hedger suffers a loss in the futures market and achieves an offsetting gain in the cash market. Again, she achieves a net loss of $C-F$. Thus, in a normal backwardation market, the pure short hedger eliminates the risk of price fluctuations, but pays for this reduction by sustaining a loss on his hedging operation.

Futures markets provide hedging opportunities for those who employ a pure long hedge as well. The financial manager who desires to borrow money for 90 days from a foreign subsidiary is an example of a pure long hedger. She sells foreign exchange in the cash market and simultaneously buys foreign exchange in the futures markets for delivery in 90 days. By reexamining Figures 12.1 and 12.2, the reader should be convinced that the pure long hedger can lock in a profit in a market characterized by a normal backwardation, whether the price goes up or down. In a contango market situation, the pure long hedger locks in a loss on his hedging operation. This loss is the price the financial manager must pay for risk reduction.

Table 12.1 summarizes the various situations we have discussed in the preceding paragraphs. It shows the results of pure long and pure short hedges in six circumstances, corresponding to whether the futures price is above or below the cash price on the initiation date and whether the cash price goes up, down, or stays the same.

Examples of Pure Hedges

The economic principles of the pure hedge may be illustrated with the help of several examples. These examples also provide some appreciation for the economic conditions for which a hedge strategy may be useful.

Pure Hedge Example 1   A financial manager has excess cash of $5 million to invest for the next 91 days. Since the discount yield on 182-day T-bills is currently 9.40%, while the discount yield on 91-day T-bills is 9.00%, he is tempted to invest in the 182-

Table 12.1   Summary of Economics of Pure Hedging

Relation of Cash and Futures Prices	Direction of Price Change in Cash Market	Action	Result
Contango	Down	Sell futures, buy cash	Net gain = $F - C$
Contango	No change	Sell futures, buy cash	Net gain = $F - C$
Contango	Up	Sell futures, buy cash	Net gain = $F - C$
Normal backwardation	Down	Sell futures, buy cash	Net loss = $C - F$
Normal backwardation	No change	Sell futures, buy cash	Net loss = $C - F$
Normal backwardation	Up	Sell futures, buy cash	Net loss = $C - F$
Contango	Down	Buy futures, sell cash	Net loss = $F - C$
Contango	No change	Buy futures, sell cash	Net loss = $F - C$
Contango	Up	Buy futures, sell cash	Net loss = $F - C$
Normal backwardation	Down	Buy futures, sell cash	Net gain = $C - F$
Normal backwardation	No change	Buy futures, sell cash	Net gain = $C - F$
Normal backwardation	Up	Buy futures, sell cash	Net gain = $C - F$

day T-bill. Since the financial manager does not want to accept the risk of interest rate fluctuations, he sells five 91-day T-bill futures contracts for delivery in 91-days at the same time that he buys the 182-day T-bills in the cash market. The 91-day T-bill futures contract is currently yielding 9.60%.

As shown in Table 12.2, there are two possible outcomes to the financial manager's hedging strategy. If the interest rate on the 91-day T-bill rises to 10.00%, the financial

Table 12.2   Results of Hedging Strategy

Outcome 1

Date	Cash	Futures
Aug. 3	Buys $5 million of 182-day T-bills in cash market at 9.40% ($P = 95.30$)	Sells 5 November 91-day T-bill contracts at 9.60% ($P = 97.60$)
Nov. 1	Sells $5 million of 182-day T-bills in cash market at 10% ($P = 97.50$)	Buys 5 November 91-day T-bill contracts at 10% ($P = 97.50$)

Bond equivalent yield: $\dfrac{97.50 + .10 - 95.30}{95.30} = 9.65\%$

Outcome 2

Date	Cash	Futures
Aug. 3	Buys $5 million of 182-day T-bills in cash market at 9.40% ($P = 95.30$)	Sells 5 November 91-day T-bill contracts at 9.60% ($P = 97.60$)
Nov. 1	Sells $5 million of 182-day T-bills in cash market at 9.00% ($P = 97.75$)	Buys 5 November 91-day T-bill contracts at 9.00% ($P = 97.75$)
	Gain = $2.45	Loss = $.15

Bond equivalent yield: $\dfrac{97.75 - .15 - 95.30}{95.30} = 9.65\%$

manager earns only 9.23% on his investment in the 182-day T-bill, but he also makes a capital gain on his T-bill contract. His total yield measured on a bond-equivalent basis is 9.65%.

If the interest rate on the 91-day T-bill falls instead to 9.00%, the financial manager earns 10.28% on his investment in the 182-day T-bill, but he also incurs a capital loss on his T-bill futures contract. His total yield measured on a bond-equivalent basis is once again 9.65%.

Pure Hedge Example 2   The firm's financial manager has approximately $1 million to invest for three months starting March 1. She would like to invest in 91-day Canadian Treasury bills, which are currently yielding 14.50%. However, she is afraid that a fall in the value of the Canadian dollar might reduce her interest earnings. To reduce this risk, she can sell ten June Canadian Dollar (CD) contracts. June Canadian dollars are currently selling at $.8234, while Canadian dollars in the cash market are selling at $.8256. The results of the financial manager's transaction are shown in Table 12.3:

Table 12.3   Results of Hedging Strategy

Date	Cash	Futures	Basis
March 1	Buy 965,018 Canadian dollars at $.8256	Sell ten June Can$ contracts at $.8234	22
June 1	Sell 965,018 Canadian dollars at $.8206	Buy ten June Can$ contracts at $.8201	5
Results	Loss: $.0050 × 965,018 = $4,825	Gain: $.0033 × 965,018 = $3,185	
		Net loss of $1,640	

Since this is a sell hedge and the futures price is initially below the cash price, the financial manager loses $1640 on his hedging operation. This loss is considerably less than the loss she could have suffered ($4825) without the hedge; however, and it is known with a fair amount of certainty at the time the hedge is initiated. Because the financial manager suffers a loss on her foreign exchange transactions, her interest in U.S. dollars is somewhat less than the yield on the Canadian T-bill. The financial manager should recognize this important fact when she makes her decision to invest.

Economics of An Anticipatory Hedge

An anticipatory hedge is the hedge strategy most suited to an individual who anticipates being either long or short in the cash market at a later date. The financial manager who expects to sell a large amount of commercial paper in two months is a prime candidate for an anticipatory hedge strategy. He can use the futures market as a temporary substitute for a later position in the cash market. At the time he takes his position in the cash market, the manager will close out his position in the futures market at a price that is equal, or nearly equal, to the then current cash price. Since the

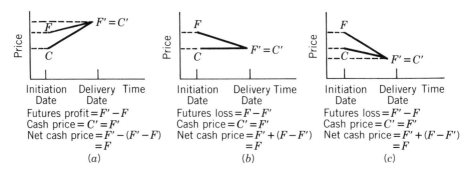

Figure 12.3   Economics of anticipatory long hedge (contango).

futures transaction on the delivery date is opposite to the cash transaction on that date, and the two prices are equal, the value of the manager's position does not change on that date. He is left with a position in the cash market at a price equal to the price at which he originally entered the futures market.

The economic principles underlying the anticipatory hedge may be illustrated with the help of Figures 12.3a–12.3c and 12.4a–12.4c. Figures 12.3a–12.3c correspond to a situation where the futures price is above the cash price on the initiation date and Figure 12.4a–12.4c correspond to a situation where the future price is below the cash price on that date.

Consider a manager who knows that he will have to purchase a commodity in three months, but wants to fix the price on that transaction now. For the sake of illustration, assume also that the futures price is initially above the cash price and that the cash price rises. This corresponds to the situation pictured in Figure 12.3a. If the manager purchases a futures contract on the initiation date and closes it out at the time he enters the cash market, he will achieve a capital gain on his futures position. To obtain the net price at which the manager enters the cash market, we must subtract this capital gain from the actual price at which he enters the cash market. We see from Figure 12.3a that, as long as the futures and cash prices are equal on the date the manager enters the cash market, he will enter the cash market at a net price equal to the futures price on the initiation date.

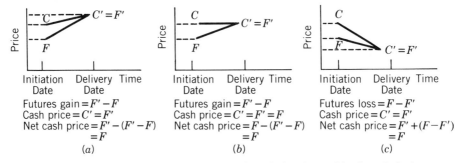

Figure 12.4   Economics of anticipatory long hedge (normal backwardation).

A careful examination of Figures 12.3 and 12.4 reveals that the above principle continues to hold regardless of the relationship between the cash and futures prices on the initiation date and no matter what the direction of the price movement in the cash market. As long as the cash and futures prices are equal on the date when he enters the cash market, the manager will be able to enter the market at a net price equal to the original futures price.

Examples of Anticipatory Hedges

The economic principles of anticipatory hedging are illustrated in the following examples.

Anticipatory Hedge Example 1   A U.S. firm has just received (on February 1) a piece of machinery from a German exporter. Payment of 450,000 Deutsche Marks (DM) is due in 30 days. To avoid the risk of an unfavorable shift in exchange rates, the financial manager of the U.S. firm purchases four March DM contracts selling on the International Monetary Market of the Chicago Mercantile Exchange for $.4268. Table 12.4 displays the results of her transaction.

Table 12.4   Results of Hedging Strategy

Outcome 1

Date	Cash	Futures	Basis
Feb. 1	DM's currently selling at $.4281	Buys 4 IMM June DM contracts at $.4268	13
March 1	Delivery commitment 450,000 DM at $.4395	Sells 4 IMM June DM contracts at $.4394	1

Results

Profit: $.4394 − $.4268 = $.0126

To calculate the net price at which the financial manager obtains the Deutsche Marks, we subtract her gain in the futures market from the March 1 price of Deutsche Marks. We see that she obtains the Deutsche Marks at a net price of .4395 − .0126 = .4269. This is only 1 basis point different from the futures price on the initiation date.

Outcome 2

Date	Cash	Futures	Basis
Feb. 1	DM's currently selling at $.4281	Buys 4 IMM June DM contracts at $.4268	13
March 1	Delivery commitment 450,000 DM at $.4167	Sells 4 IMM June DM contracts at $.4166	1

Results

Loss: $.4268 − $.4166 = $.0102

Net price of Deutsche Marks = $.4167 + $.0102 = $.4269

We see that the financial manager's ability to hedge the risk of price fluctuations is independent of whether the cash price moves up or down. In either case she has been able to obtain the Deutsche Marks at a price that is very close to the futures price on the initiation date.

Anticipatory Hedge Example 2   On June 18 the financial manager is reviewing her cash forecast for the next six months. She is quite confident that starting in the middle of September she will have excess cash of $5 million to invest for three months. Current interest rates are high on U.S. T-bills and she would like to lock-in the interest she will earn on this money. To do this, she purchases five September bill contracts with a yield of 13.50. (This is 100 minus the price of the bill contract.) The results of this transaction are shown in Table 12.5:

Table 12.5   Results of Hedging Strategy

Outcome 1 Date	Cash	Futures	Basis
June 18	T-bills in cash market currently selling at 13.90	Buys five September bill contracts at 13.50	40
Sept. 15	Buys 91-day bill trading at 12.25	Sells five September bill contracts at 12.25	0

Results

Gain: 125 basis points

Net yield on 91-day bill = 12.25 + 1.25 = 13.50

Outcome 2 Date	Cash	Futures	Basis
June 18	T-bills in cash market currently selling at 13.90	Buys five September bill contracts at 13.50	40
Sept. 15	Buys 91-day bill trading at 15.55	Sells five September bill contracts at 15.55	0

Results

Loss: 205 basis points

Net yield on 91-day bill = 15.55 − 2.05 = 13.50

As shown in Table 12.5, the financial manager has been able to lock in the yield of 13.50 because the basis was zero on the date she entered the cash market. In Outcome 2 the T-bill yield increased and the financial manager may have regretted her decision to hedge. However, she should be comforted by the fact that she has also eliminated the risk of a decline in yields.

THE RELATIONSHIP BETWEEN CASH AND FUTURES PRICES

It is apparent from our earlier discussion that the relationship between the futures price of a commodity and its cash price plays an important role in the analysis of futures contracts. A discussion of futures contracts would be incomplete without a brief description of the prevalent theories regarding this relationship.

The simplest theory about the cash-futures price relationship is called the Expectations Hypothesis. It says that the futures price is equal to the expected cash price on the delivery date, or in symbols:

$$F = E(\tilde{C}),$$

where F is the futures price and $E(\tilde{C})$ is the expected cash price on the delivery date. The " ~ " indicates that the cash price is uncertain.

The logic behind the Expectations Hypothesis is that speculators will sell the futures contract whenever the futures price is above the expected cash price at delivery and will buy the futures contract whenever the futures price is below the expected cash price at delivery, since their expected profits are positive. The Expectations Hypothesis implicitly assumes that speculators are "risk neutral"; that is, they do not need to be compensated for bearing the risks of price fluctuations that hedgers want to avoid.

The eminent economist J. M. Keynes put forth an alternative hypothesis in his book *A Treatise On Money*.[2] He argues that speculators will have to be compensated for bearing the risk of price fluctuations. Furthermore, speculators will be long in the futures market on average because the typical hedger will be short. If speculators are to be compensated for bearing risk, and are assumed to be net long in the futures market, then the current futures price must be below the expected cash price on the delivery date—that is, $F<E(\tilde{C})$ for all t, except the delivery date. Keynes named this normal backwardation. Figure 12.5 shows the relationship between the futures price and the cash price under this hypothesis for the case where the expected cash price is constant over time.

Keynes' hypothesis about normal backwardation rests on the assumption that the average hedger has a future commitment to sell the commodity. In many markets, this is not true. If hedgers are net long in the futures market, speculators must assume a net short position on average. Obviously, risk averse speculators will not be willing to assume a net short position unless the futures price is above the expected cash price on the delivery date. This situation is called a contango.

The above theories ignore an important economic factor present in the futures markets for many commodities. Commodities such as corn and wheat that are harvested at periodic intervals must be stored to allow consumption in the non-harvest seasons. Since it is always possible to sell the commodity at harvest time, no one would be willing to provide storage facilities for the commodity unless they felt that the cash price would rise sufficiently to cover both the cost of storage and the interest on the investment. The Supply of Storage Theory says that the futures price must be above

---

[2] J. M. Keynes, *A Treatise of Money*, 2, Macmillan, London, 1930.

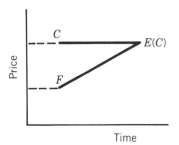

Figure 12.5 Relationship between futures price and cash price: normal backwardation.

the current cash price by enough to cover the cost of storage plus interest on the investment. This theory is thus consistent with a contango market.

FUTURES AND FORWARD RATES ON FINANCIAL INSTRUMENTS

Since futures contracts are nothing more than forward contracts traded on a formal exchange, the futures price of a commodity must bear a close relationship to its forward price in cases where the latter exists. In financial markets, it is easy to create forward contracts simply by buying and selling financial instruments of different maturities. For instance, a T-bill dealer who finances his investment in a 182-day T-bill by selling a 91-day term repurchase agreement is really creating a forward investment in a 91-day T-bill for delivery in 91 days. The implied forward rate on the 91-day T-bill is given by the following equation:

$$(1 + r_{91} \times \frac{1}{4})(1 + r_{91}^f \times \frac{1}{4}) = (1 + r_{181} \times \frac{1}{2}), \tag{12.1}$$

where r_{91} is the interest rate on the 91-day repurchase agreement, r_{91}^f is the implied forward interest rate on the 91-day instrument, and r_{182} is the interest rate on the 182-day T-bill. In financial markets, it is common to refer to the relationship between the yields on instruments of various maturities as the yield curve. We noted in Chapter 10 that the yield curve is likely to be upward sloping when forward rates of interest for a given maturity exceed the current rate on that maturity in the cash market. Likewise, the yield curve is likely to be downward sloping when forward rates are below the current cash rates.

If the above arguments are true, then it follows that the yield in the futures market exceeds the yield on the cash instrument whenever the yield curve is upward sloping, and falls short of the yield in the cash market whenever the yield curve is downward sloping. If we accept the additional assumption that the yield curve is upward sloping when interest rates are expected to rise and downward sloping when interest rates are expected to fall, then it also follows that the yield in the futures market exceeds the yield in the cash market when interest rates are expected to rise and falls short of the yield in the cash market when interest rates are expected to fall.

Example   To illustrate why the forward and futures yields must be equal, consider a situation where the 91-day T-bill is yielding 9%, the 182-day T-bill is yielding 9.56% and the futures contract on a 91-day T-bill deliverable in 91-days is yielding 9.5%.

According to Equation 12.1, the implied forward yield on the 91-day T-bill is given by the following expression:

$$\left(1 + r^f_{91} \times \frac{1}{4}\right) = \frac{\left(1 + r_{182} \times \frac{1}{2}\right)}{\left(1 + r_{91} \times \frac{1}{4}\right)} = \frac{1.0478}{1.0225} = 1.0247.$$

Thus, $r^f_{91} = 9.8\%$, which is higher than the yield on the 91-day T-bill futures contract.

In this situation, the financial manager can earn an arbitrage profit by taking the following steps:

1. Buy the 182-day T-bill in the cash market at a yield of 9.56%.
2. Sell a 91-day term repurchase agreement at 9% (we assume that the repurchase agreement sells at the same yield as the 91-day T-bill).
3. Sell a futures contract on the 91-day T-bill for delivery in 91-days.
4. Deliver the 182-day T-bill in 91-days (which now has 91-days remaining to maturity) to fulfill the futures contract.

Intuitively, the first two of these transactions serve to create a forward investment in a 91-day T-bill that earns 9.8% beginning 91-days from now. The third and fourth transactions create the financing for the forward investment in the 91-day T-bill at an interest cost of 9.5%. Thus, the financial manager is able to earn a sure arbitrage return of 30 basis points for each dollar of face value, without investing a single dollar of his own money. This is certainly a road to great wealth.

Unfortunately, the above arbitrage situation cannot last for long. The actions of investors to buy the 182-day T-bill in the cash market and sell the 91-day T-bill in the futures market will tend to reduce the yield on the 182-day T-bill and raise the yield on T-bill futures to the point where the forward and futures rates are equal.

SUMMARY

This chapter explores the economics of various types of hedging strategies frequently utilized by financial managers to reduce business and financial risks, and presents examples for further clarification. The chapter demonstrates through a graphical analysis how the tendency of the basis to move toward zero allows the hedger to reduce business and financial risks considerably. It also explains why many hedges are imperfect in practice. The chapter then gives examples of situations where the pure, imperfect, anticipatory, partial, and cross hedges can be best utilized. The chapter closes with a discussion of the theories on the existence and form of the basis in futures trading. The key to all hedging strategies is the fact that the basis tends toward zero by the delivery date.

DISCUSSION QUESTIONS

1. What are the differences between the cash, futures, and forward markets?
2. Define "basis."
3. Why does the basis tend to be zero on the delivery date?
4. Why are hedging strategies seldom perfect?
5. What is the difference between a pure and anticipatory hedge?
6. Under what circumstances is a partial hedge useful?
7. Under what circumstances is a cross hedge useful?
8. What is the difference between a long and short hedge?
9. Provide examples of situations where a financial manager would need to employ:
   (a) A pure short hedge.
   (b) A pure long hedge.
   (c) An anticipatory short hedge.
   (d) An anticipatory long hedge.
10. What is the difference between a contango and a normal backwardation?
11. In a contango market, does the pure short hedger earn a profit or a loss?
12. In a normal backwardation market, does the pure short hedger earn a profit or a loss?
13. Discuss the reasoning behind the expectations hypothesis.
14. Why did Keynes believe the futures price would normally be below the cash price?
15. What is the effect of storage costs on the relationship between cash and futures prices?
16. How can an individual create a forward contract in T-bills?
17. What does the slope of the yield curve imply about forward rates of interest?
18. What does the slope of the yield curve imply about the yield on financial futures contracts?

PROBLEMS

1. Use diagrams, such as those in Figures 12.1 and 12.2, to explain why a pure long hedger locks in a loss in a contango market and a profit in a normal backwardation market.
2. Use diagrams, such as those in Figures 12.3 and 12.4, to explain the economic results of an anticipatory short hedge.
3. The financial manager of J. Grenfell Associates has excess cash to invest for the next 182 days. The discount yield on 1-year T-bills is currently 10.30%, while the discount yield on a 182-day T-bill futures contract is currently yielding 9.80%. Explain how the financial manager can increase the yield on her investment over the next 182 days, without incurring any risk of interest rate fluctuations.
4. Does the situation described in Problem 3 offer any opportunities for arbitrage profits? If so, explain how the financial manager can achieve these profits.

SECTION V

RECEIVABLES MANAGEMENT

CHAPTER 13

Managing Receivables

Accounts receivable arise when the firm grants credit to selected individual and business customers.[1] The problem of managing accounts receivable then is essentially the same as the problem of managing the firm's credit policies. In particular, it involves three kinds of decisions: choosing the appropriate level of the firm's investment in accounts receivable, selecting credit and non-credit customers, and monitoring credit performance.

CHOOSING HOW MUCH TO INVEST IN RECEIVABLES

The average amount of accounts receivable shown on the firm's books is the product of its average credit sales per day and its average collection period. If the firm has annual credit sales of $365,000 and the average collection period is 60 days, then its accounts receivable will average $60,000.

The volume of average credit sales per day and the average collection period depend on both the level of economic activity and the firm's credit terms. A discussion of how the level of economic activity affects the volume of the firm's credit sales and its average collection period is beyond the scope of this chapter. The following subsection demonstrates how the firm's credit sales and its average collection period are affected by the firm's credit terms.

---

[1]Parts of this chapter are taken from James H. Vander Weide, "Financial Management in the Short Run," in Dennis E. Logue, ed., *The Handbook of Modern Finance,* Warren, Gorham & Lamont, New York, 1984.

Credit Terms

Credit terms are the terms of the agreement whereby the firm extends credit to individual or business customers. It involves an agreement about the credit period, the form of the credit arrangement, the discount, and the discount period.

The credit period is the total time for which credit is extended. In practice, this is frequently measured by the length of time between the date on the invoice and the date on which payment is due. Although the length of the credit period depends on many factors—including competitive conditions in the industry, the costs of maintaining inventories, the cost of capital, and the economic conditions of the customer—it is common practice in many industries for the credit period to be either 30 or 60 days. In some industries, such as clothing, however, the common practice is to use what is called seasonal dating. This allows the customer to accept goods from wholesale, and pay for them only after they have been sold at retail.

The form of the credit agreement is usually a matter of industry practice, but it also depends on the credit standing of the customer. The most common practice is to grant credit "on open book," meaning that the seller will invoice the buyer and record the amount on his accounts receivable ledger. However, in international business and some domestic industries, a more formal credit agreement, known as a trade acceptance is common. The trade acceptance is actually a time draft on the buyer's bank account that is frequently originated by a letter of credit (from the buyer's bank) guaranteeing the amount. When the buyer's bank accepts this draft, it becomes known as a banker's acceptance, which then may be traded in the money market until it becomes due. Finally, for customers of unknown or poor credit risk, the seller may only extend credit against a promissory note.

To encourage customers to pay promptly, firm's may offer a discount if payment is made within a certain prescribed period, known as the discount period. For instance, the seller might state that the buyer will get a 2% discount if payment is made within 10 days of the receipt of invoice, otherwise, the full amount is due in 30 days. These terms are written in shorthand as: 2/10, net 30.

Evaluating Changes in Credit Terms

The firm's investment in accounts receivable may be evaluated using standard capital budgeting techniques. When using these techniques, the manager must identify both the relevant cash flows and the cost of capital. We shall explore how to evaluate the firm's investment in accounts receivable through several examples.

Example 1. Suppose that a firm, Amco, Inc., sells 110,000 widgets per year at $70 per unit. Amco's variable cost is $60 per unit, and all of its sales are on credit, with terms of net 30 days. However, the average collection period is 40 days, because some customers are slow in paying. Under these assumptions, the average amount of receivables on Amco's books is $7,700,000 \times 40/365 = \$843,836$.

Now suppose that Amco is considering extending credit to customers with a slightly lower credit standing, a decision that it believes will produce an increase in sales of

10,000 units and an average collection period of 50 days. (For convenience, it is assumed that there will be no bad debts.) Since Amco's plants are producing below capacity, there will be no increase in fixed costs associated with the increase in sales. Under the new policy, the average amount of receivables carried on Amco's books is $8,400,000 \times 50/365 = \$1,150,685$.

Before we analyze whether or not Amco should extend credit to these additional customers, we need to make a distinction between the average amount of receivables on the firm's books and its average investment in receivables. As noted above, the average amount of receivables is the product of its average credit sales per day and its average collection period. However, the firm's investment in accounts receivable is the product of its average variable costs per day and its average collection period. This is because variable costs are the best measure of the dollars tied up in receivables. Thus, Amco's investment in accounts receivable will increase under its new policy by $(\$1,150,685 \times 6/7) - (\$843,836 \times 6/7) = \$263,013$.

An analysis of additional profits from Amco's proposed new policy are shown in Table 13.1. Since Amco expects to increase its profits by $34,247, it should clearly adopt the proposed new policy.

Example 2.   Suppose that Amco, Inc. is also considering offering a discount of 2% for payment within 10 days. Amco believes that 60% of its customers will take advantage of the discount, and that the average collection period for the non-discount customers will be 50 days.

Recall that Amco's investment in accounts receivable is less than the amount of accounts receivable shown on its books because of the difference between its selling price and its variable costs. Under its original policy, we showed that Amco's investment in accounts receivable is given by $\$7,700,000 \times (40/365) \times (6/7) = \$723,288$. If Amco adopts the discount policy, its investment in accounts receivable will be given by

$$.6 \times .98 \times \$7,700,000 \times (6/7) \times (10/365)$$
$$+ .4 \times \$7,700,000 \times (6/7) \times (50/365)$$
$$= \$467,967.$$

Thus, its investment will be reduced by $255,321.

An analysis of the profits from the introduction of a discount is shown in Table

Table 13.1   Profit Analysis of Relaxing Credit Standards

Additional sales	$700,000
Profitability of additional sales	$100,000
Additional investment in receivables	$263,013
Opportunity cost of additional investment at 25%	$ 65,753
Net profits	$ 34,247

Table 13.2   Profit Analysis of Discount Policy

Opportunity savings from reduced investment:
  $0.25 \times \$255,321 = \$68,830$
Cost of discount:
  $.02 \times .6 \times \$7,700,000 = \$92,400$
Net savings $= -\$23,570$

13.2.[2] Since the cost of the discount is expected to exceed the opportunity savings from the reduced investment in accounts receivable, Amco is ill advised to adopt the discount policy.

SELECTING INDIVIDUAL CUSTOMERS

Traditionally, credit granting decisions to individual customers have been based on the five C's of credit: character, capacity, collateral, capital, and conditions. Information relating to the five C's was generally obtained from personal interviews and a reasonably exhaustive analysis of the customer's financial condition. In this section, we define the five C's of credit, and then discuss the weaknesses of this approach to credit granting decisions. Two approaches that address these weaknesses are described in some depth.

The Five C's of Credit

The first, and most important, of the five C's, character, is related to personal characteristics such as honesty and integrity. It is meant to measure the individual's intent, or willingness, to pay. Information on this characteristic is obtained from personal interviews and credit references.

Capacity is a measure of the individual's ability to pay. An assessment of capacity is based on an analysis of the individual's income in relation to expenses. For corporate customers who can use the accrual method of accounting, one would also want to investigate how income and expenses are translated into cash flows.

The third C of credit, collateral, has to do with assets that the individual might be able to pledge against the extension of credit. This is an extremely important characteristic in bank loans, but is relatively unimportant in the extension of trade credit. The assignment of assets is not a frequent practice in trade credit because the legal, accounting, and storage costs are simply prohibitive.

Capital is related to the resources that the customer can draw on in the event that income or cash flow proves inadequate. For business customers, capital is generally measured by the amount of equity on their balance sheet, while for individual custom-

---

[2]Amco's discount policy decision could also have been analyzed using the present value approach described in Hill and Reiner [5]. However, the present value approach is more complex and, as Weston and Tuan [15] have shown, it produces the same accept/reject decision as the simpler approach described here.

ers capital is defined by the individual's net worth. Information on equity, or net worth, is also obtained from the customer's financial statements, but here the analyst is more interested in the balance sheet than the income statement.

The final C, conditions, has to do with the economic climate in which the customer operates. If economic conditions are depressed, the individual's current income may be high, but there is little likelihood that this level of income will continue. Thus, economic conditions are used to judge the sustainability of the customer's income.

Weaknesses of the Five C's

The traditional five-C framework ignores two important aspects of the credit granting decision. First, it ignores the significant costs of obtaining all the information required to evaluate character, capacity, collateral, capital, and conditions. As noted above, assessments of character require either a personal interview or credit references, while assessments of capacity and capital require detailed analysis of the customer's financial statements. As shown below, the cost of obtaining this additional information may well exceed its value.

Second, the five-C framework doesn't specify how the information obtained can be translated into a credit granting decision. For instance, it doesn't say what the financial manager should do if the customer is strong in character and capacity, but weak in capital. The credit scoring models discussed below are designed to alleviate this second weakness of the five-C framework.

A Sequential Approach to the Credit Granting Decision[3]

In situations where the cost of obtaining information is large compared to the amount of credit granted and the profit on the sale, the financial manager may want to take a sequential approach to the credit granting decision. In this approach, the financial manager obtains information in stages, beginning with a low cost source and, if necessary, moving to higher cost sources.

The financial manager may begin by checking the company's credit history with this customer. If the credit history is either unequivocally good or unequivocally bad, the financial manager can make the accept or reject decision immediately without obtaining additional information. If the credit history is either mixed or nonexistent, however, the financial manager may find it worthwhile to obtain additional information such as credit references or financial statements. At each stage, the financial manager weighs the benefits of additional information against the costs. Only if the benefits clearly outweigh the costs is the additional information obtained.

Illustration

To illustrate this approach, suppose that the financial manager of Amco, Inc. has just received an order for 10 widgets that depends on his decision to grant, or not grant, credit. To make this decision, the financial manager must calculate both the acceptance

[3]This section is based on the research of Dileep Mehta described in [9] and [10].

cost and the rejection cost, where the acceptance cost is defined as

Acceptance cost = (Probability of bad debt) (Variable costs)
+(Required rate of return)
× (Average collection period) / 365
× (Variable costs) + Average collection costs

and

Rejection Costs = (1−Probability of bad debt) (Profit on the sale).

He will then choose that action with the least expected cost.

The financial manager knows that the profit on each widget is $5, the variable cost is $25, and the firm's required rate of return is 20%. He also knows from his past experience with all credit applicants, that, without any customer specific information, the average collection period is 41 days, the average collection cost is $2.15, and the probability of bad debt loss is .061.

However, the financial manager can improve his estimates of the average collection costs and the probability of bad debt by obtaining information relating to this specific customer. For a cost of $2, he can investigate whether the firm has had previous experience with this applicant and what it has been. For a cost of $18, the financial manager can request financial statements from the customer and analyze them carefully.

If the manager investigates the firm's previous experience with the customer, his estimate of the average collection period, average collection cost, and probability of bad debt loss depends on whether the past experience has been good(G), poor(P), or nonexistent(N). His particular estimates are summarized in Table 13.3.

After investigating the past experience, the financial manager may decide that it is not worth the additional $18 to obtain and analyze the customer's financial statements. To make this decision, he must estimate how much the additional information is worth. It will only have positive value if it causes him to change his decision.

Suppose that the financial manager can classify financial statements as being sound(S) or unsound(U). After analyzing the financial statements, the financial manager's estimates of the average collection period, average collection costs, and probability of bad debt loss are shown in Table 13.4.

Table 13.3 Estimates of Average Collection Period, Average Collection Costs and Probability of Bad Debt After Investigating Past Experience

Classification	Probability of Occurrence	Average Collection Period	Average Collection Costs	Probability of Bad Debt Loss
G	.4	30 days	.84	.031
P	.4	170 days	11.30	.645
N	.2	41 days	2.15	.061

Table 13.4   Estimates of Average Collection Period, Average Collection Costs and Probability of Bad Debt After Analyzing Financial Statements

Good Past Experience

Classification	Conditional Probability of Occurrence	Average Collection Period	Average Collection Costs	Probability of Bad Debt Loss
S	.8	25 days	$ .30	.001
U	.2	50 days	$3.00	.15

Poor Past Experience

Classification	Conditional Probability of Occurrence	Average Collection Period	Average Collection Costs	Probability of Bad Debt Loss
S	.1	75 days	$5.00	.15
U	.9	180 days	$12.00	.7

No Past Experience

Classification	Conditional Probability of Occurrence	Average Collection Period	Average Collection Costs	Probability of Bad Debt Loss
S	.7	28 days	$0.50	.01
U	.3	70 days	$6.00	.18

With the help of this information, we can now break the manager's decision problem into three stages. At Stage 1, the financial manager has no customer specific information. He can make one of three decisions: accept the applicant, reject the applicant, or incur the $2 cost to investigate past experience. If the manager chooses to investigate past experience, he proceeds to Stage 2. At this stage, he again has three alternatives: accept the applicant, reject the applicant, or incur the $18 expense to investigate the customer's financial statements. If the manager chooses to investigate the customer's financial statements, he proceeds to Stage 3, where he only has two alternatives: accept or reject.

A visual depiction of the financial manager's sequential credit granting decision problem is shown in Figure 13.1. The squares in this diagram represent decision alternatives facing the financial manager and the circles represent chance events. The diagram is meant to be read from left to right. The three alternatives at Stage 1 are shown at the far left. If the manager chooses to accept or reject at this stage, there is nothing else to do. If, however, the manager chooses to investigate past experience, he encounters a chance event; namely, whether the past experience is good, poor, or nonexistent. The manager then moves to a Stage 2 decision, shown by the squares in the center of the diagram. If the manager chooses to accept or reject at Stage 2, there is nothing else to do. If, at Stage 2, he chooses to investigate further, however, he encounters another chance event; namely, whether the financial statements are sound

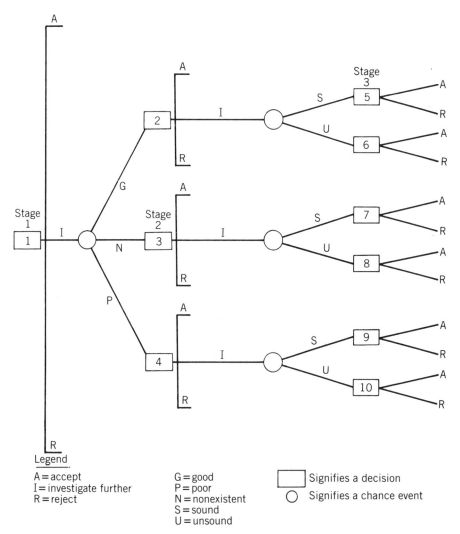

Figure 13.1 Decision tree diagram of credit granting decision.

or unsound. After observing the value of the second chance event, the financial manager must make the final decision to accept or reject.

Although the diagram shown in Figure 13.1 provides a useful overview of the financial manager's decision problem, some additional calculations are required before we can determine what the financial manager's best decision actually is. In particular, we need to calculate the costs associated with each decision at each stage of analysis.

Let us start at Stage 3. We see from Figure 13.1 that there are six different decision situations, labeled 5 through 10, depending on the information obtained in the two previous stages. We need to calculate both the acceptance cost and the rejection cost for all six decision situations. Using our previous formulas for the acceptance and rejection costs and the values shown in Table 13.4, we obtain the values shown at the right of Figure 13.2. We see that it is best to accept the applicant in decision situations 5 and 7, while it is best to reject the applicant in decision situations 6, 8, 9, and 10.

Turning to Stage 2, we need to evaluate the cost of all three alternatives for decision situations 2, 3, and 4, a total of 9 different outcomes. The costs of accepting and rejecting for decision situations 2, 3, and 4 can be calculated in a straightforward manner by substituting the appropriate information from Table 13.4 into the formulas for acceptance cost and rejection cost. However, the cost associated with the decision to investigate further at Stage 2 is more difficult to calculate, because it is only an expected value.

Consider decision situation 2. If we decide to investigate further at this point, we have a .8 probability of assessing the financial statement to be sound and a .2 proba-

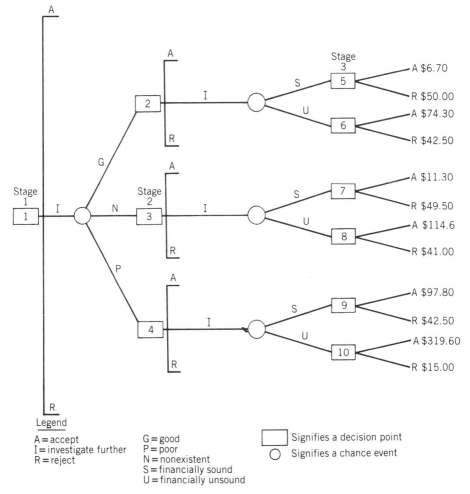

Figure 13.2 Numerical analysis of credit granting decisions at Stage 3.

bility of assessing the statement to be unsound. We have already noted that it is best to accept the applicant if the financial statement is sound and reject the applicant if the financial statement is unsound. Thus, the expected cost of investigating further at decision point 2 is given by

$$
\begin{matrix} \text{Cost of} \\ \text{Investigating Further} \end{matrix} = .8 \times \begin{pmatrix} \text{acceptance cost,} \\ \text{when statement sound} \end{pmatrix} + .2 \times \begin{pmatrix} \text{rejection cost,} \\ \text{when statement is unsound} \end{pmatrix}
$$

$$
+ \text{(cost of analyzing financial statement)}
$$

$$
= .8 \times 6.70 + .2 \times 42.50 + 18
$$

$$
= 31.86.
$$

The expected cost of investigating further at decision points 3 and 4 are calculated in a similar manner.

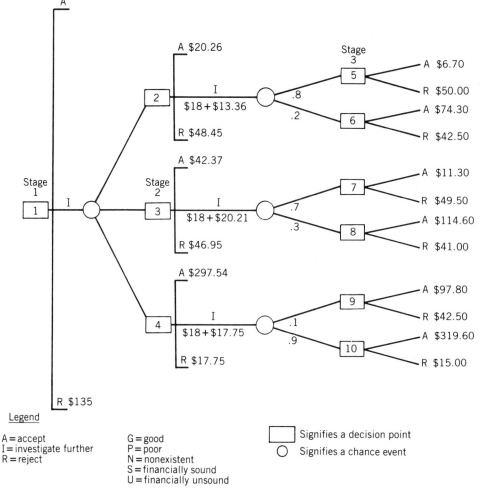

Figure 13.3 Numerical analysis of credit granting decisions at Stage 2.

Legend

A = accept
I = investigate further
R = reject

G = good
P = poor
N = nonexistent
S = financially sound
U = financially unsound

☐ Signifies a decision point
○ Signifies a chance event

The nine cost calculations for Stage 2 are shown in Figure 13.3. We see that it is best to accept the applicant at decision point 2; it is best to investigate further at decision point 3; and it is best to reject the applicant at decision point 4.

Turning finally to Stage 1, we now calculate the expected costs of the three alternatives: accept, reject, or obtain additional information. The costs of accepting and rejecting are calculated in a straightforward manner. The cost of investigating further is equal to

$$(.4 \times 20.26) + (.2 \times 38.21) + (.4 \times 17.75) + \$2 = \$24.84.$$

The complete decision tree diagram and the final calculations are shown in Figure 13.4. We see that it is best to incur at least the $2 cost of investigating past experience, rather than granting or rejecting credit automatically at Stage 1. Obviously, this conclusion depends on the numbers chosen for this example; the reader should be aware

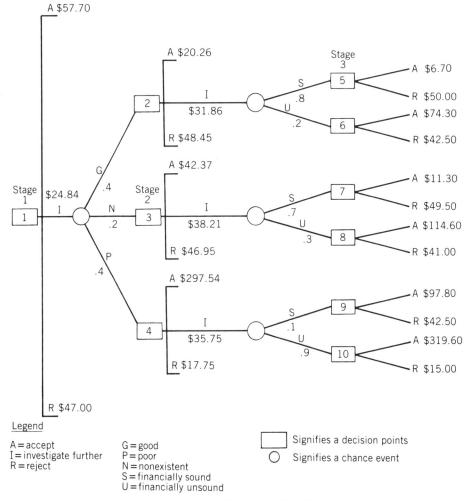

Legend

A = accept   G = good

I = investigate further   P = poor

R = reject   N = nonexistent

    S = financially sound

    U = financially unsound

□ Signifies a decision points

○ Signifies a chance event

Figure 13.4 Complete numerical analysis of credit granting decisions.

that it may not generalize to other credit granting decisions. However, the lesson that information costs must be compared to the value of obtaining additional information, as well as the sequential decision approach taken here, is applicable to other situations.

CREDIT SCORING MODELS

Suppose that a financial manager has obtained financial information on a particular credit applicant, and found that the customer's financial leverage is above the industry average, its operating leverage is below the industry average, and its liquidity is approximately the same as the industry average. Should the financial manager grant credit to this customer or not? The answer is that it is difficult to say, without knowing how the customer's financial leverage, operating leverage, and liquidity relate to his ability to ultimately pay for the goods.

Because of the above difficulty, many firms have begun to use credit scoring models to help them relate financial, demographic, and other information about the customer to the ability to repay. These models rely on a sophisticated statistical technique called discriminant analysis to determine a set of weights and a set of explanatory variables that best distinguish "good" customers from "bad" customers.

To develop a credit scoring model, the analyst first must decide what distinguishes a good account from a bad account. Suppose she decides that a good account is one that is paid within three months and a bad account is one that is paid beyond three months or not at all. The analyst must then develop a profile of characteristics that might be used in distinguishing good and bad accounts. For instance, she might find that good and bad accounts have the profiles shown in Table 13.5.

Looking at these figures, we see that the profile for good accounts is certainly quite different than that for bad accounts, suggesting that this is an appropriate set of characteristics to use in distinguishing accounts. However, we still do not have a set of weights that will help us determine a single credit score for each customer. This is where discriminant analysis is especially helpful.

Discriminant analysis works very much like a regression, where the dependent variable y takes on the value 1 or 0 depending on whether the account is good or bad. The

Table 13.5 Profiles of Good and Bad Risks

Characteristics	Average Value for Each Group	
	Good Risks	Bad Risks
Average income (in 1,000's)	$ 34.73	$16.56
Average net worth (in 1,000's)	$116.45	$41.98
Years in present job	9.8	5.4
Number of dependents	1.6	3.3
Total debt/total net worth (%)	21%	48%
Average age	43	37

Table 13.6 Characteristics
of Credit Applicants

Characteristics Possessed	**Weights**
Income (in 1,000's)	7.31
Net worth (in 1,000's)	5.26
Years in present job	16.85
Number of dependents	−47.19
Total debt/total net worth (%)	−20.76
Average age	4.9

goal is to determine a set of weights $a_1, \ldots, a_n$ that, when multiplied by the values of the independent variables $x_1, \ldots, x_n$ and summed, will best predict the y values. Thus,

$$y = a_1x_1 + a_2x_2 + \cdots + a_nx_n,$$

where the a's are chosen to minimize the cost of forecast errors.

Returning to our example, suppose that through the use of discriminant analysis, the analyst has found the set of weights found in Table 13.6. To determine a particular credit score then, the financial manager would simply multiply the above weights by the value of each characteristic. When this is done to the set of customers in the study sample, the resulting credit scores will typically follow the distributions shown in Figure 13.5.

Since these distributions overlap, there will be some misclassifications no matter what score, F^*, is used to distinguish good from bad customers. The final step then is to choose a cutoff score, F^*, that minimizes the total cost of misclassifications. Because of the judgement involved, many firms choose two cutoff scores. If the customer's score exceeds the upper cutoff, the account is automatically classified as "good"; if it is below the lower cutoff, the account is automatically classified as "bad"; and if it falls between, further analysis is required.

There is no doubt that credit scoring models have been found to be useful in many applications. The principal advantage of credit scoring models is that they specify the

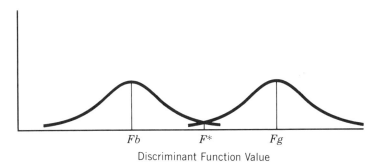

Discriminant Function Value

Figure 13.5 Credit scores of good and bad customers.

relationship between customer characteristics in an objective, verifiable, and statistically sound manner. The principal disadvantage is that, like any statistical method, they are based on the assumption that future customers will behave in the same way as previous customers. Since this is not always true, credit scoring models must obviously be used with a great deal of care.

MONITORING RECEIVABLE PERFORMANCE

The third major activity of the financial manager in regard to accounts receivable management is to monitor the firm's accounts receivable performance. The two most widely used methods of performing this task are: calculating the receivable turnover or its reciprocal, the Days' Sales Outstanding, and calculating the Aging Schedule of Receivables.

Days' Sales Outstanding

We noted above that the amount of accounts receivable shown on the firm's books is equal to the product of the average credit sales per day and the average collection period; that is,

$$\text{Total Accounts Receivable} = (\text{Average credit sales per day}) \times (\text{Average collection Period}).$$

Dividing both sides of this equation by the average credit sales per day, we see that the average collection period is given by

$$\text{Average Collection Period} = \frac{\text{Total receivables}}{\text{Average credit sales per day}}.$$

When looked at in this fashion, the average collection period is sometimes called the Days' Sales Outstanding (DSO). It is used as a primary method of monitoring whether the firm's collection experience is improving or deteriorating.

To illustrate how the use of the Days' Sales Outstanding can provide misleading signals about the status of the firm's credit policy, consider a firm whose credit sales are shown below:

Jan.	Feb.	March	April	May	June	July	Aug.	Sept.	Oct.	Nov.	Dec.
100	200	300	400	400	400	500	600	700	600	500	400

Assume that 20% of a given month's credit sales are collected in the current month, 40% are collected in the subsequent month, 30% in the following month, and 10% in the third month following the date of the credit sale. The set of numbers: .2, .4, .3, and .1 represent the payment pattern for the firm's customers, and under the above assumption, this pattern is stable. Since, for any given month's credit sales, receivables are just the proportion of the credit sales that have not been paid, a payment pattern of .2, .4, .3, and .1 implies a receivable pattern of .8, .4, and .1. Thus, the credit sales in January produce $80 of receivables in January, $40 in February, and $10 in March; the credit sales of $200 in February produce receivables of $160 in February, $80 in March, $20 in April, and so on.

From the above discussion, we see that the receivables shown on the books of our firm in any month are given by:

$$REC_t = .8CS_t + .4CS_{t-1} + .1CS_{t-2},$$

where

REC_t is the receivable balance in month t

$\quad CS_t$ is the credit sales in month t

$\quad CS_{t-1}$ is the credit sales in month t-1

$\quad CS_{t-2}$ is the credit sales in month t-2.

Applying this relationship to the credit sales shown above, we obtain the following level of receivables by month:

Jan.	Feb.	March	April	May	June	July	Aug.	Sept.	Oct.	Nov.	Dec.
290	240	330	460	510	520	600	720	850	820	710	580

Using the above figures for receivables and credits sales, we can now calculate the Days' Sales Outstanding at the end of each quarter. The resulting figures are shown in Table 13.7 for averaging periods of 30, 60, and 90 days.

Although the firm's payment pattern was assumed to be constant, the use of the Days' Sales Outstanding indicates a volatile collection experience. If we use a 30-day

Table 13.7 DSO by Quarter for Different Averaging Periods

Quarter	Averaging Period		
	30 Days	**60 Days**	**90 Days**
1	$\frac{330}{10} = 33$	$\frac{330}{8.3} = 40$	$\frac{330}{6.7} = 49$
2	$\frac{520}{13.3} = 39$	$\frac{520}{13.3} = 39$	$\frac{520}{13.3} = 39$
3	$\frac{850}{23.3} = 36$	$\frac{850}{21.7} = 39$	$\frac{850}{20} = 43$
4	$\frac{580}{13.3} = 44$	$\frac{580}{15} = 39$	$\frac{580}{16.7} = 35$

period for averaging credit sales per day, we conclude that our credit experience deteriorates from quarter 1 to quarter 2, improves from quarter 2 to quarter 3, and deteriorates again from quarter 3 to quarter 4. The opposite results obtain if we use a 90-day averaging period. Only if we use a 60-day averaging period do we reach a conclusion that is consistent with our assumption of a constant payment pattern.

The Aging Schedule   The Aging Schedule of Accounts Receivable displays the percentage of the firm's current accounts receivable that fall in different age categories. Under the above assumptions, the Aging Schedule of Accounts Receivable at the end of each quarter is given in Table 13.8.

These figures indicate a deterioration in the payment patterns of the firm's credit customers. Once again, however, the original data were based on the assumption of a constant payment pattern. Thus, the Aging Schedule may also provide incorrect signals to the financial manager.

To illustrate why the two methods, DSO and AS, produce misleading signals, consider the actual cash collections and accounts receivable balances that are generated from each month's credit sales under the assumption of a stable payment pattern of .2, .4, .3, and .1. These are shown in Tables 13.9 and 13.10. It is clear that the rows of these two tables contain the best payment pattern information, because they reflect what percentage of a given month's credit sales are collected in subsequent months.

The two traditional methods of monitoring accounts receivable performance sometimes produce misleading signals primarily because they focus on the columns of Tables 13.9 and 13.10 instead of the rows. The Aging Schedule at the end of March is calculated by looking at the receivable balance shown at the bottom of the March column of Table 13.10, and determining what percentage of this total is one month old, two months old, and three months old. Looking at the March column, we see that a relatively high percentage (240/330 = 73%) is one month old, but this is due primarily to the fact that credit sales in March are large compared to those of the previous two months.

The Days' Sales Outstanding takes the total accounts receivable at the bottom of the March column and relates this to the average credit sales over the last 30, 60, or 90 days. Since credit sales are rising, it is not surprising that the answer is sensitive to the length of the averaging period.

Table 13.8   Aging Schedule of Accounts Receivable by Quarter

Interval	1st Q	2nd Q	3rd Q	4th Q
0–30 days	73%	62%	66%	55%
31–60 days	24%	31%	28%	35%
61–90 days	3%	8%	6%	10%

Table 13.9 Monthly Cash Collections from Credit Sales

Month	Credit Sales	Jan.	Feb.	March	April	May	June	July	Aug.	Sept.	Oct.	Nov.	Dec.
Oct.	600	60											
Nov.	500	150	50										
Dec.	400	160	120	40									
Jan.	100	20	40	30	10								
Feb.	200		40	80	60	20							
March	300			60	120	90	30						
April	400				80	160	120	40					
May	400					80	160	120	40				
June	400						80	160	120	40			
July	500							100	200	150	50		
Aug.	600								120	240	180	60	
Sept.	700									140	280	210	70
Oct.	600										120	240	180
Nov.	500											100	200
Dec.	400												80
Total		390	250	210	270	350	390	420	480	570	630	610	530

Table 13.10 EOM Accounts Receivable Balances

Month	Credit Sales	Jan.	Feb.	March	April	May	June	July	Aug.	Sept.	Oct.	Nov.	Dec.
Oct.	600												
Nov.	500	50											
Dec.	400	160	40										
Jan.	100	80	40	10									
Feb.	200		160	80	20								
March	300			240	120	30							
April	400				320	160	40						
May	400					320	160	40					
June	400						320	160	40				
July	500							400	200	50			
Aug.	600								480	240	60		
Sept.	700									560	280	70	
Oct.	600										480	240	60
Nov.	500											400	200
Dec.	400												320
Total		290	240	330	460	510	520	600	720	850	820	710	580

272

Payment Pattern Approaches

From the above discussion, it is apparent that, if we want a correct signal of the payment patterns of the firm's customers, we must relate either cash collections or accounts receivable balances back to the credit sales that generated them; that is, we must gather data similar to that shown in the rows of Tables 13.9 and 13.10. Two approaches for accomplishing this have been recommended. The first, based on a payment pattern matrix, was developed by Llewellen and Johnson[4], while the second, based on a payment pattern regression, was developed by Stone.[5]

Suppose that the financial manager separates the accounts generating credit sales by the month in which the credit sale occurred. She then determines what percentage of the accounts generating credit sales in January are paid in January and each of the subsequent months. She also does this for February, March, and so on, and displays the results in the form of the matrix shown in Table 13.11 (called a payment pattern matrix).

A perusal of this matrix would provide the financial manager with accurate information on trends in payment patterns. If, as shown here, the percentages collected in months 0 and 1 are declining, while those collected in months 2 and 3 are increasing, the financial manager is fairly safe in concluding that her customers' payment pattern is deteriorating. Of course, she must be careful that the change is of sufficient magnitude to represent a true trend, rather than a statistical abberation.

The payment pattern matrix requires that the manager be able to segregate accounts based on the month in which the credit sale occurs. In cases where this is not possible, Stone suggests the use of a payment pattern regression equation of the following form:

$$CC_t = P_0 CS_t + P_1 CS_{t-1} + P_2 CS_{t-2} + \cdots + P_H CS_H + C_t,$$

where

CC_t is aggregate cash collections in month t

CS_t is aggregate credit sales in month t

CS_{t-1}, CS_{t-2}, and so on are aggregate credit sales in previous months

$P_0, \ldots P_1$, and so on are regression coefficients that indicate the payment pattern of the firm's customers

C_t is an error term.

Stone suggests that the coefficients P_0 to P_H be estimated from a regression equation involving data from previous periods. The regression equation should then be used to forecast cash collections in future periods. As the actual cash collections are observed, the financial manager can calculate the forecast error in each future period. If these are persistently negative (positive) for several months, the financial manager would be justified in concluding that his payment pattern had improved (deteriorated).

---

[4]Wilbur G. Llewellen, and Robert W. Johnson, "Better Way to Monitor Accounts Receivable," *Harvard Business Review*, May–June, 1972, pp. 101–109.
[5]Bernell K. Stone, "The Payment Pattern Approach to the Forecasting and Control of Accounts Receivable," *Financial Management*, Autumn 1976, pp. 65–82.

Table 13.11 Payment Pattern Matrix

Month of Credit Sale	Percent Collected in Same Month (0), 1 Month Later (1), etc.			
	0	**1**	**2**	**3**
Jan.	.2	.4	.3	.1
Feb.	.19	.39	.31	.11
March	.18	.38	.32	.12
April	.17	.37	.33	.13
May	.16	.36	.34	.14
June	.15	.35	.35	.15

SUMMARY

The financial manager makes three kinds of decisions in regard to the firm's accounts receivables: she chooses how much the firm should invest in accounts receivable, she screens individual customers who are candidates for credit, and she monitors the firm's credit experience.

The choice of how much to invest in accounts receivable can be made much like any other capital budgeting decision. The manager simply identifies the cash inflows and outflows associated with the investment decisions, and evaluates them using present value analysis. In estimating the firm's investment in accounts receivable, however, the manager must be careful to use variable production cost rather than product price as the estimate of the amount of cash tied up in each credit sale.

When selecting individual credit customers, the financial manager must evaluate whether the customer will ultimately repay the loan. Traditionally, this evaluation was based on the five C's of credit: character, capacity, collateral, capital, and conditions. However, the traditional approach neglected the high cost of obtaining all the necessary information to perform a thorough five-C analysis and it provided almost no guidelines for translating the information obtained into a specific credit decision. The sequential approach to the credit granting decision described in this chapter addresses the first of these weaknesses of the traditional approach, while the credit scoring approach, also described in this chapter, addresses the second.

Monitoring accounts receivable is sometimes a difficult task. When credit sales are changing significantly over time, the two most widely used methods of monitoring accounts receivable, the Days' Sales Outstanding and the Aging Schedule, provide misleading signals about the credit behavior of the firm's customers. Fortunately, the financial manager can use either the payment pattern matrix or the payment pattern regression to obtain correct signals. Although these two approaches require more information to implement than the two more widely used approaches, this information cost is not significant in the computer age.

DISCUSSION QUESTIONS

1. What are the major activities of the firm's credit manager?
2. Discuss how the firm's credit terms affect its average credit sales per day and its average collection period.
3. How should a change in credit terms be evaluated?
4. Why is the firm's investment in accounts receivable less than the accounts receivable shown on its books?
5. Describe the major weaknesses with the Five-C Approach to the credit granting decision.
6. Discuss the concepts of acceptance cost and rejection cost as they relate to the credit granting decision.
7. How does one determine the value of additional information about the credit customer?
8. When using the decision-tree approach to the credit granting decision, why is it best to evaluate the tree from right to left?
9. What are the major advantages of using credit scoring models to make credit granting decisions?
10. Describe the steps one would go through in developing a credit scoring model.
11. What are some of the problems involved with using credit scoring models?
12. Are credit scoring models purely objective, or is there a subjective element as well?
13. Describe the Days' Sales Outstanding method of monitoring accounts receivable performance.
14. What is the Aging Schedule of Receivables and how is it used to measure accounts receivable performance?
15. Why do the Days' Sales Outstanding and Aging Schedule methods sometimes produce misleading signals of accounts receivable performance?
16. What is a payment pattern matrix?
17. Describe how the payment pattern matrix can be used to monitor accounts receivable performance.
18. Discuss how the payment pattern matrix differs from the payment pattern regression approach to monitoring accounts receivable performance.

PROBLEMS

1. Suppose that Pearson's Department Store has annual credit sales of $12.6 million, with an average collection period of 42 days. What is the average amount of accounts receivable on Pearson's books?
2. Now suppose that Pearson's is considering relaxing its credit standards, a decision that it believes will increase annual credit sales by $1.4 million and increase the average collection period to 55 days. If variable costs represent 85% of sales, how much will Pearson's investment in accounts receivable increase under the new policy?

3. If the opportunity cost of capital to Pearson's is 25%, should they adopt the new credit policy?
4. Consider Tables 13.3 and 13.4. How do the probability values shown in Table 13.3 relate mathematically to those shown in Table 13.4?
5. Consider Figure 13.2. Demonstrate how the cost values for the accept and reject decisions ($6.70 and $50.00, respectively) at decision point 5 were derived.
6. Consider Figure 13.3. Explain why it does not pay to obtain additional information at decision points 2 and 4.
7. Mr. Friedman, the credit manager at Computer World, has decided to use a credit scoring model to help him make credit granting decisions. He has performed a discriminate analysis of credit data from previous customers and obtained the weights shown in Table 13.6. He is now reviewing a new applicant with the following characteristics: income—$27,500, net worth—$88,000, years in present job—6, number of dependents—2, total debt/net worth (%)—35%, and average age—49. If the cutoff score for a good credit risk is 200, should this applicant be accepted?
8. Mr. Johnson, the credit manager at Software Systems, Inc., has determined from previous experience that 10% of a given month's credit sales are collected in the current month, 40% are collected in the subsequent month, and 50% are collected in the second month following the date of the credit sale. Credit sales were $250,000 in January, $125,000 in February, $300,000 in March, and $200,000 in April. What is the level of accounts receivable at Software Systems, Inc. in April?

ADDITIONAL READINGS

1. Altman, Edward, "Financial Ratios, Discriminant Analysis, and the Prediction of Corporate Bankruptcy," *Journal of Finance,* Sept. 1968.
2. Altman, Edward, "The Z-Score Bankruptcy Model: Past, Present and Future," Chapter 5 in *Financial Crises: Institutions & Markets in a Fragile Environment,* Ed. Altman and Arnold Sametz, eds., John Wiley & Sons, New York, 1977.
3. Boggess, William P., "Screen-Test Your Credit Risks," *Harvard Business Review,* Nov.–Dec., 1967, pp. 113–122.
4. Dyl, Edward A., "Another Look at the Evaluation of Investment in Accounts Receivable," *Financial Management,* Winter 1977, pp. 206–216.
5. Hill, Ned C. and Kenneth D. Riener, "Determining the Cash Discount in the Firm's Credit Policy," *Journal of Financial Research,* Spring 1979, pp. 68–73.
6. Johnson, Robert W., "Management of Accounts Receivable and Payable," Chapter 28 in *Financial Handbook,* 5th ed. Edward I. Altman, ed., John Wiley & Sons, New York, 1981.
7. Llewellen, Wilbur G. and Robert W. Edmister, "A General Model for Accounts-Receivable Analysis and Control," *Journal of Financial and Quantitative Analysis,* March 1973, pp. 195–206.

8. Llewellen, Wilbur G. and Robert W. Johnson, "Better Way to Monitor Accounts Receivable," *Harvard Business Review,* May–June, 1972, pp. 101–109.

9. Mehta, Dileep, "Optimal Credit Policy Selection: A Dynamic Approach," *Journal of Financial and Quantitative Analysis,* Dec. 1970, pp. 421–444.

10. Mehta, Dileep, "The Formulation of Credit Policy Models," *Management Science,* Oct. 1968, pp. 30–50.

11. Sartoris, William L. and Ned C. Hill, "Evaluating Credit Policy Alternatives: A Present Value Framework," *Journal of Financial Research,* Spring 1984, pp. 81–89.

12. Sartoris, William L. and Ned C. Hill, "A Generalized Cash Flow Approach to Short-Term Financial Decisions," *Journal of Finance,* May 1983, pp. 349–360.

13. Smith, Keith V., *Guide to Working Capital Management,* McGraw-Hill, New York, 1979, pp. 115–140.

14. Stone, Bernell K., "The Payment Patterns Approach to the Forecasting and Control of Accounts Receivable," *Financial Management,* Autumn 1976, pp. 65–82.

15. Vander Weide, James H., "Financial Management in the Short Run," Chapter 23 in *The Handbook of Modern Finance,* Dennis E. Logue, ed., Warren, Gorham & Lamont, New York, 1984.

16. Van Horne, James C., *Financial Management and Policy,* 5th ed., Prentice-Hall, Englewood Cliffs, N.J., Chapter 15.

17. Weston, J. Fred and Tuan, P.D., "Comment on the Analysis of Credit Policy Change," *Financial Management,* Winter 1980, pp. 59–63.

SECTION VI

INVENTORY MANAGEMENT

CHAPTER 14

Inventory Models

The firm's investment in inventories is frequently as large as, if not larger than, its investment in receivables. It is the financial manager's responsibility to monitor the firm's inventory investment to assure that the return on investment continues to exceed the cost of capital. This chapter describes several techniques that have been found useful for this purpose.[1]

NATURE OF THE INVENTORY MANAGEMENT PROBLEM

The nature and scope of the inventory management problem may be illustrated in terms of Figure 14.1, which describes the flow of goods and the typical delays in a system for producing and distributing high volume, standardized products. At the right of the diagram, we see that demand is generated by consumers who enter a retail outlet with an order. Competitive conditions require that the manager of the retail outlet maintain an inventory so that the order may be filled instantaneously. Periodically, the manager reviews his inventory levels and transmits an order to the distributor that will replenish his stock. If the retailer reviews his inventory every ten days, it takes three days for the order to reach the distributor, and it takes seven days for the order to be filled and delivered to the retailer, then the retailer must maintain, at a minimum, sufficient inventories to cover demand for twenty days.

---

[1]Parts of this chapter are taken from James H. Vander Weide, "Financial Management in the Short Run", in Dennis E. Logue, ed., *The Handbook of Modern Finance*, Warren, Gorham & Lamont, New York, 1984.

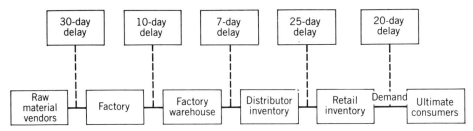

Figure 14.1 Delays in the production–inventory system.

As the distributor fills orders from retail, his inventories are depleted as well, and so he must periodically place orders to replenish his stock from the factory warehouse. If the distributor reviews his inventory every fifteen days, it takes three days for the order to be prepared and sent to the factory warehouse, and it takes seven days for the order to be filled and shipped to the distributor, then the distributor must maintain sufficient inventories to satisfy demand for the next twenty-five days.

Moving further back in the production process, we see that inventories at the factory warehouse are replenished from the goods produced in the factory. Since the production process takes time, the factory manager must begin the production process in advance and produce sufficient quantities to satisfy demand for inventory at the warehouse during the coming period. To produce the required levels, however, the manager must have sufficient inventories of raw materials. Thus, the ultimate demand of consumers finally impacts the demand for raw materials.

From the above descriptions, it is clear that the nature and scope of the inventory management problem depends on the boundaries of managerial control. If the manager is in control only of the retail outlet, her management problem is relatively simple: she needs to forecast customer demand, obtain information on her inventory level, and order the appropriate amount of inventory. The inventory management system of this manager is frequently called a "pure inventory system" because it involves no production decisions.

On the other hand, if the manager is in control of the entire production-inventory-distribution system, her management problem is quite complex: she must forecast ultimate customer demand, determine how this demand affects each stage of the distribution system, and schedule production and employment levels at each stage of the system.

Given the variety of production-inventory problems that managers face, it is not surprising that there is no one inventory management technique appropriate for all problems. Later in this chapter, we describe inventory models that address different aspects of the inventory management problem. These models make certain assumptions about the nature of customer demand, the boundaries of managerial control, and the cost of inventory management. To assess the relevance of these techniques to her particular inventory problem, the manager must judge whether the assumptions are appropriate in light of her situation.

RATIONALE FOR INVENTORIES

Firms hold inventories for five reasons. First, firms require some inventories to fill the pipelines of the production and distribution system. For instance, goods in the process of production and goods in the process of shipment are part of the firm's inventory investment. Although this aspect of the firm's inventories is relatively invisible, it frequently is such a large part of the total inventory investment, that it cannot be ignored.

Second, firms hold some inventories to minimize the substantial fixed costs associated with the order or production of additional inventories. As noted later, these costs include production setup costs, inventory review and ordering costs, and transactions or transportation costs that are independent of the size of the order. The effort to minimize these costs encourages firms to make larger and less frequent orders, and to hold larger average inventories. For lack of a better name, inventories in this category are sometimes called "lot size" inventories.

Third, firms in industries with seasonal demand, frequently hold inventories to achieve the economies associated with a stable production schedule. If the firm can forecast the demand for its goods with reasonable accuracy, it can reduce the cost of changing work force levels, overtime pay, and frequent production setups by producing at a constant level throughout the year. However, this means that the firm's production will exceed its sales in periods of low demand, causing its inventories to increase.

Fourth, in situations where demand is uncertain, firms hold inventories as a buffer against the possibility of stockouts. Although the cost of an inventory shortage is difficult to measure precisely, there is little doubt that it is substantial, especially in cases where customers have alternative sources of supply. In addition to the inventories held as a buffer against demand uncertainties, there are also inventories, usually of raw materials, held as a buffer against supply uncertainties. These inventories are especially large in industries subject to the threat of strikes or work stoppage.

Finally, firms hold inventories as a means of decentralizing decision-making authority in complex organizations. In some cases, the cost of these additional inventories is less than the cost of coordinating activities at many stages of the production process. Inventories in this last category are sometimes called "decoupling inventories" because they allow the manager to decouple decisions at one stage of the production-distribution process from those at another.

INVENTORY COSTS

The firm that decides to hold inventories incurs a variety of costs, which may be grouped into four categories: acquisition costs, holding costs, shortage costs, and management costs. As the name suggests, acquisition costs include all of the costs of acquiring the item to be held in inventory. These include the purchase price, the transportation or production cost, and the cost of maintaining the purchasing activity, including management time, telephone expenses, and so on.

Holding costs include all costs of holding the item in inventory until it is sold. The cost of storage, shrinkage, security, and interest are all included in the holding cost category.

Shortage costs are the multitude of costs that the firm incurs when customers order an item that is out of stock. These include customer ill will, lost profits on sales, and higher than usual production or transportation costs. Because shortage costs are high, some firms hold inventories of sufficient magnitude that shortage never occurs. Since this too involves substantial costs, however, the firm is better advised to treat the cost of shortage explicitly in its analysis.

The final cost of inventory management is the cost of management itself. For firms with thousands of different items in inventory, management costs may be significant. In an effort to reduce management costs, many firms have developed sophisticated computer-based inventory information and control systems. It is certainly worthwhile to consider such systems carefully.

INVENTORY DECISION MODELS

The goal of inventory management is to minimize the total cost of the firm's inventory investment. Several models that help the manager accomplish this task are described below. These models are distinguished by the assumptions they make regarding customer demand, inventory cost, management policies, constraints on the system, and conditions of supply. We will briefly review the various choices concerning these assumptions before we discuss several inventory models in detail:

1. *Demand.* The model builder has several choices regarding his treatment of the customer demand. First, he must decide whether he will treat the demand as deterministic (i.e., known with certainty) or stochastic (i.e., subject to the laws of probability). The choice is usually made to treat demand as deterministic because this greatly simplifies the mathematical formulation; however, some simple stochastic specifications are used in some circumstances. Second, he must decide whether the demand is stationary or seasonal. If it is stationary (in the deterministic case, the term stationary has the same meaning as constant), the problem can, in many cases, be treated as a single period rather than a multiperiod problem, and hence the mathematics is much reduced in complexity.

2. *Cost.* With regard to cost, the model builder must decide both which costs are relevant and the form these costs take. The simplest assumption is that there are two types of cost: those that depend on the quantity ordered and those that depend on the number of orders. The simplest assumption about the form of the cost functions is that they are linear. Nonlinear cost functions make the inventory problem considerably more difficult.

3. *Management Policy.* Three assumptions about management policy appear in inventory models. One concerns the frequency at which the inventory level is re-

viewed. The choice is to treat it as continuously reviewed or only reviewed periodically. Another refers to the boundaries of managerial control. In terms of Figure 14.1, the model builder can assume that the manager controls only the level of inventory, as might be appropriate in a pure inventory system, or the model builder can assume that the manager is in charge of scheduling production and manpower levels as well. The third assumption pertains to the type of inventory management strategy that the manager can employ. In Chapter 10, we described an inventory approach to the cash-marketable securities decision that employed a control limit policy. This is a frequent assumption in stochastic inventory models.

4. *Constraints.* In some circumstances, the model builder may wish to place constraints on the values of the manager's decisions. These come into play in cases where there is a fixed warehouse capacity or where the amount produced or stored of one item is affected by the amounts produced or stored of others.

5. *Supply.* The final category of assumptions concerns the conditions under which inventory is replenished. First, there is a need to specify whether inventory is replenished instantaneously, or only with delay. Second, there is a need to specify whether inventory is replenished through production or through order. Third, there is the need to specify whether the supply is certain or uncertain. Finally, there is the need to specify the price at which inventory is replenished.

The model builder's choices concerning the above assumptions affect both the relevance and the complexity of the inventory decision model. The ideal situation is where a simple set of assumptions captures the essential characteristics of the manager's real world decision problem. This occurs in some retail inventory situations where the simple EOQ model described below is frequently applicable. However, in many other circumstances, the model builder has to make an uncomfortable trade-off between realism and complexity. Hopefully, the discussion below will better prepare the manager to make his tradeoff.

The EOQ Model

The economic order quantity (EOQ) model is a simple, but widely used, approach to minimizing inventory costs. To illustrate its use, consider the inventory problem of the Triangle Beverage Co., a company that distributes approximately 156,000 cases of Butch Beer per year to over 12,000 retail outlets in the Southeast. Triangle purchases Butch Beer from the manufacturer at a cost of $4.50 per case, including transportation. The company believes that it incurs two kinds of inventory costs. Holding costs, including interest, breakage, warehouse cost, pilferage, insurance, and taxes, amount to 25% of the firm's average inventory investment over the year. Acquisition costs—including management time, paper, postage, telephone, and transportation—are about $25 per order.

The problem is to decide how many units to order at a time. If the firm chooses to order large quantities, it will incur a large investment in inventories, and thus its holding costs will be relatively high. However, if the firm seeks to minimize holding costs by making frequent orders for small quantities, it will incur excessive acquisition costs. The least cost order quantity will clearly be one that balances the excessive holding costs associated with large orders with the excessive acquisition costs associated with small orders.

To analyze the inventory problem of the Triangle Beverage Company, it is helpful to be able to express the total inventory costs as a function of the order quantity. Let us begin with the holding costs. As shown in Figure 14.2, if the firm orders Q cases of Butch Beer at time 0, its inventory will be Q at time 0 and will receed gradually to zero by the time the next shipment arrives. Thus, the firm's average inventory level will be one-half Q and its annual holding cost, which is equal to the average inventory times the annual holding cost per unit, will equal one-half $C_H Q$, where C_H is the holding cost per unit. For the Triangle Beverage Company, the holding cost per unit equals .25 × $4.50, and so the annual holding cost is equal to $.56 × Q.

Turning to the annual ordering costs, we know that it is the product of the number of orders per year and the cost per order. Let D denote the annual level of demand (156,000 cases). Then the number of orders per year is equal to the annual demand divided by the quantity per order; that is, it is equal to D/Q. Thus, the annual acquisition cost equals

$$D/Q \times C_A,$$

where C_A is the acquisition cost per order. Since C_A is $25 for Triangle Beverage, the annual acquisition cost is $(156,000/Q) \times \$25 = \$3,900,000/Q$. Furthermore, since the total inventory cost is simply the sum of the annual holding cost and the annual acquisition cost, the desired expression relating total costs to the quantity ordered is now at hand. It is

$$TC = 0.56Q + 3,900,000/Q.$$

Using the above expression for total cost as a function of Q, we can obtain the least cost order quantity in one of two ways. First, we can use the total cost equation to calculate total costs associated with a number of different values of Q. For the case of Triangle Beverage, we have done this for 9 values of Q ranging from 1000 to 5000. The results are shown in Table 14.1. We see that total costs are lowest when 2500 cases are ordered at one time. Under this policy, the firm would make approximately 62 orders a year, or one order every 5.9 days.

The second method in finding the least cost order quantity is to find the minimum

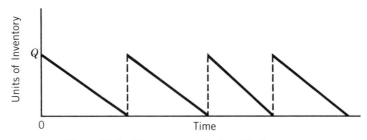

Figure 14.2 Time pattern of triangle's inventory.

Table 14.1   Total Costs for Different Purchase Orders

	Holding Cost 0.56Q	Acquisition Cost 3,900,000 Q	TC
1000	560	3,900	4,460
1500	840	2,600	3,440
2000	1120	1,950	3,070
2500	1400	1,560	2,960
3000	1680	1,300	2,980
3500	1960	1,114	3,074
4000	2240	975	3,215
4500	2520	867	3,387
5000	2800	780	3,580

value of the total cost function, using calculus. When this is done, we find that the least cost order quantity Q is in general given by the expression

$$Q^* = \sqrt{\frac{2DC_A}{C_H}} \,.$$

In this case, this yields

$$Q^* = \sqrt{\frac{7,800,000}{1.13}} = 2,627.$$

Although this appears to be somewhat more accurate than the first approach, the difference in cost between a policy of ordering 2500 units at a time compared to 2627 units at a time is small, especially in light of the two simplifying assumptions that the demand and cost values are known with certainty and the demand occurs at a steady rate throughout the year.

Lead Time in the EOQ Model

The above analysis of the Triangle Beverage Co.'s inventory problem should be modified slightly to recognize the delay between the order and receipt of beer. We noted above that Triangle's best policy is to order roughly 2600 cases every six days. Suppose now that it takes three days for the beer to be shipped from the manufacturer to Triangle's warehouse. Then, it is evident that, rather than waiting until its inventories are depleted, Triangle should place an order whenever its inventories reach a level of 1300 cases. This is the number of cases that will just be consumed during the shipment period. Since Triangle's inventory is depleted at the rate of roughly 2600/6 cases per day, this is the same as saying that Triangle should place an order three days before receipt of a new shipment. The time between the placement of an order and the receipt of a new shipment is called the lead time in inventory analysis.

Table 14.2 Total Costs for Different Purchase Orders with Purchase Discounts

Quantity	Holding Costs	Acquisition Costs	Discount Cost Saving	Total Inventory Costs—Discount Savings
1000	560	3,900		4,460
1500	840	2,600		3,440
2000	1120	1,950		3,070
2500	1400	1,560		1,960
3000	1668	1,300	7800	−4,832
3500	1946	1,114	7800	−4,740
4000	2200	975	15,600	−12,425
4500	2475	867	15,600	−12,258
5000	2750	780	15,600	−12,070

Quantity Discounts

It may be optimal for Triangle Beverage Co. to order more than 2600 units at a time, if its supplier offers discounts for large orders. Suppose now that Triangle's supplier offers a discount of $.05 per case for orders between 3000 and 4000 cases, and a discount of $.10 per case for orders greater than 4000 cases. This discount must be reflected in the analysis of Triangle's least cost purchase quantity. The analysis shown in Table 14.2 reveals that an order quantity of 4000 cases produces the optimal tradeoff between the purchase cost savings of larger quantity orders and the increased inventory costs of these orders.

Safety Stock

The assumption of known demand has been critical to our analysis so far. Demand uncertainty can be handled within the EOQ model framework through the inclusion of a safety stock. In terms of the graph shown in Figure 14.3, the firm would never let its inventory get down to zero. Instead, it would keep a safety stock of S cases to protect against larger than expected demands. Of course, this would also increase its average investment in inventory.

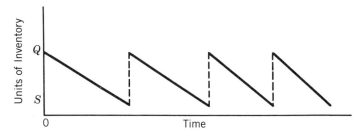

Figure 14.3 Time pattern of Triangle's inventory with safety stock.

To see how the firm might determine the optimal safety stock to hold, suppose that Triangle Beverage believes that the demand for beer over a 6-day period is as shown below:

Demand:	1,000	1,500	2,000	2,500	3,000	3,500	4,000
Probability:	.05	.10	.20	.30	.20	.10	.05

Suppose also that Triangle incurs a $2 cost per unit in lost sales or customer ill will every time demand exceeds the amount of inventory on hand.

Table 14.3 displays an analysis of the expected costs associated with safety stocks of 1500, 1000, 500, and 0 units. If the firm holds a safety stock of 1500 units, there is no chance of a stockout, and so the firm's stockout costs are zero. However, the holding costs of the extra 1500 units in inventory equals $840. If the firm holds a safety stock of 1000 units, there is a 5% chance that it will incur stockout costs of $1000. Adding the $50 expected stockout cost to the $560 additional holding cost, we obtain a total of $610. Repeating a similar analysis for safety stock levels of 500 and zero, we see that the optimal safety stock is 500 units.

AGGREGATE PRODUCTION–INVENTORY PLANNING

Firms that experience seasonal fluctuations in sales have three choices for satisfying customer demand:

1. They can vary production levels to coincide with demand.
2. They can keep production at a constant level, and satisfy peak demand out of inventories of goods produced in previous periods.
3. They can follow an intermediate policy somewhere in between these two extremes.

Table 14.3 Expected Costs Associated with Various Safety Stocks

Demand for 6-Day Period

Demand:	1,000	1,500	2,000	2,500	3,000	3,500	4,000
Probability:	.05	.10	.20	.30	.20	.10	.05

Safety Stock	Stockout	Stockout Cost (at $2)	Probability	Expected Stockout Cost	Additional Holding Cost	Total Cost
1500	0	0	0	0	840	840
1000	500	1000	.05	50	560	610
500	1000	2000	.05	100		
	500	1000	.10	100		
				200	280	480
0	1500	3000	.05	150		
	1000	2000	.10	200		
	500	1000	.20	200		
				550	0	550

If the firm chooses to adopt alternative 1, it will likely incur high costs for changing production levels, hiring and firing workers, overtime premiums, and extra maintenance for excessive use of machines in peak periods, but its inventory costs will be minimal. If the firm adopts alternative 2, its inventory costs will be high, but its costs of changing production and work force levels will be low. Alternative 3 is a compromise that involves intermediate levels of production, inventory and labor costs.

The process of analyzing and choosing production, inventory, and manpower levels that satisfy demand at minimum cost is called aggregate production–inventory planning. The management science literature describes a number of models that are designed to improve the aggregate production–inventory planning process. These models have been applied in many industries, including oil refining, shoe manufacturing, and paint manufacturing. These industries are characterized by continuous production of a highly standarized commodity. The problem of production–inventory planning for job shop processes is considerably more difficult to solve, and so planning for production–inventory levels in these processes frequently occurs on a more heuristic level.

The financial manager is interested in the firm's aggregate production–inventory plan because the results of this plan serve as input to her financial plan. If the firm adopts a level production policy in order to minimize production and labor costs, its inventories will increase sharply in some months, thus increasing the firm's financial requirements. The financial manager should understand how the production–inventory plan is put together so that she can assess whether the interest costs of the additional financing exceeds the benefits of the plan. To help the financial manager understand the issues in production–inventory planning and to introduce her to the available decision tools in this area, we present a linear programming formulation of the production–inventory planning problem in Appendix A.

SUMMARY

This chapter reviews the reasons why firms hold inventories and describes a set of methods that have been found to be useful in managing inventories. The appropriate method to use in a particular instance is a function of the nature and scope of the firm's inventory system. Frequently, the techniques require special assumptions that may not hold exactly in practice. Thus, in applying these techniques, the user must understand the nature of his own inventory system, and judge whether the assumptions of one or more techniques are applicable to his system. Although this is a difficult task, the firm's investment in inventories is frequently so large that considerable effort devoted to this task is well worthwhile.

DISCUSSION QUESTIONS

1. Why is the firm's financial manager interested in the firm's inventory policies?
2. Describe the different kinds of inventory problems that arise in a production-distribution system for high volume standardized products.

3. What are the major tasks involved in managing the firm's inventories?
4. Discuss the reasons why firms hold inventories.
5. What are the major costs of holding inventories?
6. What are the major considerations in building an inventory management model?
7. What are the major assumptions of the EOQ model?
8. In what situations is the EOQ model most likely to be helpful?
9. What are the factors that affect the firm's need for a safety stock of inventory?
10. Describe how the optimal safety stock can be found.
11. What strategies can the firm employ to satisfy a seasonal demand for its product?
12. Describe the major costs associated with each strategy.
13. How does the firm's monthly production plan affect the firm's financial requirements?
14. What techniques are available for planning production–inventory–manpower levels?
15. Describe some of the complications that might arise in practice to make inventory models less valuable.

PROBLEMS

1. The inventory manager at Weiss Machine Parts is concerned that his current policy for ordering a certain brand of spark plug may be cost ineffective. The manager purchases 120,000 boxes of spark plugs per year at $11.70 per box. The manager believes that he incurs holding costs equal to 20% of the firm's average inventory investment and acquisition costs of about $100 per order. What is the optimal order quantity for these spark plugs?
2. Suppose now that the supplier offers a discount of 25¢ per box for orders between 3000 and 4000 boxes and a discount of 50¢ per box for orders greater than 4000 boxes. How do these discounts affect the optimal order quantity?
3. Assume that the demand for spark plugs has the following distribution over the next ten days:

Demand:	2,000	2,500	3,000	3,500	4,000	4,500	5,000
Probability:	.05	.10	.20	.30	.20	.10	.05

Assume also that there is a $5.00 cost per box in lost sales or customer ill will every time demand exceeds the amount of inventory on hand. Determine the optimal safety stock for the inventory manager to hold utilizing an optimal order quantity of 3200.

ADDITIONAL READINGS

1. Anderson, David R., Dennis J. Sweeney and Thomas A. Williams, *An Introduction to Management Science: Quantitative Approaches to Decision Making,* 3rd ed., West Publishing Company, St. Paul, Minn., 1982.

2. Baker, Kenneth R. and William W. Damon, "A Simultaneous Planning Model for Production and Working Capital," *Decision Sciences*, Jan. 1977, pp. 95–108.

3. Brown, Robert G., *Decision Rules for Inventory Management*, Holt, Rinehart and Winston, New York, 1967.

4. Buffa, Elwood S. and William H. Taubert, *Production-Inventory Systems: Planning and Control*, Richard D. Irwin, Homewood, Ill. 1972.

5. Hanssman, F. and S. Hess, "A Linear Programming Approach to Production and Employment Scheduling," *Management Technology*, Jan. 1960, pp. 46–52.

6. Johnson L. and D. Montgomery, *Operations Research in Production Planning, Scheduling and Inventory Control*, John Wiley & Sons, Inc., New York, 1974.

7. Magee, John F., "Guides to Inventory Policy," I–III, *Harvard Business Review*, Jan.–Feb., 1956, pp. 49–60; March–April, 1956, pp. 103–116 and May–June, 1956, pp. 57–70.

8. Magee, John F. and David M. Boodman, *Production Planning and Inventory Control*, McGraw-Hill, New York, 1966.

9. Magee, John F. and Harlan C. Meal, "Inventory Management and Standards," Chapter 23 in *The Treasurer's Handbook*, J. Fred Weston and Maurice B. Goudzwaard, eds., Dow Jones-Irwin, Homewood, Ill. 1976.

10. Orlicky, Joseph A., *Material Requirements Planning: The New Way of Life in Production and Inventory Management*, McGraw-Hill, New York, 1975.

11. Plossl, G. W. and O. W. Wright, *Production and Inventory Control: Principles and Techniques*, Prentice-Hall, Englewood Cliffs, N.J., 1967.

12. Smith, Keith V., *Guide to Working Capital Management*, McGraw-Hill, New York, 1979, pp. 141–172.

13. Smith, Keith V., *Management of Working Capital*, Sec. 4, West Publishing, New York, 1974.

14. Vander Weide, James H., "Financial Management in the Short Run," Chapter 23 in *The Handbook of Modern Finance*, Dennis E. Logue, ed., Warren, Gorham & Lamont, N.Y., 1984.

15. Wagner, Harvey M., *Principles of Operations Research*, 2nd ed., Prentice-Hall, Englewood Cliffs, N.J., 1975.

APPENDIX A

Linear Programming Formulation of Production–Inventory Planning Problem

The aggregate production–inventory planning problem may be formulated in terms of the following variables:

Decision variables:

WF_t = workforce level during month t

RP_t = regular time production output, in dollars, in month t

OP_t = overtime production output, in dollars, in month t

IN_t = inventory level, in dollars, at end of month t

H_t = employees hired at the start of month t

F_t = employees fired at the start of month t.

Model parameters:

$t = 1,2, \ldots , N$ = month index

S_t = dollar sales in month t

m = technological limit on workforce size

α = productivity in dollars of output per employee per month

β = overtime productivity in dollars of output per employee per month.

Cost Components:

p = regular time monthly payroll cost per employee

c = nonlabor production cost per output dollar

o = overtime payroll cost per output dollar

h = out-of-pocket inventory holding cost per dollar per month

a = hiring cost per employee

b = firing cost per employee.

Using these variables, the production–inventory planning problem can be stated as the following linear program:

$$\sum_{t=1}^{N}(pWF_t + cRP_t + (c + o)OP_t + hIN_t + aH_t + bF_t) \qquad (14.1)$$

subject to

$$IN_t = IN_{t-1} + RP_t + OP_t - S_t \qquad 1 \leq t \leq N \qquad (14.2)$$

$$WN_t = WN_{t-1} + H_t - F_t \qquad 1 \leq t \leq N \qquad (14.3)$$

$$RP_t \leq \alpha WF_t \qquad 1 \leq t \leq N \qquad (14.4)$$

$$OP_t \leq \beta WF_t \qquad (14.5)$$

where $0 \leq WF_t \leq m$ and $RP_t, OP_t, IN_t, F_t, H_t, \geq 0$.

The objective in this formulation is to minimize the total cost of the firm's operating plan over the planning horizon, including wage cost, nonlabor expenses, inventory holding costs, and the cost of changing work force levels. Constraint set 14.2 says that inventories at the end of period t must equal inventories at the beginning of the period plus new production minus sales.

Constraint set 14.3 says that the work force in period t is equal to the work force in the previous period plus new hires minus fires. Constraint sets 14.4 and 14.5 define the maximum amounts that can be produced on a regular and overtime basis, given the firm's work force levels in that period.

The above linear programming formulation is typical of the many formulations that have appeared in the literature. In particular applications, the formulation will almost certainly have to be altered somewhat to take account of the firm's operating environment. In most firms, the operating environment is such that the final formulation will be considerably more complex than that above. In some instances, the added complexities merely increase the number of variables and constraints in the linear programming formulation. In others, the added complexities change the nature of the problem to such an extent that a linear programming formulation is no longer possible. Even in these cases, however, analytical methods are frequently helpful.

GLOSSARY

acceptance cost   the expected cost to the firm of granting credit.

acquisition costs   the cost of acquiring an item to be held in inventory. Depending on the situation this may include the purchase price, transportation cost, production cost, or the cost of maintaining the purchasing activity.

aggregate production–inventory planning   the process of determining the production, inventory, and manpower levels that minimize the cost of satisfying a seasonally fluctuating demand.

algorithm   a set of logical procedures that may be used to arrive at a solution to a decision problem such as the lockbox location problem.

anticipatory hedge   a situation where an individual or firm takes a position in the futures market that is a temporary substitute for an anticipated position in the cash market at a later date.

arbitrageur   an individual who seeks to profit from a situation where the same commodity is trading at different prices.

automated clearing house   a corporation operated either by the Federal Reserve System or a group of private banks that allows funds to be transferred from one bank account to another without the costly movement of paper that characterizes a traditional check payment system.

availability time   the delay between the time a check is deposited in a firm's bank account and the time the bank is willing to credit the account with additional funds. The delay arises because of the time required to present checks to the drawee bank; however, it does not correspond to this time exactly.

bankers acceptance   a time draft drawn on a bank that is frequently used to finance international trade.

basis   the difference between the cash price and the futures price of a commodity.

basis point a term used in interest rate calculations to refer to a difference of 1/100 of 1% in interest.

batch production process a production process where machines produce a variety of items in batches; that is, a fixed quantity of the first item is produced, then a fixed quantity of the second item is produced, and so on.

carry the difference between the financing costs of money market dealers and their return on investment.

cash budget a projection of the firm's cash position over the near term future that is based on the firm's projected cash receipts from sales and cash disbursements for such items as raw materials, labor, dividends, and interest.

cash concentration system a system for transferring funds on deposit in regional banks to a central cash pool where they may be managed more efficiently.

cash items in the process of collection check items in the process of collection that have been credited to the bank of deposit but not yet collected from the drawee bank.

cash management information system a computer-based system that allows the cash manager to obtain timely information on the amounts of funds on deposit at the firm's bank accounts.

certificate of deposit a large denomination, negotiable, fixed-term time deposit that is generally issued in bearer form so that the investor can sell it prior to maturity if he so desires.

clearing system slippage the difference between the clearing time experienced by the check issuer and the availability time granted to the check depositor.

collection period the time from when the bill is due to when it is paid.

commercial paper an unsecured promissory note sold at a discount to the public.

compensating balances idle balances in a firm's checking account that are used to compensate the bank for making a line of credit available or for other services the bank may provide.

computer-based financial planning model a mathematical representation of the firm's financial statements that, because it is programmed on a computer, can be helpful in exploring the financial implications of alternative corporate policies and economic scenarios.

contango a situation where the cash price of a commodity is below its futures price.

continuous production process a production process where goods move at a constant pace along an assembly line.

controlled disbursing account a disbursing account at a bank that receives check presentations at an early hour in the day, and is willing to notify the firm of the amount presented so that it can fund the account before the end of the day.

correspondent banking relationship a relationship whereby one bank keeps deposit balances in another in return for services such as check clearing, consulting, trust, and securities trading.

credit period the total time for which credit is extended.

credit scoring model a statistical model that is useful in distinguishing good and bad credit risks on the basis of certain objective characteristics of the credit applicant.

cross hedge a situation where an individual or firm uses a futures contract in a commodity other than the one she holds in the cash market to hedge the risks of price fluctuations in her cash market commodity.

Days' Sales Outstanding a method of monitoring trends in customer payment patterns. It is equal to total receivables divided by average credit sales per day.

decision tree   a diagram of a decision problem that displays the decisions that can be made in their proper sequence, the possible outcomes of uncertain events and the payoff that occurs for each decision-chance event combination. The diagram is used to help the manager make the best decision at the first stage of analysis.

delivery date   the date in a futures contract when the seller is obligated to deliver the commodity to the buyer at the price specified in the original contract.

depository transfer check   a check used solely for the purpose of transferring deposits from one of the firm's accounts to another; a depository transfer check is non-negotiable.

discount period   the length of time that the customer has to pay his bill if he wants to get a discount on the price for prompt payment.

distribution approach   a statistical approach to cash forecasting that uses a dummy variable regression equation to estimate the typical pattern of cash flows over the days of the week and days of the month.

drawee bank   the bank at which the check issuer has funds on deposit that will be transferred to the payee at the time of presentment.

EOQ model   a mathmatical model used to determine the order quantity that minimizes the sum of the acquisition and holding cost of inventory.

electronic funds transfer   a means of transferring value from one account to another in which information is transmitted electronically either via computer tape or computer-to-computer direct communication, rather than by means of paper (e.g., checks).

endogenous variables   variables in a financial planning model whose values are determined by the model itself rather than being set externally.

error term   a variable in a statistical model that represents the effect of a large number of independent factors that the model builder is unable to specifically identify but which contribute to the value of the forecast variable.

Euro-dollar deposit   a dollar denominated deposit in a bank or bank branch located outside the United States.

exogeneous variables   variables in a financial planning model that are determined external to the financial planning environment.

federal agency securities   money market instruments representing the debt obligations of the federally sponsored credit agencies.

Federal Deposit Insurance Corporation   a federal agency that provides insurance on deposits up to a maximum of $100,000 at commercial banks.

Federal Funds   federal funds are unsecured overnight loans from one financial institution to another. Federal Fund borrowings are exempt from reserve requirements. Value is transferred by changes in correspondent bank accounts or by changes in bank balances at the Federal Reserve. Federal funds are immediately available funds.

Federal Open Market Committee   a committee within the Federal Reserve that sets the system's targets for growth in the money supply, interest rates, and the availability of credit.

Federal Reserve System   a federal agency whose purpose is to promote a high level of economic activity and assure the health of the nation's banking system.

float   in a general sense the term refers to the dollar amount in the process of collection. Specific definitions of float vary depending on the user's concept of when the collection process begins.

forecast input   the information that is used in making a forecast.

futures commission merchant   a broker in futures contracts who provides many services to customers, one of which is the execution of trades on the floor of the exchange.

futures contract   a standardized contract calling for the exchange of a commodity for cash at a later date. Futures contracts are traded on a formal exchange under a specified set of rules.

hedger   an individual who uses the futures market as a means of offsetting risks associated with his basic line of business.

heuristic algorithm   a procedure for solving the lockbox and disbursement location problems that makes use of a commonsense rule of thumb to continually search feasible combinations of sites until an optimal or near optimal solution is found.

holding cost   the cost of keeping an item in inventory.

homogeneous customer group   a group of customers that are relatively similar in regard to their total collection (mail plus availability) or presentation times.

immediately available funds   funds deposited into an account that may be withdrawn immediately.

imperfect hedge   a situation where an individual firm cannot guarantee the complete elimination of risk by taking opposite positions in the cash and futures markets.

job shop   a production operation where goods are produced to order rather than standardized.

lead time   the length of time between the date inventory is ordered and the date it is received.

liability management   a term used to refer to the bank practice of actively seeking funds in the money market rather than passively accepting time and demand deposits.

linear programming   a mathematical formulation of a decision problem that specifies an objective and a set of constraints that are linear functions of variables under the decision-maker's control (decision variables). In terms of this formulation, the decision problem is to find a set of values for the decision variables that gives a maximum (or minimum) value to the objective and yet satisfies all of the constraints.

line of credit   an agreement that allows a firm to borrow any amount from its bank up to a stated maximum at any time during the year.

liquidity   the ability to generate cash at short notice. Assets are said to be liquid when they can be sold for cash at short notice with little or no loss in value. Liquidity is also provided by the ability to borrow at short notice.

local bank   a bank that relies primarily on deposits as a source of funds and lends almost exclusively to individuals and firms in its local area.

lockbox   a postal address maintained by the firm's bank that is used as a receiving point for checks sent from the firm's customers.

long hedge   a situation where the hedging individual or firm buys a futures contract.

margin   a deposit made by a participant in a futures trade whose purpose is to help assure fulfillment of contractual obligations.

mismatched book   a portfolio of assets and liabilities where the average maturity of the assets is not equal to the average maturity of the liabilities.

money center bank   a large bank that funds investments, loans, and securities by purchasing large quantities of funds in the money market through such vehicles as federal funds, repurchase agreements, CD's, and commercial paper. In addition to its lending activities, money center banks offer a wide array of financial services that appeal to corporate financial managers throughout the country.

money market   the place where short-term financial instruments are bought and sold.

money market broker   an individual or institution that arranges money market trades for a fee. Brokers do not trade from their own portfolio.

money market dealer   a participant in the money market who buys and sells securities for his own portfolio.

normal backwardation   a situation where the cash price of a commodity is above its futures price.

open book account   a credit practice where the seller invoices the buyer and records the amount owed on her accounts receivable ledger.

open market operations   open market operations are the primary means by which the Federal Reserve controls the supply of money and credit. It increases the supply of money and credit by purchasing securities from a government securities dealer through its agent at the market trading desk at the Federal Reserve Bank of New York. It decreases the supply of money and credit by instructing its agent to sell securities.

optimization algorithm   an algorithm for solving the lockbox and disbursement location problems that guarantees the best solution will be found.

order quantity   the amount of inventory that is ordered each time an order takes place.

partial hedges   a situation where an individual or firm takes a position in the futures market that is smaller than his position in the cash market.

payee   the individual for a firm designated on a check as the recipient of value.

payment pattern approach   a statistical approach to cash forecasting that relates a component of the cash stream, such as cash collections, back to the source that generates it through a regression equation.

payment pattern matrix   a method of monitoring trends in customer payment pattern. The matrix displays the percent of each month's credit sales that are collected in one month, two months, and so on.

perfect hedge   a situation where an individual or firm is able to completely eliminate the risk of price fluctuations by taking opposite positions in the cash and futures markets.

planning horizon   the length of time over which the firm plans its activities.

preauthorized draft   a check used to periodically withdraw funds from an individual or firm's account. The draft is initiated by the payee instead of the payor. It is preauthorized in the sense that the payor has signed an agreement allowing the payee to draft its account for this amount.

presentation time   the delay between the date a check is written and the date the check is presented to the drawee bank for collection; sometimes the term clearing time is used as a synonym.

production inventory system   an inventory system where the level of inventory depends on the level of the firm's production; thus, production and inventory decisions are made simultaneously.

pro forma financial statements   a projection of the firm's financial statements at some future point or points in time.

pure hedge   a situation where the individual or firm assumes a position in the futures market that is equal and opposite to his current position in the cash market.

pure inventory system an inventory system where items are replenished by order rather than by production.

quantity discount a reduction in price for ordering large quantities.

regional banks banks having some characteristics of money center banks and some characteristics of local banks. Their clientele is based primarily within their region of the country, but they offer many of the services of money center banks and are active in acquiring funds in the money market.

Regulation Q a Federal Reserve regulation that specifies the maximum rate of interest that financial institutions may pay on time and savings deposits.

rejection cost the expected cost to the firm of rejecting a credit applicant.

remote disbursing account a disbursing account at a bank located at a point where check presentation times are long.

repurchase agreements an agreement to buy a security, usually a Treasurey bill, and to resell it at a specified price at a later date.

reserve requirement a Federal Reserve requirement that all depository institutions maintain a certain percentage of their customer deposits in the form of cash or deposits at a Federal Reserve district bank.

safety stock inventory that serves as a buffer against unexpected fluctuations in demand.

short hedge a situation where the hedging individual or firm sells a futures contract.

shortage cost the cost of not being able to fill customer demand for an inventoriable item.

speculator an individual who seeks to make a profit by predicting trends in market prices.

stationary a statistical word that refers to a forecasting situation where historical patterns repeat themselves in the future.

term loan a bank loan with a maturity greater than 1 year that is repaid in periodic installments.

The Aging Schedule a method of monitoring trends in customer payment patterns. The schedule displays the percentage of current accounts receivable that are one month old, two months old, and so on.

Treasury bill a money market instrument that represents the short-term borrowings of the United States government.

unique zip code a zip code that is assigned to only one firm or bank. The unique zip code allows the post office to sort the bank's lockbox items more rapidly, which results in faster deposit of lockbox items.

variable rate loan a loan where the rate of interest is adjusted periodically to conform more closely with prevailing interest rates in the money markets.

wire transfer a means of effecting the immediate transferring of funds from an account at one bank to an account at another bank; instructions for this transfer are transmitted over one of two wire systems—one maintained by the Federal Reserve and one maintained by a group of private banks.

yield curve a graph of the relationship between the maturity of a security and its yield.

INDEX